Conte

Introduction

Introduction

The book has several different objectives and in a way attempts to be all things to all readers. The fundamental approach which is basic to all sections of the book is that it is aimed at the beginner. It includes some general introductory chapters on hardware, word processing, spreadsheets and data processing. Interspersed with this general material are detailed worksheets which exercise the particular facilities of the chosen software packages.

The other main objective is that the material is designed for the independent learner, whether reading through the more bland descriptive chapters, or working through the details of the worksheets. The level and pace of the material is meant to be suitable for someone working on their own without any additional assistance.

There are many different types of beginner. There is the complete beginner who may not even have a machine available yet, who wants to assess the possible usefulness of a micro system, and consider how the various processing techniques could be useful to his or her business activities. At the other extreme there could be the business person, whose office already uses a micro system as a word processor perhaps, but who now wishes to extend the use of the system into other areas such as accounts, or into general data–file handling.

It is possible to use the book in this flexible way: to explore a particular technique as quickly as possible, such as using a data–base for a particular application, and then returning to read the rest of the book to get a more general view of the whole area of data processing later. So the book presents a flexible package which allows a 'pick'n mix' approach so that you can choose your own particular path through the material.

If nothing else, the book is a source of well tried practical exercises. The material or very similar material to that presented in the worksheets has been used on a wide range of courses at Orpington College for several years. The courses range from normal evening classes for the general public on information technology and introductions to business computing, through to in–service training courses both for teaching and administrative staff. The material has been used on more traditional further education courses such as BTEC First Diploma courses in Business Studies, Certificate of Pre–Vocational Education courses, Youth and Adult (TOPS) Training Scheme courses. The material is suitable for preparation for the Royal Society of Arts (RSA) CLAIT examination (Computer Literacy and Information Technology), for London Chamber of Commerce and Industry (LCCI) examinations and for general complementary or background studies for a whole range of students in information technology. The exercises and worksheets will also be suitable introductory material for the new GCSE course in information technology, and would more than cover the ground of the core of TVEI related to information technology.

The treatment in the worksheets is not exhaustive of all of the available techniques of the various packages, but covers the basic material which usually takes the student through the initial stages, thoroughly enough for him/her to reach the stage of being able to continue independently to use the elements of a package which are required to tackle a particular application. Generally it does not take much effort to become proficient in using any one of the packages.

So the book is aimed at the independent learner who is working on his/her own and maybe just wishes to extend his/her knowledge of information processing. The material will also be useful to someone working in a business environment who has had some experience of using a microcomputer system, but would like to extend this experience to other software packages, and to obtain a general background for these activities.

The structure of the book also makes it useful to a student in a school or college, where the exercises could be carried out in the 'IT room', and the remainder of the book used to broaden out the background to these practical activities. Also many teachers of information processing are learning as they go, 'picking themselves up by their own boot straps', being familiar with some aspects of the syllabus, but possibly not all — and so the book is aimed to help a teacher in that situation. The background information is provided, together with a supply of worksheet material which may be modified to suit the teacher's particular need. The worksheets produced here for the independent learner tend to be slightly too wordy for instant use in the classroom situation, unless that situation is 'open access' and aimed at more independent learning.

For the worksheets I have assumed that the hardware available to the reader is a standard IBM PC or clone. In Chapter 1, I have explained enough about the hardware for you to appreciate some of the general technicalities of such a system. The objective for that chapter is that at the end of it you should be able to look through the advertisements in the computing press and understand what most of the terms used there mean, and to be able to take part in meaningful conversations with colleagues and/or sales and maintenance personnel.

It is the programs which make a computer system come alive, and they are collectively referred to as software. The software packages which I have chosen for the worksheets are WordStar for word processing, SuperCalc3 as a spreadsheet, and dBASEII as a database package. These are among the earlier versions of software of their type, but have become in many ways almost classic benchmarks against which more recent packages are compared. The features of these packages used in the exercises in the book are common to all versions of the packages including the earlier editions. They are now also three of the cheapest packages which are commercially available for the PC and clones. I have also assumed that these packages are operating within the Microsoft Disk Operating System (MS-DOS), but this is not essential, for the packages work just as well under other operating systems, such as CP/M and the details of entry into the packages would have to be changed only very slightly to reflect changes of operating system.

In the same way, it would be a relatively easy task to change the word processing worksheet section to suit the WORD word processing package, the spreadsheet exercises to suit either Multiplan or Lotus 123.

Most books on computing tend to be out of date almost by the time they are published, and as I mention in Chapter 1, there is a new generation of 32–bit micro systems appearing on the market currently. I do not however think that the software will change at the same rate as the hardware. It seems to be most likely that the same sorts of packages or possibly more integrated versions of these three will appear for this new generation of machines. In fact there seems to me to be a gap developing between the rates of development of hardware and software; we do not seem to have moved on as rapidly in recent years in software development proportional to rate of innovation in hardware.

The book then falls into three discrete sections. Word processing is introduced in Chapter 2 and then the worksheets follow as Chapter 3. Similarly, spreadsheets are introduced in Chapter 4 followed by worksheets on this package. Thirdly a very gentle introduction to data processing with its associated logic is presented in Chapters 6 to 8 before the dBASEII worksheets in Chapter 9. The introductory descriptive chapters are meant to stand alone so that they can be read as complete entities in their own right. They are not merely introductions to the worksheets which follow them. In the same way the worksheets can be used independently of the descriptive chapters. One of the shortcomings of this attempt of making the sections independent, is that there is some repetition of material.

In Chapter 1 I have tried to give an introduction to hardware which takes you from the very first elementary concepts, right through to taking a glance at more up-to-date developments, such as those associated with the 32–bit INTEL 80386 chip. The style here varies from straight textbook descriptions, to homely advice about hardware systems, with a glimpse of what the future may have in store. Do not feel that you need to wade through all of this chapter before proceeding with the rest of the book, just return to it for background details or general reading, as required.

I make no apology for trying to introduce some programming with dBASE II in Chapter 10. After a good word processor I have found a good data–base program to be the most useful administrative and educational package. dBASE II is powerful in immediate interactive mode, but is much more powerful in its command mode provision. This dBASE II facility has been largely neglected by the educational world so far, so I hope that the material in Chapter 10 will, not only be useful, but also serve to kindle an interest in dBASE II programming for its own sake. There are many GCSE and GCE A Level computing 'projects' which would be better and more easily written in dBASE II than in BASIC!

I have already used some jargon which may be slightly confusing to the beginner. 'Hardware' is used to describe the actual physical components of a computer system, while 'software' is reserved only to refer to programs or collections of programs. The term 'packages' is used to denote a collection or suite of several programs which has been designed to carry out a specific task, such as word or data processing. By the word 'data' I just mean 'facts and figures' and by 'data processing' I refer to those activities such as sorting, searching, listing, editing, which are carried out on data which has been stored in bulk. Bulk data is usually stored magnetically on disk and each collection of data is referred to as a 'file'.

There are generally two types of data. You will be very familiar with numbers which come in two basic types, counting numbers or integers, and decimal numbers which are usually derived from some sort of measurement. The second data type is referred to as a 'string', and is applied to a group of characters, which could be a word and therefore considered as just a string of letters, or it could also be a number i.e. a string of digits, possibly including either a comma or a decimal point; but it could be just a collection of other characters, the characters that you see on the standard keyboard, such as exclamation mark, asterisk, the ampersand and so on. So the term string is just a general term meaning any collection of characters.

The glossary is more than a collection of terms used in the book and it is more than just a list of 'buzz' words. It is meant to define more carefully how some of the specialised words are used, and to act as a source of reference for you when you are reading through the book. You will readily agree that if you do choose to read the book in a random way, picking out those parts which you need first and then returning to other parts later, then you will not necessarily have read the definition of a technical term which will be given when it is first introduced. So, the glossary should be a valuable help in overcoming the 'jargon' problem.

The worksheets are task-orientated, but the various packages have very different natures and this means that the worksheet material for the different packages is not presented in a totally standard way. One way of looking at the three packages is to see them in terms of the difference in structure of the data they process, for example a word processor is manipulating textual data in a very free and unstructured form, whereas a data–base also deals with textual (string) and numeric data; but here there is an overall more clearly defined structure in terms of fields and records to data in this form. The spreadsheet at the other end of the spectrum is quite rigid in its structure, divided up into cells according to rows and columns and, not only is the data structured, but its appearance is also heavily structured.

So you can view the three as representing a spectrum of data–handling kits, with the word processor being very free in its data structure, down to the spreadsheet, which is quite rigid in its data structure. This is of course a very broad generalisation, and in newer packages there is a much greater overlap between the three packages. To this end I have included in the SuperCalc3 and dBASE II worksheets details of how data may be transferred from these packages into WordStar documents.

To start with it is often easier to see things in discrete categories, for example spreadsheets are often seen as being exclusively used for accounting purposes, but they do allow logical comparisons and so are suitable for general statistical exercises, for scheduling and timetabling. In the same way dBASEII has wider uses than is indicated in the text. It is also quite suitable for carrying out statistical analyses and as most dBASEII manuals will illustrate, it is possible to use the system to design stock control or accounting systems; these are however only accomplished by using the command programming language which is included in dBASEII which I have not had space to explore to any great depth in this book, but which is a very powerful facility in its own right.

The material, in different shapes and forms, has been inflicted on students at Orpington College for several years. It has also been used for in–service sessions for both teaching and support staff. The feedback from students and staff over the years has been invaluable, and I am indebted to them for their suggestions and contributions. In particular I must thank Pauline Edwards and Carol Baylis for providing the word processing worksheets, and Pauline again for much of the material for the spreadsheet worksheets. I am also grateful for the many hours which my daughter Elena spent keying in text for me.

I hope that you will enjoy reading the book and find the worksheets helpful in developing your expertise in using the tools of information Technology, so that the microcomputer system will become a more effective feature in your daily life.

1 The microcomputer system

1.1 Introduction

You need to know very little about the details of the hardware of a microcomputer system to be able to use it effectively. If your sole interest is to get on and use the system as a word processor or to help you with your business accounts, then all you really need to know is how to switch on, load the various disks, use the keyboard effectively and save the results of your work safely on disk. You will also wish to output some of these results onto paper so that people without a computer may have access to your data.

This approach begs several questions. Why are you using a computer at all? What micro system are you using? How effectively are you using it? Who decided that it was suitable for your particular application? If you are part of a large organisation, where the choice of hardware and software was a corporate decision made by experts, then all should be well. But if you have been, or will be expected to take part in decisions about the choice of hardware or software now or in the future, then you will be able to do so if you are slightly better informed. Furthermore, if you are more knowledgeable you will be able to make more effective use of the system.

If you are on your own, then you will eventually have to consider some technical questions. Does the printer give you the quality of output you want? A printer suitable for letter output is not necessarily ideal for printing balance sheets. Does your application really need a colour screen display? Is the memory large enough to hold the software without frequent disk saving operations which will slow down your work? Do you need a hard disk, or will you be able to get by using several floppy disks? Is a standard keyboard ideal for your particular work? Can your machine be linked to others to form a network sharing common data and can it link into Prestel or act as a telex system? If it is not totally satisfactory, what is needed to enhance or upgrade the system? I suggest that you will be better able to take a more meaningful part in discussions with your colleagues, maintenance engineer or computer salesperson if you know at least what some of the basic software and hardware terms mean.

1.2 The system

Figure 1.1 shows the five essential hardware components of a basic business microcomputer system such as the IBM PC or its clones: keyboard, screen or Visual Display Unit (VDU), printer, processor and disk drives together in one unit. These physical components are linked by cables, but they are organised into a functional system by the programs which originate and operate largely in the processor, which are collectively referred to as 'software'.

It has been usual in the past to show the hardware system diagrammatically as:

Input ----> Processor ----> Output

↓ ↑

Backing Store

Useful as that simple picture is, it does rather blurr how you view the activity of inputting from and outputting to disk of programs and data. In other words the movement of data to and from disks (the backing store) must also be seen as output and input activities, which are not fundamentally different from outputting to screen or printer, or inputting from the keyboard.

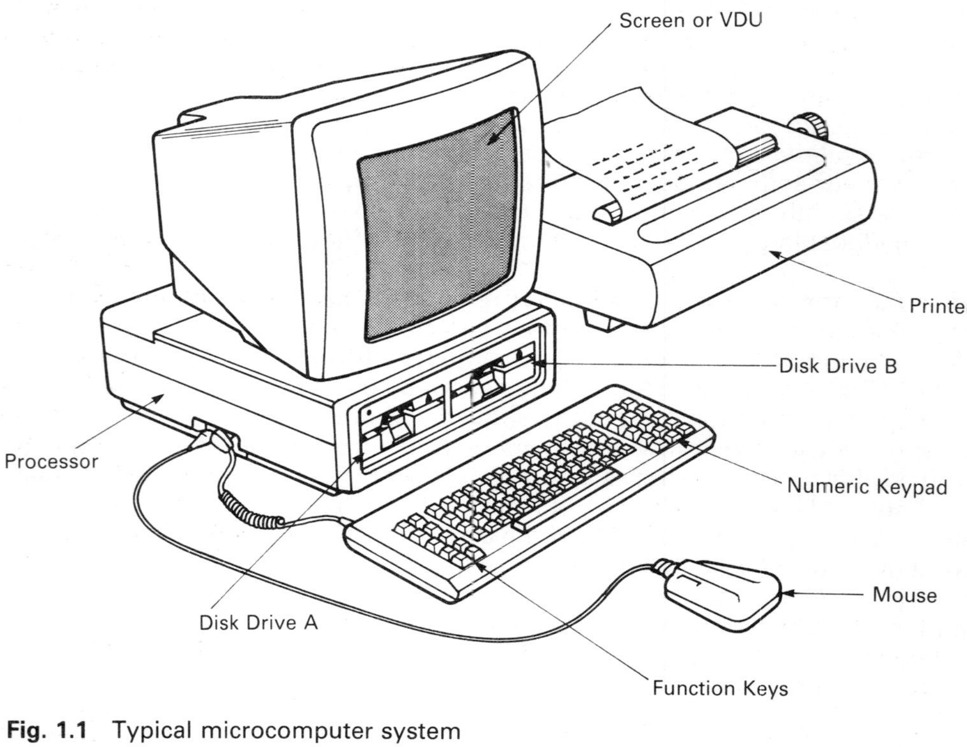

Fig. 1.1 Typical microcomputer system

1.3 The keyboard

The IBM PC or clone has a standard 80–key keyboard, with ten function keys to the left side, a numeric keypad to the right, and standard QWERTY keyboard in the centre. The keypad has cursor keys (the arrowed keys), and other keys e.g. Page–up and Page–down, Tab and Print Screen, which can be programmed ('configured') to have special uses with a particular software application such as word procesing. In the same way the left function keys may be configured to have special uses, all designed to save time and effort when using a particular software package — and you should ensure when you buy software, that it uses all of the specialist features of the keyboard, or vice versa that your keyboard is able to make use of all of the facilities of the software. You can get 'professional' keyboards for use with IBM clones which have more specialist keys, giving you 100 keys to use if your work really needs this additional provision.

You can also get specialist keyboards. The 'concept' keyboard consists of pressure pads under pictures or ikons, similar to the keypads used on some High Street tills, and is used in junior classroom software applications. In the retail trade it is common place to use a bar–code reader as an input device for a portable micro. It is possible to use the Quinkey type keyboard as input, which is a special keyboard with only five keys. There is no need to remind you of the growing importance of the Mouse, which is now widely used in organising and controlling a micro system through the operating environments like GEM or MS-WINDOWS. This draws attention to the fact that if you want a special keyboard, you also have to have special software to allow you to use it. However most business data processing involves intensive input from a standard QWERTY type keyboard.

1.4 Screen

Great care should be taken over the choice of monitor (VDU) because you are going to spend a lot of time staring at its screen. It must be the right size for your particular application. The standard size being 25cm and 80 characters wide, and 20cm and 25 characters top to bottom — often described as having 80 columns and 25 rows. If you intend to use your system mainly for accounting purposes, then you might think about getting a wider screen so that you can view more columns of numbers than you can fit into the 80-character width. Similarly if you intend to use the system mainly for word processing then a screen with more than 25 rows may be more convenient and comfortable to use for larger documents — or it may pay you to consider obtaining a dedicated word processor and not to use a micro system at all!

Many micro systems are sold on the strength of their attractive colour graphics. If you are going to use software packages which have been designed round the use of varied colour displays then you must have a suitable colour monitor — it would be illogical and uneconomic to buy software whose effects you could not use fully. The opposite also applies. It is illogical to buy a colour monitor if, for most of the time, you are going to use the system for processing only text or numbers. I'd go further and assert that for example, using a word processing package which has been designed for monochrome use, will give a much less distinct appearance of the text on a colour screen than on the monochrome monitor for which it was designed — much to the irritation of the user after some time of staring at it.

A technical term which you will meet when discussing monitors is 'resolution'. You know that the image on the screen is caused by spots of fluorescence caused by an electronic beam striking the chemical covering on the back of the screen. The more spots which strike the screen per unit area of it, the clearer the image should be. The more spots per unit area, the higher the resolution, the sharper the image will be. Monochrome monitors tend to have a higher resolution than colour monitors. On the newer range of micros based on 32–bit processors you can get very high resolution graphics by having an 'Extended Graphics Adaptor' (EGA) board fitted as an optional extra.

Other practical considerations are the type of monochrome monitor which you prefer, black and white, amber or green. Colour monitors are still at least twice the price of monochrome. Swivel and tilt of the monitor are desirable options if the system is to be used extensively by people of differing stature. The exercises in 3.4 of the WordStar section reinforce some of the health aspects of computing.

1.5 The processor

To understand some of the essential jargon used to describe the key features of the processor, you have to consider a few straightforward technical details. First you must remember that the machine has to represent your data or instructions as sequences of electronic pulses. You are most likely aware of how numbers can be represented in binary form, and so will not be surprised that letters, punctuation marks and the special symbols used in data processing can also have a binary form. I will look at the ASCII code of character representation later but for now state that the character A is represented in this code by the binary number 1000001 (decimal number 65), and B by 1000010 (decimal 66), C by 1000011 (decimal 67) and so on. The full code is shown in Appendix 3. You can imagine how 1000010 can be represented inside the machine by seven electronic circuits which are either 'on' shown by a 1, or 'off' shown by a 0. Every piece of information entered into a computer is ultimately stored and processed as a binary number.

Each 1 or 0 is referred to as a 'bit', so we can say that the letters chosen above A, B and C etc. can be represented by a 7–bit code. There are very good technical reasons why an extra bit is added as a check or 'parity' bit, so this form of representation uses an 8–bit code. This method can be used to represent 256 (2 to the power 7 or $2\times2\times2\times2\times2\times2\times2$) different characters. Each packet of 8 bits is referred to as a 'byte'. The first main generation of microcomputers was based on 8–bit chips, and the 256 different characters proved to be adequate enough to represent most forms of data. The capacity of such a chip is stated in kilobytes or thousands of bytes. In fact in this case 'kilo' is used to mean 2 to the power 10 or 2×2× . . . 10 times which equals 1024, a little more than 1000 — just an interesting point of detail!

The processor consists of a large collection of chips. Some of these chips have been permanently programmed, and hold routines which are essential to the organisation of the micro system. You cannot write data or instructions into these chips and so they comprise part of the memory of the processor which is referred to as the Read Only Memory or ROM, because you can only read data and instructions from them. That part of the processor's memory from which you can both read and write data and instructions is called the RAM or Random Access Memory. Random Access is rather opaque jargon which implies that you can put and get data anywhere you choose in this area of memory, hence for 'random' read 'free'. Your software package word processor, spreadsheet or data–base is loaded, all or in part into, and is active with its current data in, RAM. When you switch off or even reset the system, the RAM is wiped clean and the information contained there lost, unless you have saved the contents of the RAM previously to disk or some other permanent store. Thus the RAM is referred to as being 'volatile'.

I took the 8–bit representation as a starting point to illustrate the general principles of binary coding. The technology has moved on in leaps and bounds since those early days. The IBM PC and its clones which I have taken as typical of the hardware available to businesses generally at present, and would be the type of machine running the software described in detail in this book, are based on a 16–bit design. Now, where is the advantage to be gained from 16– rather than 8–bit? Well, first of all you could design a more comprehensive code giving a wider range of characters. Secondly you could pass information round the system in bundles of two 8–bit characters thus doubling the speed by more comprehensive packaging — this is not quite accurate, but shows you the trend! A more subtle point is that 8–bit chips were only capable of addressing and controlling a maximum of about 64 kbytes of RAM. Now the 16–bit chips found in the IBM PC and clones are capable of addressing a much larger RAM, and the standard RAM size now is 512 to 640 kbytes — about ten times larger. The most recent generation of micros cloning the IBM PS/2 are based on 32–bit chips. I will return to this mind boggle shortly.

The other important factor is the speed with which the processing can be carried out. You have to imagine the whole system being controlled and managed by a clock, and each basic operation a comparison of registers, a transfer of the contents of one memory location, to be carried out in time with a clock which controls the whole system. The faster the clock goes, the faster the whole processing is carried out. The newer chips allow processing at higher speeds. In the 8–bit era 1 million processes per second were quoted as the norm — to accomplish this the clock would have to be pulsing at 1 million pulses per second or 1MegaHertz. Current speeds are approaching 20 MHertz or 20 pulses per microsecond.

The obsession with speed is caused largely by the limitation that current micros are still basically serial processors. There is a section of the processor which is called the ALU (Arithmetic and Logic Unit) through which all of the instructions which the machine has to obey are passed byte by byte in their correct operating sequence. It is these 'byte–by–byte' and 'in sequence' features which are referred to when micros are described as processing 'serially'. Until a new generation of machines is designed to use 'parallel' processing, where different aspects of the processing can be carried out simultaneously, the size of byte and speed through the ALU will limit the overall performance of the system.

I have talked about chips, but individual chips have got lost in the overall more complicated design of current micros. Additional chunks of memory are added as whole boards of chips devoted to a particular purpose. The EGA board, to give you extra graphics facilities has already been mentioned. Often the literature refers to hard cards which include hard disks and circuitry all on one board.

Finally let us look just outside the range of IBM PC clones into the current next price bracket at machines based on Intel 80386 processor. This chip has a genuine 32–bit ALU, with the ability to fetch data from memory in 32–bit packets, and runs at clock speeds of 16 MHertz. It can address 4096 Mbytes of RAM directly, and is capable of genuine 'multi–tasking', having the capacity to allocate each program its own Megabyte of memory to work independently of other programs. The difficulty at present is that it has to remain compatible with currently available software, and the rest of the hardware of a sytem, disks, screens and printers, which are still of the older generation. In fact at the time of writing it is true to say that the software houses have not yet developed software comprehensive enough to take full advantage of the potential of this chip. Is the hardware at last outstripping our programming ability?

1.6 Disks

It is essential that when you switch off your micro you do not lose all of the text, data or programs which you have worked so hard to create. For the IBM PC and its clones the 5¼ inch floppy disk is the standard form of permanent storage.

You are familiar with magnetic storage, in the form of tape for audio, and video tapes are made by coating plastic tape with iron oxide, which can be magnetised and thus store magnetically sound and electronic images from your hifi system or television. Magnetic tape can be used to store the output from a computer, and in the early days of the micro, domestic tape recorders were used for this purpose. The drawback of using tape is that you can only get at the data by searching in sequence through a length of tape, and this puts severe restrictions on the speed with which you can find the data.

The floppy disk, as shown diagrammatically in Figure 1.2 consists of, a circular disk of plastic coated with iron oxide, inside a protective envelope made of paper or plastic. When the disk is inserted into the disk drive, the drive spindle clamps down on the central hole cut in the disk, and when it receives electronic instructions to do so, the disk spins at high speed inside its plastic envelope. As it revolves, a magnetically sensitive head hovers over the slot in the sleeve called the access slot or read/write window, and reads or writes the data in magnetic form from/to the surface of the disk.

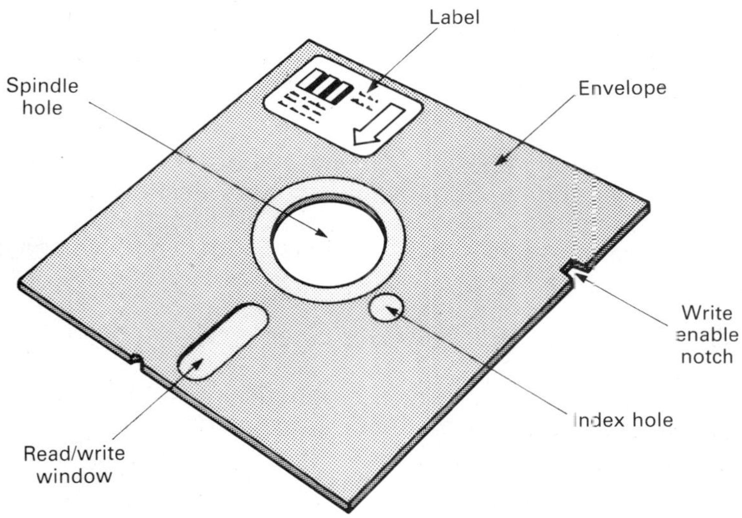

Fig. 1.2 A 5¼ inch disk

The data is organised on the disk in tracks and sectors as shown in Figure 1.3. The magnetically sensitive head of the drive moves in and out radially along the access slot, until it finds the track where the data is stored, and then it has to wait a split second for the right sector of the disk to rotate, until it arrives at the window where it can be read. You will now see the advantage of disk over tape as a form of storage, for instead of having to search through a length of tape, the read/write head can be told to go and look for a track, and then a sector on that track. So the time taken to access any part of the surface of the disk will be the time for the head to move across an inch or so of the slot plus the time for the sector to rotate into the read/write position. You can search quite freely over the surface of the disk to find data, and this facility is referred to as 'random' or 'direct' access, whereas with tape you only have 'serial' access. Special tape units (tape streamers) are used to back-up hard disks, where all the contents of the disk may be dumped to the tape at high speeds.

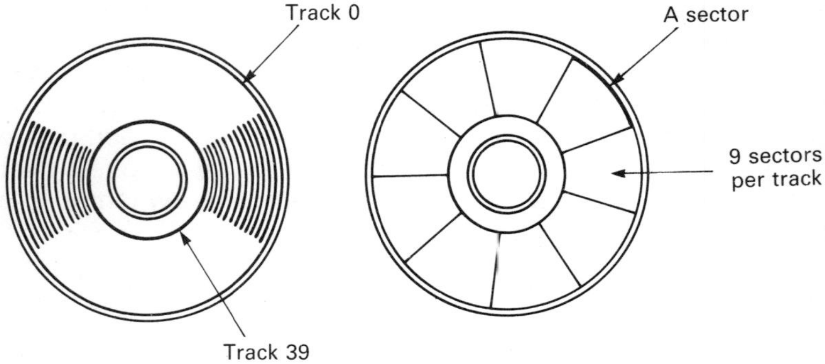

Fig. 1.3 The magnetic format of a disk

By using both sides of the floppy disk you can store about one third of a Megabyte (350k plus bytes) of data. Some simple sums will show you this. Figure 1.3 shows a 40 track disk, divided up into nine sectors. If the sector associated with each track is thought to hold 512 bytes of data then you have a total of:

$$2 \text{ (sides)} \times 9 \text{ (sectors)} \times 39 \text{ (tracks)} \times 512 \text{ bytes} = 368640 \text{ bytes}$$

The disk is divided up into tracks and sectors magnetically, not by any mechanical means. The activity of giving the disk this magnetic picture is called 'formatting' the disk. The disk has to reserve some of its available storage space to store details of the way it itself is formatted, and some more space to store details of the files which are eventually to be stored on the disk. So, all of the 368,640 are not free for your data. In fact when you format a disk you may see a response on the screen which says something like '362496 bytes free'. This is still more than one third Megabyte for your use.

The 5¼ inch floppy disk is a delicate object and in the manual for your micro you will be given lots of homely advice about treating it gently, not letting it get too hot or too cold and keeping it away from electrical devices which generate stray magnetic fields e.g. loudspeakers of your audio system, telephone and television. Never insert a disk into the drive before you switch your micro on, and always take it out before you switch off, because there are stray magnetic fields generated when all electrical equipment is switched on or off. Never take the disk out when the system is writing to it (the drive light will be on), because if the writing process is not completed then the end of your file will be missing and all of the file created will be unreadable.

Despite all of these more obvious warnings the likely causes of a disk disaster are: corrupting a piece of valuable software or data file by leaving off the tag over the read/write notch, or even more likely by not saving data frequently enough or even at all before you switch off the machine and thereby losing all of a file, and most likely by not taking care to create and store safely a second or 'back–up' copy of all of your disks. Make a rule for yourself right from the start, to save text, data or program coding after you have created about a page, irrespective of whether the job is complete or not, then at most you will only lose a page's worth of valuable time and inspiraton. At the end of every job or important part thereof, make a back–up copy, put a tag over the read/write noch and store it away somewhere safe. Be generous with disks, do not fill one disk with a great variety of files, some data–file data, some spreadsheet data, some text, some programs — keep separate disks for your different activities. Label them carefully and keep a list of what is stored on each disk. Using the MS–DOS command LABEL, you can give each disk a name or label which is stored on it magnetically, and is listed when you ask to see the disk's directory with the DIR command. If you make this name or label the same as the one you have written in felt tip pen on the actual label of the disk, life becomes infinitely tidier and simpler when you accumulate many files on a number of disks.

I have described the 5¼ inch floppy disk because it is standard with the IBM PC and clones. With newer micro systems such as the IBM PS/2 using it, the 3½ inch disk is becoming popular. Its principles of operation are similar to those described above. Although the disk assembly is smaller it is more robust because it is cased in rigid plastic, and average storage capacities are higher than those of the 5¼ inch. Typically the 3½ inch disk will store 720k bytes, but some systems are already offering 1.44 Mbytes. With the weight of IBM behind the 3½ inch disk it is likely that it will become the standard for the next generation of machines. For obvious reasons this type of disk is becoming almost standard in portable micro systems or 'laptops'.

A 'hard disk' works like a rigid assembly of floppy disks, with several disk surfaces available each with its own read/write head. The disk rotates continuously while the machine is switched on, and is fixed permanently in the processor only to be replaced by skilled engineers. Hard disks have high capacities, typically at present in the range 10–40 Mbytes, and are therefore capable of holding all of the software and data which you are likely to be considering using, and it is very easy to switch from one task to another. Micros usually have one hard and one floppy disk, so new software can be bought on floppy and then loaded onto the hard disk, and the floppy can be used to take back–up copies of data.

1.7 Printers

The day of the electronic office is approaching but it is likely that there will always be a need to communicate the results of your processing to others by means of printing them on paper. At the time of writing it is estimated that there are about 400 printers available for use with a PC. I will attempt to explain the general principles on which they work, and leave you to assess the true merits of each type for a particular task. The choice of printer will always be to some extent based on personal preferences about the eventual appearance of a document. There are two main types of printer in general use, one based on a dot matrix and the other on a daisy wheel mechanism.

Fig. 1.4 The daisy wheel

The daisy wheel printer

Figure 1.5 shows the different types of print styles which may be obtained from daisy wheel and dot matrix printers. The first paragraph was produced by a daisy wheel printer and its appearance is identical to that which would be produced by a typewriter. Figure 1.4 shows the actual daisy wheel print head, which consists of a range of print characters on the ends of the radial stalks giving the appearance of petals on a daisy, and is usually made of plastic, but metal in more expensive versions. The wheel is fixed to a spindle and rests close to the surface of the paper, and a ribbon like a typewriter ribbon (inked or carbonised) is held between the print characters and the paper. When the spindle receives an electronic signal from the computer, it turns the daisy wheel until the right character is adjacent to the paper, when a pin or small hammer is punched forward and the character strikes the paper through the ribbon, leaving its imprint. The whole head assembly moves on one space across the paper where the process is repeated for the next letter, and so on.

With a newish daisy wheel and high quality ribbon a very high print standard may be obtained similar to that of a good typewriter. Print speeds of 25 characters per second for a modestly priced machine are standard, but speeds of up to 60 characters per second are possible with more expensive models. Some printers are said to be 'intelligent' in that they print in both directions, going left to right normally and then printing the next line backwards right to left; and if the text or data stops mid–line then the print head goes to the end which is nearest to start the next line. You have to accept the quoted speeds with a pinch of salt though, because they are often only obtained in special circumstances, e.g. printing the same character right across a single line of maximum carriage width. For normal print material you should expect average speeds over a whole document of about one half or even one third of that quoted.

The daisy wheel is inflexible in being limited only to its given character set — it cannot print graphics even of the rudimentary bar chart form satisfactorily. It is a relatively cheap form of printing for replacement daisy wheels, ribbons and paper are not expensive. It is easy to feed in single sheets of paper manually for individual page documents, but sheet feeding devices for multiple copies or larger documents does put up the price.

The dot matrix printer

Here the print head just consists of a column of pins arranged along the direction of paper travel, or top to bottom as you would write on the paper. The pins are close to the paper surface but with a ribbon between head and paper, and when electronic signals are sent to the head from the processor the pins are fired at the paper as the head moves across the page. Thus. patterns of dots made by the pins through the ribbon make the characters on the paper. If you look closely at the dot matrix printouts in Figure 1.5 you will see these dots.

From the same sort of arguments which we used when talking about image resolution on the screen of the system, you will understand that the more dots you can get per unit area of paper the clearer and better defined will be the printout characters. Cheaper dot matrix printers have only nine pins in the print head, and better quality printers now feature 18 or 24 pin heads. Because the time taken just to fire the pins is much less than rotating a daisy wheel and then firing a pin, basically dot matrix printers can claim to be much faster. Obvious comparisons can be rather misleading. The quality of the printout in the basic use of the machine is rather poor, being 'dotty' or 'grainy'.

You can improve the quality if the printer makes several passes, printing part of the character in greater detail on each pass, or by printing just to the side of the previous set of dots to darken the character. Dot matrix printers can achieve 'near letter quality' (NLQ) by using such stratagems. But of course, the more passes the printer has to make the slower will be the net speed for a document. If you compare the speed which would be achieved by a dot matrix giving NLQ, and that of a daisy wheel printer for the same quantity and approximate quality of text, then the daisy wheel would not look so slow.

For draft copies of documents, and documents when quality is not so important: internal memos, orders and invoices, lists of stock held in a store and so on, then the dot matrix is more than adequate and is faster and cheaper. It is by far the most popular type of printer, and prices range from less than £200 up to £3000 for a very fast, robust machine capable of printing high quality graphic displays.

You can have the best of both worlds fairly cheaply, by buying a very cheap dot matrix printer which would be used for drafting, for those documents which do not need such a professional appearance, and on which you could display reasonable quality graphics. You can get electronic typewriters which can be connected to a computer to act as a printer and give you good quality print. You then have the opportunity to use the typewriter 'off–line' in its normal mode, and a second person could be using it, and you would not be tempted to use a word processor for simple jobs which are better left just to a typewriter. Electronic typewriters are also made with quite substantial memories of their own, so the second user could also do word processing preparation which could be later fed into the micro. This is a combination worth considering carefully if you have a small busy office which produces a lot of varied textual material and data. If you are in a small busy office you will also have to think carefully about whether you will fit your printer with an acoustic hood, because all impact printers are noisy.

Figure 1.5 also shows italic styles of printing with a dot matrix printer, and although you can see that such styles are possible by arranging the pattern of dots, you will also have realised that your printer must be provided with the appropriate software to allow these patterns to be formed. Not all dot matrix printers will automatically yield these print styles, so you should check with your printer supplier before committing yourself to a particular machine.

This is an example of computer generated text
printed by an electronic daisy wheel printer.
You can get different typefaces by changing
the daisy wheel.

This text is printed using a dot
matrix printer which can be programmed
to produce various effects such as:

Different type faces
Bold type
Condensed type
Expanded type
Italics
Superscript type
Subscript type
Underlining

and even graphics.

Fig 1.5 Printouts from daisy wheel and dot matrix printers

Some newer printers

One way of achieving colour printouts is to have a multi–coloured ribbon on a specially designed dot matrix printer. Ink jet printers are available which have a print head like a dot matrix printer except that, instead of pins, they have nozzles through which ink is squirted onto the paper. More sophisticated ink jet printers allow different coloured inks to be used to give coloured documents. The appearance of text from an ink jet printer is of a very high quality, but they are expensive and seem to be gradually overtaken by the advent of laser printers. Thermal transfer printers are also similar to matrix printers in general design but they use hot pins to melt dye from a special ribbon onto ordinary or sometimes special paper. These printers may require special paper, or ink and ink reservoirs, or ribbons and so the initial price and running costs go up.

Laser printers tend to be 'page printers' so called because the whole page, text, data and graphics, is produced before it emerges from the printer. First the printer has to receive all of the data from the processor, then its image is written on a drum, and then lastly this image is transferred to paper. Its mode of operation is very similar to that of a photocopier. With the laser printer it is possible to achieve a high quality output, with a journalistic mix of pictures, text and numerical data. The rate of production is rather slow as you would expect, with ten pages per minute being an optimistic speed, especially if the material is varied in nature.

The laser printer seems to be at the heart of the Desk Top Publishing revolution, but a fairly sophisticated computer system is necessary as the following sums will point out. The images on the page are 'grainy' with the resolution being of the order of 300 dots per inch, giving 300×300 or 90,000 dots per square inch, and so approaching 9 million dots per page. Now if a dot takes up a byte of storage, then to define a whole page in memory before printing takes place would require a memory of nine Megabytes devoted solely to building up this image for printing. This is not quite how it works and is taking an extreme case, but it is obvious that a substantial memory of at least 1 Megabyte would be required if the page image were to be built up in several partitions. So we are now saying that the printer itself will have to have its own RAM (buffer) in the order of Megabytes. This is a far cry from the standard dot matrix printer with its 2k buffer. Like the dot matrix printer it will also have to have its own software to cope with these complex printing requirements.

Such printers are expensive and are used in fairly large business organisations, and would have to be used intensively so that their facilities may be shared by several microsystems working on separate jobs, to make economic use of such a costly resource. The price of printers will eventually fall and the idea of a combination of printer and photocopier seems to point the way to a potent office machine in the very near future.

Final details about printers

The processor box is connected to the printer box by means of a cable and plug assembly. Two main types of connection are used. When signals are passed, one by one in a long stream of packets of bytes to the printer, the communication is said to be 'serial', and the serial interface, cable and plug assembly is being used. It is possible to pass signals simultaneously to the printer, for example if you have a cable with eight wires then you can pass a signal down each wire at the same time, so one 8–bit byte could be passed in one pulse, and this method of communication is referred to as 'parallel' and the parallel interface, cable and plug assembly would be in use. Most printers now have both parallel and serial plugs and interfaces available. Printers usually have a range of dip switches which can be set to allow the printer to link up with a variety of processors, and can be adjusted to permit different paper sizes, print fonts and so on.

Compatibility means not only that the hardware, plugs, cables and interface of printer and processor should match, but also that there are software routines in the processor's operating system which can pass the correct signals through the hardware, which will be 'recognised' and 'interpreted' accurately by the printer. The system must be 'configured' to recognise the type of printer in use. Operating systems usually have a CONFIG program into which you can enter data so that your system will interact correctly with the printer. To be certain, you should make sure that the printer you want is fully compatible with the micro system before purchase, i.e. actually witness it performing the features of all the tasks you may require of it.

1.8 Software

Operating systems

Software is the collective name for programs. The programs turn a collection of metal, wire, plastic and circuit boards into a functioning system. A very complicated range of software is available and needed to run even a small business micro such as the IBM PC and its clones. The purpose of this book is to give you a practical glimpse at the range of business software which is available for a PC, but even before a word processing, spreadsheet or data–base program can be entered into the system a lot of software has been activated.

For a start, consider what happens when the machine is switched on. Usually a message greets you telling you the date and time, and the previous time when the system was used, and invites you to load a 'system disk' into the disk drive known as the A–drive. From this point on, if things are going well, anything you type at the keyboard appears faithfully on the screen. How did the message get on the screen? How did it recognise the disk when it was entered and activated? Many similar questions could be asked!

When the system is in operation there is a continuous flow of electronic traffic round it. This traffic of information is controlled basically by a set of programs which are permanently in the system. These very basic programs form the 'operating system' of the computer, and reside permanently in ROM, where they can only be read and not overwritten. The operating system routes signals from processor to screen, keyboard to processor, processor to printer or telephone modem, and recognises information stored on disk and so on. As the tasks you want your system to perform become more complicated, your operating also has to become more sophisticated to organise and control them.

We have reached the point when you have loaded a systems disk into the machine and pressed any key, as you were instructed, the drive whirred and if you are using the standard IBM PC system an 'A>' appeared on the left side of the screen. This illuminating message tells you that the disk in the A–drive is the active disk and that the system is ready and waiting for further instructions. When a system includes a disk drive, and offers the capabilities of reading from and writing to disk, and generally coping with the housekeeping details of a disk system, then the operating system has to become that much more powerful to cope with these tasks. When you loaded the disk, pressed any key as requested, and the disk drive came into action, what happened was that more instructions were being read from the disk and added to the basic operating system.

These additional instructions are part of what is referred to as the 'disk operating system' or DOS. They are very complicated and are held in a series of files on the so called 'systems disk'. Microsoft Corporation is a US software company which has become famous for the disk operating system which it designed primarily for the IBM PC, and so MS–DOS (MicroSoft DOS) has become the standard DOS for the 16-bit generation of machines. If you wish to use an application program like WordStar, SuperCalc3 or dBASE II in an MS–DOS system, then you need to have some key MS–DOS routines always available on the program disk with the particular applications package which you are using, which are capable of utilising all of the specialist features of the package.

These routines are stored in a file called COMMAND.COM , and it was that file which was linked into the processor when you responded to the 'press any key' instruction on loading in the systems disk. If you look at the list of files on the systems disk you will find COMMAND.COM , and you will be surprised to see that it takes up more than 17 kbytes of storage space — so there must be some fairly complex sets of instructions contained within that file!

So you have reached the point when the **A>** appears on the left side of the screen to say that the disk operating system is ready and waiting. If you wish to load in the word processing package WordStar, you would select the disk with that package on it, insert it in the A–drive and probably continue by entering **WS** (short for WordStar) and then pressing the **Enter** key, and the disk system would be activated and you would find the first menu of the

WordStar program on the screen. Look how far you have gone already! First you had the basic operating system of the micro from ROM then you linked MS–DOS either from the systems disk, or possibly from COMMAND.COM which had been stored on the WordStar disk, and finally you loaded in the word processing program itself. You can summarise all this by saying that WordStar lives in an MS–DOS envirnoment, which in turn links into the basic operating system. You have already got involved in three sets of programs and haven't yet started any work with the system.

Languages and packages

Thank goodness it is easy to lose sight of the fact that all of the data, instructions and general traffic of information round a computer system consists of a complex system of electronic switching. The software engineers who design the systems must be able to give instructions to the electronic components of the system which correspond to this switching activity. Simply, each basic operation of the system must have, associated with it, a specific coded instruction. A code in which each instruction represents a basic electronic function within the machine is called a 'machine code', and is an example of a 'low–level' programming language. 'Low' is used to signify close to machine functioning, 'high' close to human functioning.

The ultimately 'low' machine code would be in binary form, but there is a slightly higher form of machine code where the instructions are coded in alphanumeric form, but still with the one–to–one correspondence between instruction and electronic function, and this is called an 'assembly code' or simply an 'assembler'.

It is difficult, inconvenient and tedious to program in a low–level language, so over the last 15–20 years several languages have been developed with the prime intention of making it easier for those who are not software engineers to do some programming, and with handling a specific type of processing. FORTRAN short for FORmula–TRANslator was designed largely for use by engineers and scientists. COBOL short for common Business Orientated Language was designed for use in business. BASIC, Beginners All–purpose Symbolic Instruction Code, was designed largely for the education market, to be an easy route into programming for the real non specialist. PASCAL, short for the French scientist, is a more recent language which attempts to be a compromise universal language, suited to scientific as well as business and educational processing. These are 'high–level' languages because they allow programs to be written in codes which are closer to human language, with a mixture of ordinary English words, and mathematical symbols, and thus more easy for us to use.

COBOL has remained primarily a mainframe computer language, although there are versions available for the larger business micro system, and still dominates the world of commercial programming. FORTRAN and BASIC had inherent limitations and weaknesses, but have both been modified considerably during recent years, and certainly quite a lot of programming for small business systems is still carried out in enhanced forms of BASIC. Programming is a professional occupation, and producing software for a particular application is a specialised and expensive process. Unless your application is very individual, it should be unnecessary to 'write your own', or commission it to be written, because there are so many application packages which have already been written and almost certainly could be easily modified to suit your purposes.

Finally you arrive at the main theme of this book. There are several very large suites of programs usually referred to as 'software packages', which have been designed to handle a broad class of applications. The word processor is designed for handling text, the spreadsheet for handling numeric data such as business accounts and the data–base for handling structured numeric or textual data. Many different commercial packages are available to perform these tasks, and the ones which we have chosen to present in detail, WordStar, SuperCalc3 and dBASE II, have become 'classics' of their type.

2 An introduction to word processing

Whether you are thinking about using a micro for business or leisure purposes, one of the first applications which comes to mind is to produce printed information i.e. to use it as a word processor.

You may wish just to produce business letters in a more presentable form, or more specifically a list of products or services which you offer and their prices; or you may wish to attract existing clients with news of special offers; you may wish to produce invoice letters, or orders to your supplier, or a letter enquiring about a product or service which has taken your interest. If your leisure activities involve your being the secretary of a sports club or parent teachers association you may need to produce an information sheet about the association's activities, or a list of the season's fixtures for the club's teams, or a weekly letter to team members with details of the arrangements for fixtures.

A word processor can be invaluable in helping you to produce accurate, clear and even attractively finished textual information. It can save you hours of routine and possibly frustrating typing. Its use gives you confidence that your labour is going to result in a well finished document, without sheaves of wasted paper along the way, and liberal daubings of correcting fluid. In addition, a clear, accurate document is more likely to be read, understood and acted upon than one which is badly produced.

Clarity and accuracy are important features, but its potential for saving you time and drudgery will emerge from this chapter, I hope, as the most significant advantage of the word processor.

If you are a competent typist already and have never used a word processor before, you may feel that you can do the job more quickly on your typewriter. Learning to use the word processor system will take a little time, and even a trained typist will take a little longer than usual to produce a document — initially! But many documents are very repetitious with standard sentences and paragraphs used over and over again, with only slight changes. If these passages are identified, and stored away on disk for future use, in a very short while the word processor can produce a finished document much more quickly than starting with a blank sheet of paper in a typewriter. The standard

standard passages can be called up from the disk, and used repeatedly, changed slightly to suit the current document.

2.1 The software package

In this book the term 'word processor' is used to mean a software package devoted to the task of processing textual information. The package may consist of a single program or a whole suite of 'modules'. In some early home micros the package was stored in a ROM which was inserted into the processor in addition to the BASIC and DOS ROMs and those for other facilities. The 16–bit range of machines which are currently available expect the package to be held on disk, and for the individual modules to be read into RAM as required: the RAM being now large enough to accommodate program and the textual data being input.

Strangely enough, with the new range of processors based on the 80386 and similar range of chips, it is likely that the whole word processing package could be read into its own section of RAM, and reside there all the time the machine is switched on even while the micro is being used for other purposes. There isn't all that much difference operationally between the old ROM–based package and the newer RAM–disk based systems.

So, the system which you are most likely to meet is a twin disk one where the suite of programs or modules are held together with the disk operating software on the 'program' disk in the A–drive of the micro, and the B–disk is the work disk which holds the data or text which results from your processing.

If you are completely new to word processing, as a general guide it may help if you look at word processing as two related but separate activities. When you are immersed in keying in new text, amending old text in some way, experimenting with its general layout, screen reading it looking for errors, you will be in what is usually referred to as 'edit' or 'infile' mode. Having got the text to your satisfaction, you may wish to print it out, or save it on disk, or take some text from another disk and add it on to your current text. You are now concerned with how the text as a single block of data relates to the rest of the system. So, the two states can be thought of as being 'in the file' and being 'outside the file', if we refer to the block of textual data as a 'file'.

Most word processing packages, even those for home micros now provide all of the editing or infile facilities, which you are likely to require to produce high–quality text with few tears. What distinguishes one system as being better than another is its outfile facilities — how easily the text as a whole may be handled by the system.

2.2 Getting started

With an IBM PC or compatible system all you have to do is switch the system on, load in the MS–DOS system and get to the A–prompt, and then enter the name of your word processing package, which as I have said may be on the same disk as MS–DOS or on a separate one. In chapter 3, I have assumed that the package you will be using is WordStar, and if at the A–prompt you continue 'A>WS' followed by striking the Enter key, you will be faced with the screen shown in Figure 2.1, and when you say you wish to open a document Figure 2.2, and then when you are actually in that document Figure 2.3 will appear.

```
          editing no file
                          O P E N I N G   M E N U
 ——Preliminary  Commands——     | —File  Commands—  | —System Commands—
L  Change logged disk drive    |                   |  R  Run a program
F  File directory    off (ON)  |  P  Print a file  |  X  EXIT to system
H  Set help level              |                   |
 ——Commands to open a file——   |  E  RENAME a file | —WordStar Options—
   D  Open a  document  file   |  O  COPY   a file |  M  Run MailMerge
   N  Open a non-document file |  Y  DELETE a file |  S  Run CorrectStar

directory of disk B:
 ANS           ANS.BAK       APP2          CH6           CH6.BAK       CH7
 CH7.BAK       DBO           GLOSS         PIT           PIT.BAK       SCLARG1.PRN
 SCLARG2.PRN   SCSMAL1.PRN   SCSMAL2.PRN




1INDENT 2SET LM 3SET RM 4RELMAR 5REFORM 6DEL 7BUNDLIN 9BLDFCE 10MORE
```

Fig. 2.1 First WordStar Menu

```
          editing no file

  Use this command to create a new document file,
  or to initiate alteration of an existing document file.

     A file name is 1-8 letters/digits, a period,
     and an optional 0-3 character type.
     File name may be preceded by disk drive letter A-D
     and colon, otherwise current logged disk is used.

  ^S=delete character   ^Y=delete entry   ^F=File directory
  ^D=restore character  ^R=Restore entry  ^U=cancel command

     NAME OF FILE TO EDIT?

 directory of disk B:
  ANS           ANS.BAK       APP2          CH6           CH6.BAK       CH7
  CH7.BAK       DBO           GLOSS         PIT           PIT.BAK       SCLARG1.PRN
  SCLARG2.PRN   SCSMAL1.PRN   SCSMAL2.PRN
```

Fig. 2.2 To open a Document from First Menu

```
        B:PIT    PAGE 1 LINE 1 COL 01                          INSERT ON
                                M A I N   M E N U
    —Cursor   Movement—      | -Delete- |   -Miscellaneous-    |  -Other Menu
^S char left ^D char right  |^G  char  | ^I Tab   ^B Reform   |  (from Main c
^A word left ^F word right  |DEL chr lf| ^V INSERT ON/OFF     |^J Help   ^K B
^E line  up   ^X line down  |^T word rt|^L Find/Replce again  |^Q Quick  ^P F
      —Scrolling—           |^Y  line  |RETURN End paragraph  |^O Onscreen
^Z line down ^W line up     |          | ^N Insert a RETURN   |
^C screen up ^R screen down |          | ^U Stop a command    |


PRACTICAL INFORMATION TECHNOLOGY


by


Clive Prigmore







1INDENT 2SET LM 3SET RM 4RELMAR 5REFORM 6DEL 78UNDLIN 9BLDFCE 10MORE
```

Fig. 2.3 Inside the Document B:PIT

You will get used to going through this sequence after using WordStar a few times. To symbolise the types of options presented to you, I assume that you will be presented with the simpler Menu shown as follows:

1 Edit mode
2 Load new text
3 Load text to cursor
4 Save whole text
5 Save marked text
6 Search and replace
7 Print text

Please enter your choice.

Fig. 2.4 Menu options

Option 1 invites you to enter the Edit mode, that is to enter and edit new text. The remaining options are concerned with operations which you may wish to perform on the text as a whole: to load in information which you have already saved, or to save text which you have entered, or to print it out –

operations which relate the text to the outfile mode, i.e. which involve links with the rest of the system.

2.3 Editing

The cursor, which is shown as a dash immediately after 'Please enter your choice', may be a dash or a small, and possibly flashing rectangle. It marks the point on the screen at which you can enter information. If in the above case you enter 1, followed by pressing the Enter key, then the screen will change and you will find yourself in the Edit mode, with some sort of invitation to enter text. You can usually get back to the menu mode again by pressing one of the special control keys on your machine, possibly the Escape key.

In the Edit mode the screen is not blank even at the start. A line either at the top or the bottom of the screen (called the status line) gives information about the state of the screen itself, and tells you about your position in the text in rows (lines down the screen) and columns (characters across the screen), how many characters or words you have used in your file so far, and other useful information. Often the status line is divided from the text by a ruler, i.e. a graduated line across the screen which helps you to plan the layout of your text, a more complicated form of which is shown in the WordStar screen in Figure 2.3

When you type at the keyboard the characters appear at the cursor point and the cursor moves automatically to the right. When the text reaches the right side of the screen it automatically 'wraps round' to the next line with a natural break at an appropriate point between words.

If you have arrowed keys on your keyboard then you can use them to move the cursor to any point within the text. The basic movement is up or down one line at a time, and left or right one character at a time. Other combinations of keys will allow you to move across the line one word at a time, or from the far left to the far right of a line, and to the top or bottom of the screen in one or two keystrokes.

If you move your cursor to a point in the text and start typing in the usual (Insert) mode, the new text will be entered at the cursor point which itself moves to the right as before, but now displacing the existing text to the right. Whether or not you are in Insert mode is indicated on the status line. If this mode is changed then when you come to insert into the middle of existing text, the new overwrites the old.

There are also usually two types of deletion: one in which the cursor moves to the left dragging the right–hand text with it, overwriting everything in its path; and another which deletes at the cursor point, swallowing up characters as they move in from the right, but leaving the cursor still. Most packages allow you to delete whole words or whole lines at a time, rather than character by character, and also mark whole areas of text for deletion.

You can move round the text, making insertions and deletions with ease, but some packages are more cumbersome to use than others, and if you are in business each keystroke takes time and costs money. So the better package is one in which functions can be carried out with as few keystrokes as possible. The end of a paragraph is marked by pressing the Return key, and the cursor moves to the beginning of the next line.

2.4 Layout

With a word processor it is easy to be specific about the layout of the text. Most systems allow you to specify the line and page length, and to set the left and right margins of the page, either for the whole text or parts of it. You can specify whether you want single or double spaces between lines, spaces at the top and bottom of each page, headings at the top of each page, and have the pages numbered automatically while you are at it.

Some of these features can be seen in Figures 2.5 and 2.6. Both letters were set with a line width of 50 characters. Both have the club secretary's address block indented by 35 characters across the page, and Figure 2.5 shows the extra 'disco' block inserted and indented by ten characters across the screen.

Most word processing packages allow you to indent whole paragraphs after entering a simple command. They also allow you to tabulate your work, that is to lay out columns of information in the form of a table. The machine has a TAB key, which, in Edit mode, is programmed to move the cursor across the screen in steps which you may specify. The TAB function used in conjunction with the screen ruler is of great help in getting a clear text layout.

The feature which you will probably find most striking is called justification. Most typed letters leave a ragged edge down the right–hand side, where the typist stops the last word of the line at the most suitable position; this effect is seen in Figure 2.5, in which the text is unjustified. In Figure 2.6 the most right–hand character of the last word of each line is lined up at the same, in this case 50th, position across the line, in the same way as you would see a page laid out in a book. This text display is said to be justified, and the lines are padded out with additional spaces to make the line the correct length. This padding out is particularly noticeable when the line length is short. It is usually left to personal preference as to whether you justify your text or not. Many systems also allow you to use hyphens to split words at the end of the line if you wish.

The key feature when it comes to printing out your text is that what you see on your screen is what you actually get on paper. This principle of WYSIWYG (what you see is what you get) was very important a few years ago when home computer systems were used for word processing, where the screen display had a width of 40 characters, but you wanted your printout to be in

CHARLESFIELD HOCKEY CLUB

13 Finbury Road
Charlesfield
KENT
(phone 34539)

6th Feb 1984

Mr J Peters
6 Vines Close
Bramley
Kent

Dear John,

You have been selected to play for the first team against Blackheath next Saturday 11th February. This is an away game with a bully off at 2.30 pm, so please meet at our club house at 1.15 pm at the latest, so that you can sort out the travel arrangements. Standard club kit will be provided.

If you are not able.to play please inform me or your team captain (John Jarrow) as soon as possible. Otherwise I hope you have a good game and the team wins.

****
Don't forget the disco on Saturday evening. If you haven't got tickets yet, you can get them from any committee member, or from your team captain on Saturday. Come along and have a good time, and at the same time swell the funds for the new club house.
****

Best wishes,

Tom Keegan
Club Secretary

Fig. 2.5 Unjustified text

60, 70 or 80 character widths. If you have to keep reviewing your text on the screen, and making trial print runs, achieving the final printout can be quite frustrating. Although most systems now have sufficiently wide screens, it can all too frequently still occur that there is not total one-to-one correspondence between screen and printer, which can lead to irritating anomalies. It is certainly worthwhile checking for such anomalies before a new, especially cheaper word processing system is purchased.

CHARLESFIELD HOCKEY CLUB

13 Finbury Road
Charlesfield
KENT
(phone 34539)

6th Feb 1984

Mr J Peters
6 Vines Close
Bramley
Kent

Dear John,

You have been selected to play for the first team against Blackheath next Saturday 11th February. This is an away game with a bully off at 2.30 pm, so please meet at our club house at 1.15 pm at the latest, so that you can sort out the travel arrangements. Standard club kit will be provided.

If you are npt able to play please inform me or your team captain (John Jarrow) as soon as possible. Otherwise I hope you have a good game and the team wins.

Best wishes,

Tom Keegan
Club Secretary

Fig. 2.6 Justified text

2.5 Printing

The actual appearance of the printed document will depend on your type of printer. The daisy wheel printer will give your text 'letter quality', as if it has been typed on a typewriter, whereas the dot matrix printer gives a more 'computer printout', appearance. With the improved performance of dot matrix printers the difference in quality has narrowed considerably in recent years.

Both types of printer will let you underline text and embolden it if you wish. This is done usually by leaving hidden 'markers' in the text while in edit mode. You insert the markers in the text, at the beginning of the part you want underlined or emboldened, and again after the last character. The markers are control codes which are passed to the printer when it reaches that part of the text, which activate the underlining or emboldening function at the first marker, the second marker switching it off. Emboldening means darkening the characters, in order to emphasize certain passages, and involves the printer making a double strike at the paper, usually fractionally displaced to one side of the first strike of the character, thus giving a darker appearance.

It is this preparation for printing which brings out some of the differences between word processing packages. In many word processing programs, the control characters actually appear in the text on screen. (If I had wished to embolden or underline the last sentence I would have enclosed it between markers in a similar way to these brackets and that is how it would have appeared on the screen). On a dedicated word processing system, however, the sentence may just change in intensity, appearing as a dim or extra bright passage in the middle of the text; the control characters are inserted but are not themselves visible on the screen. If this additional character effect is coupled with a WYSIWYG mismatch this combination of factors will make visualising the final layout of your text quite difficult. The extra control characters often confuse a layout which has tabulations or indentations. However, you do get used very quickly to the peculiarites of your own machine, but it is essential that you assess the importance of these considerations.

2.6 Saving time and drudgery

The features of word processing which we have looked at so far can save you a lot of time in drafting out and editing a textual document, and finally printing it in an attractive and accurate form. The great saving of effort, however, comes from moving blocks of text, both inside the file of text which you have saved on disk, and from other files of text on other disks. Often word processors are used as super typewriters even in commerce and industry, and the opportunity to save and reuse standard sentences and paragraphs is sometimes neglected. It is worth looking at the work you wish to do, right from the start, with the main objective of reusing wherever possible, the text that you enter into the machine.

2.7 When in edit mode

A simple example will show you the principles of how most packages let you move text around, inside the file on which you are working. If you as the club secretary, previewed the letter in Figure 2.5, and decided that you did not like the 'disco' paragraph inserted at the point shown, but preferred it at the foot of the letter after your signature block, to move the block of text you must first mark it out. This is done in a similar way to marking out passages to be emboldened or underlined: by putting a marker at the beginning of the block and one at the end. If you then move the cursor to the point immediately below 'Club Secretary' and press the Move key, or enter the control characters which activate the 'move' operation, the marked paragraph then moves to the position of the cursor. Most word processors also let you copy chunks of text from one point to another in a similar way, except that in this case the Copy key instead of the Move key would be pressed, after which you would have the same paragraph in two different places in your text. You can also use the marker method to delete areas of the text which you no longer want.

2.8 Standard passages

The larger the chunks of text which are reusable the more efficient the system is, but the hockey example will serve to convey the general message. It is unlikely that any hockey club would want to send out personalised letters to each member of their teams; if the club had eight teams playing in one week, this would entail the printer making about 100 individual printed copies. But it is conceivable that the secretary may wish to make one copy for each of his eight teams, photocopy or duplicate one for each player and reserve, having missed out the personal address and salutation ('Dear John') and substituted 'Dear Clubmate'. We will talk later about the task of producing the labels for the envelopes. Put yourself in the place of the club secretary again. You have realised that you use repeatedly a set of standard sentences or paragraphs, so you make a file of these, which you store on tape or disk. The master file from which others may be generated will hold phrases like those shown in Figure 2.7.

For each match, you load the file into your word processor and pick the phrases, sentences and paragraphs to suit. Critical facts will change for each fixture, and these are marked with **** in the standard phrases, as shown. To get a collective letter for all members of the first team, similar to that in Figure 2.6, you would have to pick the paragraphs numbered: 1, 2, 3, 4, 6, 7, 9 and 10. If you wished to add a reminder about subscriptions which are due, you would have to move paragraph 11 to either before or after paragraph 10, to suit your taste. Remember that you still have them stored away on backing store. You will then have to go through the letter inserting the dates, times, places name of the captain etc., to get it in final form. It takes a lot of explaining but is really quite straightforward, and even before you are totally familiar with the procedure, it is much quicker than typing the letter from scratch each time.

I have taken a simple example with very short phrases to save space in the book, but the method will save even more time when the paragraphs are

1 CHARLESFIELD HOCKEY CLUB
2 13 Finbury Road
Charlesfield
KENT

(phone 34539)

3 Dear Clubmate,

4 You have been selected to play for the **** team against **** on ****

5 This is an away game with bully off at ****, so please be at the club house by **** at the latest.

6 This is an away game with bully off at ****, so please be at our club house by **** at the latest, so that you can sort out the travel arrangements.

7 Standard club kit will be provided.

8 Club shirts only will be provided, so please bring the remainder of your kit.

9 If you are not able to play please inform me or your team captain (****) as soon as possible. Otherwise I hope you have a good game and the team wins.

10 Best wishes,

Tom Keegan
Club Secretary

11 I'll take this opportunity to remind you that the annual subscriptions are due on ****, the amount for this year is ****, please send your cheques to me as soon as possible.

12 The **** team is playing in the **** competition on **** at **** why not come along and support them, a few extra cheers will help them raise their game.

13 Just another reminder that the AGM will take place on ****, and that the club needs your support both on and off the field.

14 All committee members should note that the monthly meeting will take place at **** on **** at the club house, please make every effort to attend.

Fig. 2.7 The master file of standard paragraphs

longer. The details of how it is done will differ markedly from system to system. For maximum benefit, disk storage is required with whole documents, long standard paragraphs and key clauses stored in different files. Then to build up new documents these files may be read in as required. The advantages for the amateur can be significant, but imagine how much greater the savings could be for a solicitor or estate agent.

It is most likely that you would have more than just the one file; you would have a basic file similar to the one just described, from which you would have made other files: e.g. one for a home and one for an away game. You would probably keep a separate file of special paragraphs: for meeting reminders, subscriptions, social events and other general messages; and then feed these into the home and away letters as required. You would probably keep a correspondence file with names and address of the president and treasurer of the club, because as secretary you will have to produce letters on their behalf on occasions. The possibilities are endless, and if you plan your procedures carefully, the savings can be proportionate.

2.9 Search and replace

Searching through a data file is the main preoccupation of the data-base chapters. There are clear parallels between the interrogation methods used with data-base packages and the search faciliites which are provided with word processing packages. You could use data–base methods to create and manipulate a club membership and address file, or file of customers or suppliers. You could search through for a particular name, or for those people or companies living in a particular area of the country, or requiring or supplying certain goods or services — if the file had been structured carefully enough to yield up such information. You could also set up and manage a file of business appointments, or club events in data order, which could be searched through regularly.

The search facility is available in word processing packages of any real worth. To illustrate its use imagine that on proofreading Logic and Data–bases chapter, I found that the word 'interrogate' had been used too frequently, and wanted to change it to 'question' on some occasions. Having entered the 'Find' command, the package would then ask for the word or group of words that I wish to find. The system would pass through the text and stop at the first occurrence of the word, and give me the choice of changing it or leaving it alone. It would then pass on to the next occurrence of 'interrogate', and so on through the text.

Most packages provide an automatic search and replace facility. I could have spelt the word incorrectly as 'interogate' and wish to pass right through the whole chapter changing it each time it occurred. The search and replace function would let me do that. But having made the basic spelling mistake, it is very likely that I would have spelt 'interrogates', 'interrogated', 'interrogation' and such related words incorrectly as well. So the system should allow the ambiguous, joker or 'wild card' facility here as well as in data–base work. You should be able to enter 'interogat*' to find and replace all these related words. You should also expect the system to find 'Interogat*', so that it would pick up instances where the word had been used at the beginning of sentences.

2.10 MailMerge

MailMerge is a special application of this search and replace idea. A standard letter is shown in Figure 2.8; the data to go into this letter is held in the data file shown in Figure 2.9. By merging the two files, the particular details into the general letter, you can produce an individualised mail shot; hence the name, MailMerge.

```
&NAME&
&COMPANY&
&STREET&
&TOWN&
&COUNTY&&CODE&

Dear&NAME&

We wish to inform you that, owing to the high volume of business
which we have conducted with &COMPANY& during the first half of
this financial year, we are pleased to offer you a 10% discount
on all of our prices, for the last quarter of the year.

A current catalogue is enclosed, and we look forward to receiving
further orders from you in due course.

Yours sincerely,

Paul Owen
Sales Manager
```

Fig. 2.8 Text of the MailMerge letter

The details in each individualised letter change for each company which is addressed, so these are shown in the standard Mailmerge letter as 'variable' names: &COMPANY& and so on. To produce a letter, text is held in the machine in 'word processing' mode, and then the data file with the individualised items of address data are read into the text file. When this occurs the first item of data is stored with the variable name NAME, and the next item is stored with the variable name COMPANY, and the next with STREET, and so on. So, when these variable names occur in the printing of the letter they are replaced by their actual values: 'Mr C Aitken' for NAME, 'P Hammacks Ltd' for COMPANY, '29 Portland Drive' for STREET and so on for the first letter. Wherever the variable name occurs in the text of the letter, it is replaced by the particular data value for that letter. In this case COMPANY occurs in the text of the letter as well as in the address block, and would be replaced by 'P Hammacks Ltd', in both instances.

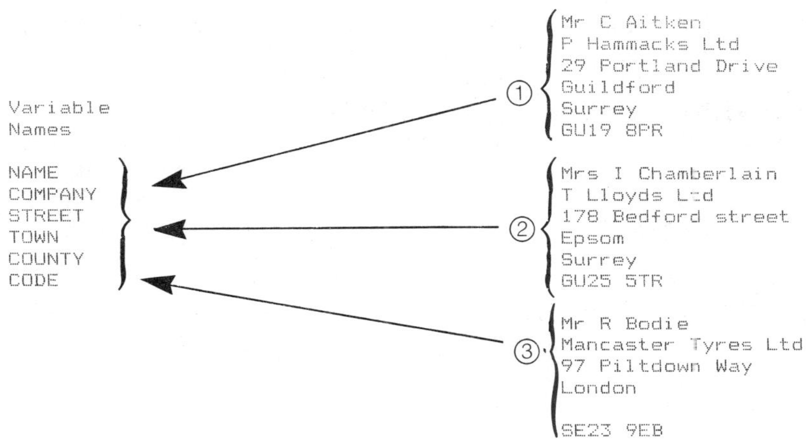

Fig. 2.9 Addressee data file

The variable names are enclosed by special symbols in the letter; in Figure 2.8 they are shown enclosed by the & character. During the production of the letter it is these symbols which indicate that the words NAME, COMPANY, TOWN etc., should be treated as variable names, and be replaced by actual data values.

As for the rest of the letter, we can assume that either it is to be printed on headed note paper, or that the heading is printed at the beginning of each letter. Similarly the date would have to be printed for each letter.

The data file of names and addresses would have to be carefully structured. We need to think of each customer as having one record, and that record having six fields and the order in which they are stored in the data file as critical factors. If an address does not require six items of data, then one of the fields must be a space. But you cannot just ignore it; you must enter the 'space' character by striking the space bar of the keyboard. Such an example is shown in the third record in Figure 2.9, where the London address does not require a value for COUNTY, so a space is shown in that field position. The address data field file can be created using a data–base file, where the variable names would be the field names; but most word processing packages let you create a data or non document file for this very purpose.

If you want it all to happen automatically, the printing process must be carefully controlled. We want such a letter to be printed on individual sheets of paper, and the printing to stop to allow us to put in a new sheet of paper for the next letter. Assuming that the paper is headed with the sender's company name, we don't want to start printing right at the top of the page — hence the instruction to insert ten blank lines at the fifth instruction in the 'program' in Figure 2.10. Furthermore, you do not want the pages to be numbered.

These instructions, which make a little program, are stored in the letter file, in such a form that they are recognised as instructions and not actual text. Here we have used the / symbol at the beginning of the line to indicate to the MailMerge package that the line is to be seen as an instruction, not a line of text. The first line of the set of instructions just forms a title for the procedure. The letter file would contain lines of instructions similar to those shown in Figure 2.10.

```
//Mail Merge Procedure
/Read six values from the data file
/Store these values in the variable names
  NAME, COMPANY, STREET, TOWN, COUNTY, and CODE
/Turn off the page numbering facility
/Start the printer
/Print 10 blank lines
/Print the letter text as in Figure 2.8
/Go to the top of next page
/Stop the printer
```

Fig 2.10 MailMerge instructions for printing individualised letters

When the printer stops you then put in a new sheet of paper, and press the correct key for the procedure to start again. If your business stationery was available in continuous perforated sheets, then the whole process could be allowed to run on its own, letter after letter. Also there are such things as automatic sheet feeders, which would let you automate the whole process, but they usually cost about half the amount of the printer itself, so before purchase you would have to be convinced that it was worth the investment. So the system still has to be minded to a certain extent by a human feeding in paper sheet by sheet, and then envelope by envelope. Envelopes can be printed straight from the 'data' or 'non document' file, by means of another procedure similar to that shown in Figure 2.10.

From the point of view of managing files on the system, the process is fairly straightforward. The address data file may not be your complete customer file; it may contain only those who have been good customers during the earlier part of the year, as the text of the letter would have you believe. So you may have to run a program through this file to pick out those companies. The customer file does not even have to be in alphabetical order, but it probably would be. The data is read from the file in strict sequential order, and so the whole process could work from a back–up file on tape, though this would slow down the process slightly. But the slowest part of the whole process is the printing, and relatively to that, reading from tape is fast, because the amount of information read into each letter is small.

2.11 Final words

I hope you have found this overview of word processing interesting and instructive, even if rather general and a bit bland. The following worksheets of WordStar exercises should firm up the details of the techniques. They do not include practise in MailMerge, but all the other techniques mentioned in this chapter including Search and Replace are covered.

3 Word processing with WordStar

3.1 Entering text

1 Switch on your equipment and load the system files to obtain a prompt e.g. **A**>.

2 Insert your **WordStar** disk in the **A** drive.

3 Key in **WS** and press the return key.

4 The WordStar program will now load: the screen will display the **Opening Menu.**

Before you begin – if you intend to save your work onto a floppy disk

5 Insert the **workdisk** into the right hand drive.

6 Key in **L** to change over to the drive in which your Workdisk is inserted.

7 In answer to the question which appears on the screen, key in **B**: followed by pressing **Return**.

You may now begin your work.

Opening a new document file

1 Press **D**.

2 In answer to the question which appears on the screen key in a **name** by which you will remember and recognize your document. You may use up to eight letters – avoid using spaces or full stops.

3 Press **Return** and prepare to key in text.

Keying in text

As soon as you have opened and named your document file, the menu at the top of your screen will change to the **Main Menu.**

Study the screen and note the following:

1 The **Status Line** at the top of the screen tells you where you are currently working.

2 Note particularly **Insert On** on the top right which means that any text keyed in between words or letters will squeeze in and move the rest of the text to the right.

3 The **Ruler Line** displays the state of the margins and tab stops.

4 The **Blank Page** — waiting for your text — with the **Cursor** also waiting at the first character space on the 1st line.

Task 1

Key in the following text.

Note: It is only necessary to press the **Return** key.

1 to create a blank line
2 to end a paragraph
3 to deliberately begin a new line.

WordStar will automatically arrange your text for you and fit it to your chosen line length. This is known as **Word Wrap**. If words will not fit on to a line, they are automatically wrapped round to begin the next.

Key in the following text:

> A word processor can be invaluable in helping you to produce accurate, clear and attractively printed text. It can save you hours of routine and possibly frustrating typing. You will feel confident that your efforts will result in a well finished document which is more likely to be read, understood and appreciated by the recipient. Learning to use a word processor system will take a little time, but the advantages will soon become clear to you. Anything which will save you both time and drudgery must be worth looking into!

Before moving on, study the text on the screen for a moment. Notice particularly the fact that both the left and right margins are straight, i.e. each line is exactly the same width as the one before; each line begins and ends at exactly the same spot. The correct term for this feature is **Justification**. We say that the lines are **Right Justified** (it is, of course, usual for them to be justified on the left, anyway).

Cursor movements

Task 2

Using the block of text which you have just keyed in at Task 1, the next step is to discover how quickly you can move the cursor around from one character to the next, one word to the next, from beginning to end of a line, from beginning to end of the whole document. If your keyboard has a block of keys on which four arrowheads are displayed, then this task is going to be easy. If not, then WordStar offers you an alternative method of cursor movement.

For users with special direction keys

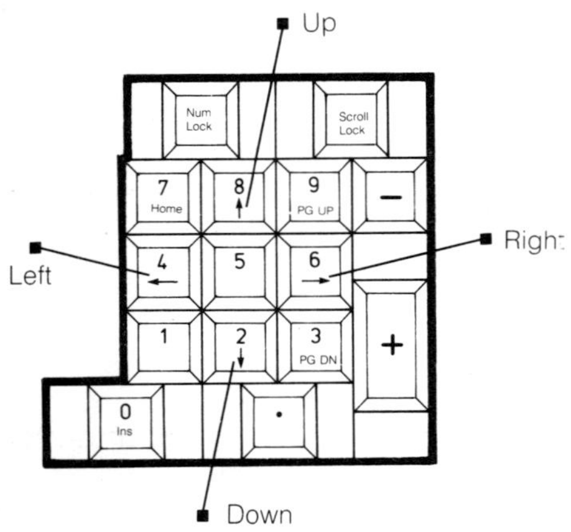

Fig. 3.1 Special Direction Keys

Try: (a) pressing each arrow key in turn to move the cursor in the direction indicated by the arrow
(b) pressing **Ctrl** + the key marked **Home** to move the cursor to the beginning of the line
(c) pressing **Ctrl** + the key marked **End** to move the cursor to the end of the line
(d) pressing **Ctrl** + → or ← to jump the cursor forward or back one word at a time
(e) pressing the **Home** key to move straight to the top of the text
(f) pressing the **End** key to move to the last line of the text

For keyboards without special cursor direction keys
To move the cursor, you must first locate the **Control** key (usually marked '**Ctrl**'). You must hold this key down whilst pressing one of the following

keys — to move the cursor in the direction indicated:

Ctrl/E	=	Cursor up	**Ctrl/A**	=	One word left
Ctrl/X	=	Cursor down	**Ctrl/F**	=	One word right
Ctrl/S	=	Cursor left	**Ctrl/QR**	=	Top of text
Ctrl/D	=	Cursor right	**Ctrl/QC**	=	End of text

Try each of the above cursor movement controls now, using the text from Task 1.

Control over the cursor is important because everything happens at the point where the cursor is currently located. If amendments have to be made to the text, the cursor *must first be positioned at the appropriate spot in the text* before any addition or deletion is made.

Continue now with Task 3 to master deletion and insertion

Deleting and inserting

Task 3

Control of the cursor is the first step when making alterations to your text. Whether you need to insert text which has been omitted or remove text which is no longer required, you begin by positioning the cursor at the spot where the alteration is to be made.

Deleting

The **Main menu** at the top of your screen is there to help you. If you study this for a while, you will see a section headed **Delete** where it tells you:

Ctrl/G	deletes a character (the one UNDER the cursor)
Del/key	**deletes a character to the left of the cursor**
Ctrl/T	deletes a whole word to the right of the cursor
Ctrl/Y	deletes one whole line (the one where the cursor is sitting)

Inserting

As mentioned before, WordStar works with **Insert On**. This means that if you have accidentally omitted some words, you can simply move to the point in the text and squeeze them in. The rest of the text will move to the right to accommodate the inserted words.

Make the following changes to your text

1. Delete at line 2 the word 'can' and replace it with the word 'will'
2. Delete at line 7 the words 'a little'
3. Insert at line 7 before the word 'advantages', the word 'main'
4. Add to the end of the text: 'At the same time, you will probably find that you enjoy using the word processor.'

A word processor can be invaluable in helping you to produce accurate, clear and attractively printed text. It will save you hours of routine and possibly frustrating typing. You will feel confident that your efforts will result in a well finished document which is more likely to be read, understood and appreciated by the recipient. Learning to use a word processor system will take time, but the main advantages will soon become clear to you. Anything which will save you both time and drudgery must be worth looking into! At the same time, you will probably find that you enjoy using the word processor.

Before we leave this particular task, it is essential that we save our work and find out how to print out a hard copy (i.e. a copy on paper). The next task tells you how to do this.

Saving documents

Task 4

When your text has been checked and finalised, it must first be saved onto disk before it can be printed:

1 Key in **Ctrl/K** — calls up the **Block menu**
2 Key in **D** — stores the document on disk

The opening menu will then reappear and your document disappears!

Printing documents

1 Key in **P** whilst at the opening menu — NAME OF FILE TO PRINT? appears.
2 Key in the **filename**. (i.e. the name you gave it at the start).
3 When the next prompt appears — just press the **Esc** key.
Your work will now be printed

Exiting from WordStar

Task 5

After saving or printing, the opening menu reappears.
To **exit** from WordStar: Key in the letter **X** . Either **A**> or **B**> will be displayed.
Remove disks and switch off

One final task follows in this section, which will give you practice in the steps which have been covered so far.

Consolidation

Task 6

1 Switch on and load WordStar.

2 Log on to the working disk.

3 Open a new document file and name it **Letter**.

4 Key in the following text. Use **Return** key **only** where indicated by >.

(Suitable date)>
>
The Principal>
Oakwood Evening Institute>
Oakwood Parade>
Southfields>
EN18 4RB>
>
Dear Sir>>
I have recently obtained a qualification which enables me to train
people to use microcomputers for information processing. I wish to
offer my services as a teacher in this area of work and would be pleased
to hear whether you have any vacancies for part-time staff at your
Evening Institute.>
>
Yours faithfully>>
>
Rebecca Jones>

5 At end of the text, check for errors and correct, if necessary.

6 Save your text on disk.

7 Print out one copy.

8 Exit from WordStar and close down.

3.2 Display features

One of the most impressive features of a word processing package is the way in which it allows the user to display text in a particularly attractive range of styles. If you do not like the look of your text when you have finished keying in, then you can change the layout — very quickly and easily. Clearly users will differ on what makes up an attractive display; this unit introduces some of the features from which to choose.

Task 1

Open a document (using the filename **Shoppers**) and key in the following text, exactly as displayed below:

THIS IS YOUR CHANCE TO

W I N

TWO LUXURY CARS IN THE

SHOPPERS PRIZE DRAW

BOTH of these top–of–the–range Fidel cars are yours if you win the free–to–enter Shoppers Prize Draw. All you have to do is return your Order Form, or make a telephone call, and your name will be included in the Prize Draw for both these luxury cars. You may enter the Prize Draw even if you do not wish to make a purchase from the Shoppers Catalogue.

Centring

1 **Save** your text on disk, using the filename **Shoppers**.

2 **Recall** the text to your screen for editing. This process is identical to opening a new document file, except that when asked for a filename, you do, of course, key in **Shoppers** whereupon the text stored under that filename will appear on your screen.

3 Our first improvement on the display will be to centre the first four lines of the text. The command for centring text appears under the **Onscreen Menu**.

(a) First move the cursor on to the line to be centred.
(b) Call up the **Onscreen Menu** by keying in **Ctrl/O**
(c) Key in the letter C to centre the line
(d) Note that the line or heading will be centred between the existing margins
(e) Repeat the process for the other three lines.

Boldface

4 The next step is to make the word 'W I N' stand out even more by getting the printer to print that particular word darker than the rest of the print. This is known as boldface and is achieved in a slightly different way to simple centring. The command is to be found under the **Print Menu** and the user must insert into the text, either side of the word or words to be affected, a pair of codes which make up a command to the printer. The effect is *not* seen on the screen, but will be carried out during printing.

(a) Move the cursor to the 'W' of the word 'W I N'.
(b) Key in **Ctrl/P** + **B**.
(c) Move the cursor to the space beyond the 'N' of the word 'W I N'.
(d) Key in **Ctrl/P** + **B** again.
The screen will show 'BW I NB'.

5 Repeat the above steps to boldface the word 'BOTH' at the beginning of the final paragraph.

6 SAVE the document again.

7 Print out one copy. Compare the result with the original display of the text (as shown on previous page) and decide for yourself which is the most attractive.

The amended version will look as follows.

THIS IS YOUR CHANCE TO

W I N

TWO LUXURY CARS IN THE

SHOPPERS PRIZE DRAW

BOTH of these top-of-the-range Fidel cars are yours if you win the free-to-enter Shoppers Prize Draw. All you have to do is return your Order Form, or make a telephone call, and your name will be included in the Prize Draw for both these luxury cars. You may enter the Prize Draw even if you do not wish to make a purchase from the Shoppers Catalogue.

Quick recap:

To centre	—	**Ctrl/OC**	
To boldface	—	**Ctrl/PB**	either side of text to be affected

In some cases, the need for a special display feature is more for emphasis than for visual appeal. Two ways in which this can be achieved are (a) by underscoring the word or words to be emphasized or (b) in cases where larger chunks of text are involved, by using different line spacing for that particular piece of text. The next task illustrates these features, using once again the document called **Shoppers**.

Task 2

1 **Recall** to your screen the document called **Shoppers**.
2 Take the cursor to the very end of the document (**Ctrl/QC**)
3 Add the following text as follows:

You have the chance to win two sensational Fidel cars — the sleek Madre XR4 and the versatile Solario. Both could be yours if you win the Shoppers

Prize Draw. Would you like to know more about them?

Fidel Madre XR4

The Madre is a sensational car. Its 4–wheel drive gives it astonishing stability, even in adverse conditions. It enables full use to be made of the powerful V6 engine.

Fidel Solario

The sleek and spacious Solario has won more awards than any other car in Fidel's history. Special features include cut–pile carpet, sun roof and superb audio system.

Remember to post your order promptly. Just fill in the details on the special order form. Anything you buy is covered by a full guarantee, so you can order in confidence.

4 Save your document and take one printout in its present form.

Underscore

Now for some more improvements! We will begin by underscoring one or two words which we wish to emphasize:

To underscore — (similar to boldface) i.e. a code each side of the word or text to be underscored

The code this time is **Ctrl/P** (study the menu) followed by **S**

5 Underscore the following words in this way:
   (a) the words 'two' and 'both' in the second paragraph
   (b) the two headings 'Fidel Madre XR4' and 'Fidel Solario'

Changing case

6 Next we will change the very last paragraph a little — just to make sure that it really stands out clearly.
7 With the cursor at the beginning of the final paragraph
   (a) we can change the whole paragraph to **Upper case** by pressing **Ctrl/Q** followed by **H** (changes one line at a time)
   (b) We will put it into double line spacing for emphasis: Press **Ctrl/O**, followed by **S**, followed by the figure **2**, then **Ctrl/B** to reform the paragraph.
8 Save the complete document and take a final printout. It should look like the following:

THIS IS YOUR CHANCE TO

W I N

TWO LUXURY CARS IN THE

SHOPPERS PRIZE DRAW

BOTH of these top-of-the-range Fidel cars are yours if you win the free-to-enter Shoppers Prize Draw. All you have to do is return your Order Form, or make a telephone call, and your name will be included in the Prize Draw for both these luxury cars. You may enter the Prize Draw even if you do not wish to make a purchase from the Shoppers Catalogue.

You have the chance to win two sensational Fidel cars – the sleek Madre XR4 and the versatile Solario. Both could be yours if you win the Shoppers Prize Draw. Would you like to know more about them?

Fidel Madre XR4

The Madre is a sensational car. Its 4–wheel drive gives it astonishing stability, even in adverse conditions. It enables full use to be made of the powerful V6 engine.

Fidel Solario

The sleek and spacious Solario has won more awards than any other car in Fidel's history. Special features include cut–pile carpet, sun roof and superb audio system.

REMEMBER TO POST YOUR ORDER PROMPTLY. JUST FILL IN THE

DETAILS ON THE SPECIAL ORDER FORM. ANYTHING YOU BUY IS

COVERED BY A FULL GUARANTEE, SO YOU CAN ORDER IN

CONFIDENCE.

Another way to give prominence to text is, of course, to indent it from each of the margins. This is covered in the next section. But first, try the following two tasks using the commands covered so far.

Consolidation

Tasks 3 and 4

Display the following two tasks, making full use of capitalisation, centring, emboldening, underscore and line spacing facilities.

1 A poster advertising the College Shop

WRITE ON

The College Shop

is the best place to buy — at amazing prices —

all kinds of stationery, secondhand course books, floppy disks, ring binders, pens, erasers, rulers — and numerous other items.

WRITE ON is your shop, run by students for your benefit. Please help by supporting it with your custom.

2 A note for all users of the College's network of microcomputers

USE OF COLLEGE NETWORK

All Users must first obtain a log–on I.D. and password from the Network Manager.

Please note: Users must maintain their own directory area. Files can only be retained for a specified period of time, after which they will be erased, unless a specific request is made.

The network is available for general use at the following times:

Mondays to Fridays — from 9.00 am until 6.00 pm.

Printouts must be collected from the Print Room within 24 hours.

3.3 Margins and tabulation

All the commands for this unit can be found on the **Onscreen Menu**, and to call this menu up onto the screen you need to key in **Ctrl/O**. Once the menu is visible you can select the command you require for setting margins, tabs etc. You will find these commands under the heading **Margins and Tabs** as follows:

L — Set left margin
R — Set right margin
X — Release margins

I — Set **N** Clear Tab
G Paragraph tab (Temporary margin)

Margins

The default margins of WordStar are Left 1 and Right 65, with tabs set every five character spaces. The ruler line automatically comes on with WordStar and if you hold the spacebar down and move across the screen you will see the column number on the status line changing. Also, as you type each line and start a new one, the line number changes on the status line.

Having called up the **Onscreen Menu** you select **L** for setting the left margin; the question **LEFT MARGIN COLUMN NUMBER (ESCAPE for cursor column)?** will appear on the screen. Key in the margin number to be set and press **Return**. To set the right margin you need to select **R** instead of L, then key in the column number required and press **Return**.

An alternative way of setting the margins is to position the cursor in the column at which the margin is required, then call up the **Onscreen Menu**, followed by keying in **L** or **R** and instead of keying in a column number you just press the **Escape** key.

Tabulation

Always clear any existing tabs first by keying in **Ctrl/O** followed by **N**. This question will appear on the screen: **CLEAR TAB AT COL (ESCAPE for cursor col; A for all)?** At this point you key in **A** followed by **Return**. If you had wanted to clear just one tab, you could key in the column number; or if your cursor was positioned in the column where the tab was set, you could press the **Escape** key.

Setting tab stops is very similar to setting margins; you call up the **Onscreen Menu** as before but you select **I** instead of L or R. With WordStar there is also the facility for setting decimal tab tops. This is done in the same way as setting ordinary tabs except that you need to key in a hash sign i.e. # before keying in the column number.

Setting Margins

Task 1

1 Open a document using a suitable file name e.g. Margins.

2 Set the left margin at 10 by calling up the **Onscreen Menu, (Ctrl/O)** selecting **L** then keying in 10 and press **Return**.

3 Set the right margin at 55 following the same instructions as for setting the left margin except selecting **R** instead of L.
Note: As an alternative you could position the cursor where you require your margins, call up the **Onscreen Menu** and select **L**, followed by pressing the **Esc** key for the left margin, and **R** followed by the **Esc** key for the right margin.

4 Key in the following text.

> The care of trees is in general not well understood, and poorly practised. The life of a tree falls into three periods: establishment, growth to maturity, and then senility. Intensive care is needed only in the first and shortest phase, and sometimes some fairly drastic work in the last phase. So if careful watch is kept for three years, the next two hundred years can be spent in just watching the tree grow.
>
> In that early period the roots have to take a hold in the new soil, spread out just below the surface for feeding, and penetrate deeper for stability. The leading shoot must get into its stride, approximately three feet a year, to spread its branches up the stem, and to establish the foundation of the future crown. A tree planted at the appropriate size, less than a metre tall, requires no stake at all. The stake is entirely to hold the roots steady to the ground until they have grown out into the surrounding soil. It is not intended to hold the stem up.
>
> Within a few years of planting we can have a tree with a good root system, standing free and sturdy, complete with the beginning of a shapely crown.

5 Save this document and take a printout.

Reforming text into new margins

Task 2

1 Recall the previous document used for Task 1.

2 Set new margins of 5 and 60. Now to reform the text into the new margins the cursor must be placed on the first letter of the first paragraph. With the cursor in position press **Ctrl/B** (you will find **B** on the main menu under the heading Miscellaneous). Watch what happens to the text. If you find that this does not work, and that the cursor is flashing near the end of the line, in the middle of a word, it means that the Hyphen Help facility is on. You have three choices as how to proceed:
- (a) You can turn **off** this facility by pressing **Ctrl/O**, followed by **H**, (Hyph-help) and then continue to reform the rest of the paragraph by pressing **Ctrl/B** again.
- (b) You can continue to use **Ctrl/B** every time the cursor flashes.
- (c) You can key in a **'-'** hyphen at a suitable position within the word that the cursor is flashing and then the reforming will continue.
  To reform the second paragraph the cursor will again have to be placed on the first letter of the paragraph before pressing **Ctrl/B**. The same applies for the third paragraph.

3 Save your document and take a printout. Compare it to your first print out.

Note: If you wanted to reform the whole document with one command you could use the command **Ctrl/QQB**, but check if the Hyphen Help facility is on. If it is, the reforming will pause at certain words asking for a hyphen. You may find it easier to switch the Hyphen Help facility **Off** before starting any document.

Indenting paragraphs

Task 3

For indenting paragraphs the same procedure is followed as for setting the margins. The paragraph is then reformed into the new margins by pressing **Ctrl/B**. As few, or as many paragraphs as you wish can be indented this way.

If you had intended to continue using this document, keying in more text, you would have to reset original margins for non–indented paragraphs.

1 Recall the document used for Task 2.

2 Reset the margins to 1 and 65 and reform the whole document. You can use **Ctrl/QQB**. Remember about Hyphen Help.

3 Position the cursor on the clear line space between paragraph one and two. Now indent the second paragraph only, by setting new margins of 4 and 61.

4 Reform the paragraph into the new margins, using **Ctrl/B**.

5 Save the document and take a printout.

Changing line spacing

Task 4

To change the line spacing from single to double: ensure that the cursor is positioned at the top of the screen and call up the **Onscreen Menu**. Select **S** (Set line spacing) and key in **2**, then press **Return**.

1 Recall the document used in Task 3.

2 Set the line spacing for double. Reform the text either using **Ctrl/QQB** or **Ctrl/B**.

3 Save the document and take a printout.

Setting tabs

Task 5

Before starting this task if you are continuing straight on from Task 4, you will have to reset the margins to 1 and 65, and put the line spacing back to 1.

1 Open a document with a suitable filename e.g. Tabs.

2 Clear all existing tabs. **Ctrl/O** followed by **N**, then in answer to the question on the screen key in **A** (for all) and **Return**.

3 Set tabs at 16, 29 and 41 as follows:
Call up the **Onscreen Menu**, key in **I**, followed by keying in the first tab number required i.e. **16**, then press **Return**. Repeat for other tabs.
To move from one tab to the next you can use the tab key ⇆ or press **Ctrl/I**.

4 Having set your tabs, key in the following table of examination dates.

EXAMINATION DATES

MONDAY	TUESDAY	WEDNESDAY
History	Biology	Maths
Computing	French	Chemistry
English	Physics	Geography
Cookery	Italian	Commerce

5 Clear all existing tab stops but do not delete the table.

Decimal tabs

Task 6

To set decimal tabs follow the same procedure as for setting ordinary tabs except that before you key in the column number you need to key in a hash sign i.e. #. This sign appears on your ruler line at the tab position.

1 First key in the heading of the table shown below. Set decimal tabs at 16, 30, and 42, then key in the following table. Watch now, as you key in the full stop, the decimal points are automatically lined up.

Decimal Tabs

1.53	2.1	3.65
10.03	9.87	12.4
12.5	20.70	21.63
101.9	123.11	135.89

2 Save the document and take a printout. Tasks 5 and 6 should be printed on the same page.

Setting a temporary left–hand margin

Task 7

To be able to use the facility of a temporary margin, first of all you need to set a tab stop. For this task we shall have a temporary margin of 15.

1 Open a document, clear all tabs and set just one at 15.

2 Key in the number at the left–hand margin (235). Now to use the temporary margin call up the **Onscreen Menu**, and then key in **G** (paragraph tab). Notice the change on your ruler line.

3 Type in the heading 'MINUTES OF PREVIOUS MEETING'. When you press **Return** to give you a clear line space, you will need to use **Ctrl/O**, followed by **G** again, before you can continue typing.

4 Continue to key in the text, but remember to use the temporary margin command, every time, after pressing Return.

235 MINUTES OF PREVIOUS MEETING

The Minutes of the Meeting held on Thursday last, in September, were approved by the Committee and signed by the Chairman.

236 HEATING IN ST GEORGE'S HALL

The Secretary reported that arrangements could be made with the caretaker for the time-switch for the heaters to operate at 10 pm instead of 9.30 pm provided that the Society agreed to meet the extra cost.

237 PROPOSED OUTING TO LONDON

The Secretary reported that there had been a good response to the proposed visit to the Mount Theatre and that tickets had been obtained. The coach would depart at 5.30 pm.

5 When you have completed the task, save your document and take a printout.

Consolidation tasks

Task 1

1 Open a document and key in the following text, with margins set at 5 and 60 and in single line spacing.

Vitamins are chemical substances present in minute quantities in plants and animals. Regular supplies of all the vitamins are essential for our proper growth and health. Only tiny amounts are needed: in fact, in the cases of vitamins A and D, too much can be harmful.

Each vitamin performs specific functions but many of these functions overlap, and several of the vitamins interact beneficially with each other and with other substances in our diet.

2 Indent the first paragraph by 5 on each margin.

3 Change the second paragraph to double line spacing.

4 Save the document and take a printout.

Task 2

1 Open a document and set an ordinary tab stop at 12 and a decimal tab stop at 42 then key in the following:

Scottish	041.2215785
Northern Ireland branch	023.8632670
North of England branch	061.9734957
South-Western branch	040.4812683
Eastern branch	037.4551514

2 Save the document and take a printout.

3.4 Block commands

Marking out a block of text

For moving, copying or deleting text with WordStar, the text needs to be marked out (highlighted) first. As you will have realised by now, WordStar has several different menus, and on the **Block Menu** you will find the necessary commands for marking out text under the heading **Block operations**, as follows:

B	Begin	To mark the beginning of the block
K	End	To mark the end of the block
H	Hide/Display	To remove the highlight or restore the highlight
C	Copy	To copy the block of text
Y	Delete	To delete the block of text
V	Move	To move the block of text

W	Write	To write the block of text to another file (e.g. a paragraph which you may want to use again in a different document)
N	Column on (**Off**)	Needs to be **On** for moving columns

All these above commands need to be preceded by **Ctrl/K**, which takes you to the block menu and then you can select the command you require.

Note: These commands must be used in the correct sequence, i.e. **B**, to mark the beginning of the block, followed by **K**, to mark the end of the block and then selecting one of the commands for copying, deleting etc.

Moving and copying text

When moving or copying text it will be necessary to place the cursor at the new position for the marked block before selecting the Move or Copy command. When you have finished moving a piece of blocked text, for example, you will need to hide the markers, i.e. remove the highlighting.

Using block commands for moving text

Task 1

Open a document and key in the following text:

<u>USE AND CARE OF DISKS</u>

1 Never touch the magnetic media directly.
2 No food or drink should be consumed when handling disks as contamination of the disk can corrupt the data.
3 Avoid dusting near disks, as dust particles may corrupt the reading or writing of data, to and from the disk.
4 Always have a back-up copy of your work on another disk.
5 Store disks away after use in their storage box.
6 Do not expose disks to any magnetic fields.
7 Magnetic disks should not be exposed to direct sunlight or extreme temperatures.
8 When labelling disks it is adivsable to write on the label before placing it on the disk. If you have to write on the label afterwards always use a felt tip pen.

1 Move paragraph 7 up to between 2 and 3 by placing your cursor on the number 7 and then calling up the Block Menu **Ctrl/K**. Mark out the beginning of the block, by keying in **B**. Now take your cursor to the end of the paragraph onto the clear line space (above paragraph 8) and mark out the end of the block **Ctrl/K** to call up the Block Menu, followed by **K**. The paragraph should now be highlighted.

2 To move the paragraph between paragraph 2 and 3 take the cursor to the new position and use the command **Ctrl/K**, followed by **V** for moving the marked block.

3 For making the next alteration you just need to place the cursor at the beginning of the next paragraph to be moved and start the sequence of commands again.

4 Now make paragraph 5 into paragraph 7, following the correct sequence. Notice that the new highlighting automatically removes the previous highlighting.

5 As you will not be making any more amendments you will need to remove the highlight (hide the markers), **Crtrl/K** followed by **H**. Remember to renumber the paragraphs and delete any extra clear line spaces.

6 Save your work to disk and take a printout. Then delete the file.

Using block commands to copy

Task 2

Open a document and key in the following letter.

Jones Furniture Co
Main Street
BRADFORD
Yorkshire
BD1 8HN

Ref RDH/CB

25 October 1987

N K Taylor PLC
28 High Street
BURTON-ON-TRENT
Staffordshire

Dear Sirs

Our representative, Mr P Morgan, will be in your district next week, and will take the opportunity of calling to see you on Wednesday at 10 am.

If this date is not suitable, please let me know when it will be convenient for you to see Mr Morgan.

Yours faithfully

1 Following the instructions for marking out text, mark out the whole letter (**Ctrl/K**, followed by **B**, then **K**).

2 Now with your cursor positioned at the end of the letter, press the **Return** key three times. **Note** This is just to give you a couple of clear line spaces between the letters.

3 With your cursor positioned at the left margin use the command to copy marked text and make a second copy of the letter (**Ctrl/K**, followed by **C**).

4 At this point it would be useful to change the name and address of the addressee. Turning the **Inset on** facility **off** by pressing **Ctrl/V** move the cursor to the first line of the addressee and overtype with a new name and address as follows: T F Finch PLC, 75 Crook Road, BROMLEY, Kent BR1 8TT .

5 Save the document and take a printout.

This facility could be useful if it was necessary to send a few people the same letter, or if you needed a duplicate copy of a particular document.

Using block commands to delete, write and move columns

Task 3

It is often useful to save a particular paragraph for use in a future letter. By marking out text using block commands it is possible to write it to another file under a different filename. You can **Write** text to another file as follows:

1 **Recall** the letter used for the previous task. Mark out the second paragraph in the letter using instructions from Task 2.

2 Call up the **Block Menu** and select the command **W** for write. The question **NAME OF FILE TO WRITE MARKED TEXT ON?** will appear on your screen.

3 Key in a suitable filename, e.g. Para 1 (for paragraph 1). Remember no more than eight characters.

At this point leave the highlight on as you can now delete this paragraph as follows:

To **delete** a paragraph you need to call up the **Block Menu** and use the command **Y** to delete. The paragraph will no longer appear on your screen.

To prove that we actually did save this paragraph to another file, we need to **read** the document 'Para 1' and call it up onto the screen as follows:

1 Position the cursor at the left margin, one clear line space below the first paragraph.

2 Press **Ctrl/K** followed by **R** and **NAME OF FILE TO READ?** will appear on the screen. Key in Para 1 and press **Return**. The paragraph which we saved and then deleted should now be back on the screen.

Lastly in block commands you can move columns of text. Still using your letter we shall move the address of Jones Furniture to the left margin for a fully blocked style letter. A column can be moved as follows:

(a) Call up the **Block Menu** and select **N** to put the **Column Mode** on.

(b) Position your cursor on the "**J**" of Jones and mark out the beginning of the address.

(c) Take your cursor to the very end of the address and, pressing the space bar, move the cursor across to the right margin. Now mark out the end of the text. The whole column containing the address will now be highlighted.

(d) Take your cursor to the left margin where the address is required and select the command for moving text.

(e) Remove the highlight. If you require a printout save the document first. If not, you can abandon the document using **Ctrl/K** followed by **Q**. You will be asked to confirm that you wish to abandon your document. Also remember to turn off the Column Mode, **Ctrl/K** followed by **N**.

Consolidation

Task 4

1 Open a document and key in the following text on Health & Safety.

2 Amend the order of the list:
Make point 3 the first point on the list
Make point 2 the last point on the list
Put point 1 below point 4
Renumber the points on the list.

3 Make a second copy of the whole list immediately below the original list, but leaving two clear line spaces between the two.

4 Write point 5 to a new file for use on a different Health & Safety document.

5 Delete the column of numbers.

6 Save the document to disk and take a printout.

Health & Safety Points For Using A Computer

1 The screen should be at approximate right angles to line of sight.

2 All wires must be kept out of the way.

3 The operator must have regular breaks from the screen to avoid headaches and dizziness.

4 The operator requires a comfortable swivel chair with adjustable backrest and adjustable height.

5 The colour of the print on the screen should be pleasant to the eye and the brightness variable.

Health & Safety Points For Using A Computer

The operator must have regular breaks from the screen to avoid headaches and dizziness.

The operator requires a comfortable swivel chair with adjustable backrest and adjustable height.

The screen should be at approximate right angles to line of sight.

The colour of the print on the screen should be pleasant to the eye and the brightness variable.

All wires must be kept out of the way.

3.5 Search and replace

The two commands for Quick Find and Quick Amend can be found on the **Quick Menu, Ctrl/Q**, under the Miscellaneous Heading.

F	Find text in file
A	Find & Replace

When using either of these commands, before you call up the Quick Menu, you *must* ensure that the cursor is positioned at the top of the text. The only time this does not apply, is when you select the option to search backwards through the text. Obviously, in this case the cursor would need to be positioned at the bottom of the text. Once you have selected the Find Command, **FIND**? appears on the screen.

At this point, you need to key in the string of characters or words you wish to find and press **Return**. **OPTIONS? (? FOR INFO)** will now appear.

Now you key in a **?** (question mark) and press **Return**, and a small **Options Menu** will come up as follows:

Normally press RETURN only, or enter one or more of:
number=repeat count, B=Search Backwards, W=whole Words only,
U=ignore case, N=replace w/o asking, G=replace in entire file

number	repeat count	having decided on the string you want to find, you can select a single occurrence of that particular string in the text, i.e. the second, third, occurrence etc. To do this you key in e.g. **2**
B	Search backwards	You can select **B** if you wish to search backwards through the text
W	whole words only	As it says, if you select **W** WordStar will only look for the whole word. An example would be 'the' but not 'there'.
U	ignore case	If you select **U**, WordStar will search for, e.g. 'the' or 'THE', i.e. upper or lower case.
N	replace w/o asking	Selecting **N** will instruct WordStar to replace your string without asking you to confirm each time. (only applicable with Quick Amend)
G	replace in entire file	Selecting **G** will instruct WordStar to replace your selected string with a new string throughout the document. Again only applicable with Quick Amend.

You can make more than one selection from the Options Menu, and once you have made your selection, you press **Return**. This will take you back to your document, and the first occurrence (unless you have selected otherwise), of the particular string you have asked WordStar to find, or amend.

To move on to the next occurrence of your string, you use the command **Ctrl/L**, and so on, through the text.

To get familiar with Search and Replace, you can try out the different facilities with just one short document, making several different choices as you will see in the following tasks.

Task 1

1 Open a document and key in the following text.

B A R G A I N S G A L O R E

at your local SUPERSTORE

Video Recorders starting at	–	£
Black and White Televisions starting at	–	£
Colour Televisions starting at	–	£
Microwave Ovens starting at	–	£

2 With your cursor positioned at the top of the text, call up the Quick Menu **Ctrl/Q**, followed by **F** (Find).

3 When **FIND?** appears on the screen, key in the **£** sign and press **Return**. We are looking for the pound sign to fill in some amounts.

4 We do not require the Options Menu for this task so you can press **Return** again, at the question **OPTIONS?** .

5 The cursor will now be flashing at the first occurrence of the £ sign. Key in 186.00 as this is the starting price of video recorders.

6 To move on to the next £ sign, use **Ctrl/L**. Key in the following amounts using **Ctrl/L** to move to on each time:

Black & White TVs	49.00
Colour TVs	195.00
Microwaves	99.00

7 When **NOT FOUND** appears, press **Escape** key to end the search.

8 Save your document and take a printout.

Task 2

1 Recall the document used in Task 1.

2 You are going to look for the third occurrence of the £ sign, as you were given the wrong price for colour televisions. The price should read £192.00.

3 Call up the Quick Menu, and select the Find Command. Key in £, followed by **Return**, but this time ask for the Options Menu by keying a **?** (for the third occurrence of the £ sign), followed by **Return**.

4 Now key in **3** (for the third occurrence of the £ sign), followed by **Return**.

5 You should now have returned to the text and the cursor should be positioned where requested, i.e. at the third occurrence of the £ sign. Turning the **Insert off (Ctrl/V)** overtype 195.00 with 192.00.

6 *Do not* save your document at this point as you can go straight into Task 3.

Task 3

1 Add the following paragraph to your document.

> No other store has such reasonable prices for all their electrical goods, not just Black and White televisions and Colour televisions but all electrical appliances for the home.

2 Place your cursor at the top of the text. This time you are going to find the word 'Televisions'. Press **Ctrl/Q**, followed by **F**, then key in **Televisions** and press **Return**.

3 Key in a **?** for the Options Menu. Now key in **U** (ignore case) and press **Return**. The cursor should now be positioned at the first occurrence of the word 'Televisions'. The word 'televisions' in the additional paragraph should have an initial capital, so using Quick Find we can search through pressing **Ctrl/L**, until the word to be changed is reached.

4 When you reach the first occurrence of 'televisions', in the paragraph, the cursor will be positioned at the end of the word. You will, therefore, have to move the cursor backwards to the correct position ready to amend it to 'Televisions', so that the document is consistent throughout. Move on through the document making the necessary amendments.

5 When **NOT FOUND** appears on the screen press the **Escape** key.

6 Save your document and take a printout but recall the document ready for the next task.

Task 4

For this task you are going to prove that WordStar will only look for the whole word when requested to.

1 Place the cursor at the top of the text. Select the **Quick Find** command. Key in **store** followed by **Return**.

2 Key in **?** for the Options Menu. Now key in **U** and **W** (ignore case and whole word). Press **Return**.

3 The cursor will be positioned on the word 'store' in the additional paragraph, having totally ignored 'SUPERSTORE' in the heading.

We can double check this, and at the same time introduce searching backwards through text.

4 Move the cursor to the bottom of the text. Repeat Point 1.

5 Call up the **Options Menu** and key in **U** and **B** (ignore case and search backwards).

6 The cursor will again be positioned on the word 'store' in the additional paragraph, but if you press **Ctrl/L** to continue the search you will find that this time, it will stop at the word 'SUPERSTORE'.

7 When finished press the **Escape key**. Leaving the document still on the screen we can continue with Task 5.

Task 5

So far you have only used the Quick Find command. You will find the Quick Amend command as useful, if not more useful than the Quick Find.

There are two additional choices on the Options Menu which apply to the Quick Amend Command; **N** — replace without asking and **G** — replace in entire file.

In this task you are going to change the words 'starting at' to 'as low as'.

1 With the cursor positioned at the top of the text, call up the **Quick Menu** and select **A** for Amend.

2 When **FIND?** appears on the screen, key in 'starting at' followed by **Return**.

3 When **REPLACE WITH?** appears on the screen, key in 'as low as' followed by **Return**.

4 You don't require the Options Menu this time, so press **Return**.

5 The cursor will be positioned at the first occurrence of the words 'starting at', also at the top right hand side of the screen the question **REPLACE (Y/N):** will appear. As you want to replace this string, key in **Y**.

6 As before to move on through the document use **Ctrl/L**. Key in **Y** to each occurrence of 'starting at' until **NOT FOUND** appears on the screen, and as usual press the Escape key.

7 Save the document and take a printout but again recall the document to the screen for the final task.

Task 6

For Task 5 you manually replaced each occurrence of the string 'starting at'. For this task you are going to replace the words 'as low as' to 'from', but you can instruct WordStar to do this automatically for you.

1 Place the cursor at the top of the text. Select the **Quick Amend command**.

2 Following previous instructions instruct WordStar to find 'as low as' and replace it with 'from'.

Call up the **Options Menu** as before, and select **G** and **M** (replace w/o asking and replace in entire file). Then press **Return**.

4 Every occurrence of 'as low as' should now have been replaced automatically with 'from'.

5 Save the document and take a printout.

B A R G A I N S   G A L O R E

at your local <u>SUPERSTORE</u>

Video Recorders from	–	£186.00
Black and White Televisions from	–	£49.00
Colour Televisions from	–	£192.00
Microwave Ovens from	–	£99.00

No other store has such reasonable prices for all their electrical goods, not just Black and White Televisions and Colour Televisions but all electrical appliances for the home.

You have only used a small piece of text to try out some of the facilities available in the Quick Find and Quick Amend Commands, but as you can imagine, if you need to find or amend a string of characters or words, in a very long piece of text, these facilities will save a lot of extra work.

3.6 Dot commands and final summary

The functions covered in the preceding five sections cover the most used aspects of word processing and once you have mastered those functions, you will be able to expand your grasp of the program by consulting a WordStar manual. Other word processing packages would also offer those features and it should prove a relatively straightforward task to find out how a comparable program carried out identical functions.

However, the extent of the program has certainly not yet been illustrated and there are many very useful aspects which well deserve investigation by the serious user. Unfortunately, there is space to introduce only one more feature, but it is one which will open up many new avenues. The following exercise is used to demonstrate how WordStar makes use of what are called Dot Commands.

Dot Commands allow the user to control various aspects of the final printed display, e.g. where to end a page, whether to number the pages or not, whether to include a footer or a header, if a different page length is required, etc. There are several such commands, but we will introduce just four of them. The same procedure is followed for all dot commands, although note should be taken of the points set out below:

1 Dot Commands always begin with a full stop (or point).

2 They *must* be positioned at the left margin, i.e. in the *first* character space on the line.

3 The letters may be in upper or lower case — some are followed by a number, e.g. MT12 = top margin of 12 line spaces.

4 They *must* be on a line on their own — i.e., always follow with a **Return**.

5 All Dot Commands will show on the screen — but are *not* printed out with the text.

6 Once keyed in, Dot commands operate on all text which follows

Task 1

The dot commands used in this task are as follows:

.MT	(followed by a number) sets the depth of the top margin for every page in the document — and *must be* at the very *top* of the file (i.e. line 1, character 1)
.OP	omits page number (otherwise WordStar *always* numbers the page)
.PA	starts a new page
.PN	(followed by a number) inserts page number

Open a document, using the filename **Outward** and key in the following text.

1 A top margin of 2 inches is required, i.e. 12 lines.

2 The first page is *not* to be numbered.

3 The second page *must* begin at the fourth paragraph (i.e. We returned to base . . . .

4 A page number *is* required on page 2.

To help with this first task, the position and display of the dot commands have been indicated on the text. Print out the two pages.

.MT12
.OP

ADVENTURE IN THE LAKE DISTRICT

I arrived at the Outward Bound Centre with some trepidation, wondering just what I had let myself in for. There were 12 trainees from all over the country on the course. After being shown our dormitories, we gathered for a cup of coffee and an introductory chat. It was comforting to realise that the other trainees were as green as I was, about most of the proposed activities. We were each issued with a variety of kit, with strict instructions on how to care for these items. I was impressed with the expensive equipment which they were handing out, whilst at the same time feeling slightly anxious about how we were meant to use some of them. There were all kinds of gear — for walking, climbing, canoeing and orienteering.

Monday afternoon was devoted to map reading and orienteering. There was an element of competition attached to these activities, making it a kind of race. I did not actually manage to win, but I wasn't last either. I thoroughly enjoyed this and was ready for the substantial meal when we got back. We had a rota for the washing up throughout the week and I was one of the first on the list! Somehow it did not seem an onerous task when there was so much to chat about to the other people on the course while we were busy 'doing the dishes'. In the evening, we had a film and a lecture on abseiling and prepared our gear, ready to try this out the very next day.

Breakfast was at 8 o'clock and by 9 o'clock on the Tuesday morning we were in the minibus on our way to the rocks. I must admit that for me this was the most frightening part of the week as I found it very difficult to launch myself over the edge on a rope, even though we had an excellent instructor who made it look very easy and assured us of our safety. I did feel a certain sense of achievement by the end of the morning but cannot say that I really enjoyed it. After a picnic lunch, we did an almost complete reverse turn, in that we climbed up the rocks rather than doing a Tarzan act over the edge! I preferred it this way, although one trainee who had been very successful at the abseiling could not bring himself to climb upwards!

.PA
.PN2

We returned to base thoroughly exhausted but feeling quite exhilarated by the activities of the day. Tuesday evening was a free evening with snooker, table tennis, darts etc. — available if we had enough energy left.

Wednesday dawned bright and sunny — a perfect day for canoeing. We spent most of the day on the lake and I enjoyed this best of all. We were taught how to roll the canoe so that we could recover from a capsize. Once we were all reasonably proficient in the calmer water, we were allowed out across the lake, all wearing the necessary lifejackets, of course. On Wednesday evening, we were shown a film by the Forestry Commission on the wild life to be found in the area and had a light-hearted quiz, at which, to my surprise, I quite excelled.

On Thursday, we were taken into the forest by two Forest Rangers who showed us how to identify where various animals had been and where they lived. We met up with our instructors in a clearing where instead of the expected picnic lunch, we were given raw sausages, tins of beans, pans and a box of matches. The instructors watched very carefully while we prepared and lit a fire and cooked our own meal. After this sumptuous feast, we had to check that the fire was put out and no litter left behind. We then divided into three groups. Each group was provided with a map and instructed to find our way back to base. My experience with car navigation and rallying stood me in good stead, and the group I was in was the first to arrive back, when we were provided with a very welcome cup of coffee and a bar of chocolate.

On Friday, we had a morning of discussions and group meetings, after which we sadly gathered our belongings together ready to depart. Everyone agreed that it had been a really great experience and not one of us wanted to leave. However, there is always another year and at least next time I will know a little about all these activities before I begin.

Study your final printout of the above task. You could try experimenting with variations on the layout, using the dot commands mentioned — or even look up in a WordStar manual, the other Dot Commands available to you.

Consolidation tasks

The remaining tasks in this chapter take the form of additional exercises which incorporate the features covered in this section of the book and can therefore be used to consolidate the WordStar commands and special features which have been introduced.

Exercise 1

The following text to be keyed in incorporates various facilities which you have learned to use during the previous sections.

You should be able to choose all the appropriate commands, but if you have any trouble you can always refer to the **Menus**, especially the **Help Menu**.

Points to notice:

1 The word 'Memorandum' is in boldface and spaced capitals.
2 The heading is underlined and centred.
3 Margins for the first paragraph are 5 and 65.

4 Tab stops have been set at 10 and 24.
5 The last paragraph has been indented by 5 each side and is in double line spacing.

M E M O R A N D U M

TO: All Switchboard Operators REF: KLS/

FROM: The Manager DATE:

THE NEW ROTA FOR MANNING THE SWITCHBOARD

AT LUNCHTIME

We have taken on more staff in the last two weeks, so it has been decided to operate a new rota for manning the switchboard at lunchtimes. Instead of operating the rota on a daily basis, it will now be as follows.

Week 1	Angela Taylor and Mary Walker
Week 2	Maureen Smith and Graham Jones
Week 3	Peter Lowe and Maria White

As you can see this is a three week cycle and is to be repeated accordingly.

Ensure you are aware of your duties and let me know if any problems should arise.

Exercise 2

1 The following text is to be keyed in as seen.

2 When finished the word 'copys' is to be amended to copies.

3 The third paragraph is to be moved up between paragraph 1 and 2.

4 The last paragraph is then to be deleted.

5 Finally make one copy of the whole text.

A copy of how the exercise should look when finished follows the text to be keyed in.

MANIFOLDING

When carbon copys are sent to persons other than the addressee, it is common practice to type at the foot of the letter, memo or report 'cc' (copy circulated to) followed by the names, in alphabetical order, of all the recipients, each starting on a new line at the same point of the scale. This information usually appears on all copys so that everyone concerned is aware of the distribution. The name for whom each copy is intended is either ticked at the side or the person's name is underscored: this practice helps to ensure correct distribution.

Many companies now consider the taking of carbon copys to be inefficient and simply photocopy the original as and when necessary. This saves the typist time in carrying out the messy procedure when corrections have to be made on many copys. If correct materials are used to correct top copys before photocopying each copy made looks perfect!

When sending a letter, for instance, the writer may NOT want the addressee to know that copys have been distributed to other persons. In this situation, the typist will remove the top copy and first carbon and reinsert the internal copys into the machine. At the foot of these copys the typist then types the names as indicated in paragraph one, removes any remaining carbons between copys and ticks the individual names for distribution within the company.

MANIFOLDING

When carbon copies are sent to persons other than the addressee, it is common practice to type at the foot of the letter, memo or 'cc' (copy circulated to) followed by the names, in alphabetical order, of all the recipients, each starting on a new line at the same point of the scale. This information usually appears on all copies so that everyone concerned is aware of the distribution. The name of the person for whom each copy is intended is either ticked at the side or the person's name is underscored: this practice helps to ensure correct distribution.

When sending a letter, for instance, the writer may NOT want the addressee to know that copies have been distributed to other persons. In this situation, the typist will remove the top copy and first carbon and reinsert the internal copies into the machine. At the foot of these copies the typist then types the names as indicated in paragraph one, removes any remaining carbons between copies and ticks the individual names for distribution within the company.

Exercise 3

1 **The following text is to be keyed in as seen and saved to disk.**

M25 VERGE ECOLOGY PROJECT

A proposal was mounted for an Ecology Project involving students at the College, principally those taking 'A' Level Biology and/or Geography, which would incorporate a detailed survey of the flora and other vegetation currently growing on the verges of the local stretches of the M25 Motorway. The main aim would be to collect data at comparable intervals over a period of three years in order to monitor the effects of increasing traffic. A subsidiary aim was the introduction of microprocessor–based storage facilities for the recording, analysis and presentation of the data.

The academic year had pressed on relentlessly, leaving little time for new Project work; the Biologists pointed out that the summer was approaching and the most suitable time for launching the Project and collecting the first sample data was when the grasses, etc. were in full bloom. Certain members of staff were approached in an attempt to build a Project Team which contained all the necessary expertise — enthusiasm was high; time was short — or almost non–existent!

Barbara, Steve and Marion went on a tour of the local stretches of the M25 to look for a suitable location. Barbara had already thought of a possible spot close to the M25/M20 Swanley roundabout, and after a tour of inspection, it was agreed that it was a possible site because it offered a test area and a nearby control site on the common land known as Broom Hill.

Meanwhile, numerous telephone calls were made to the Department of Transport, the local Regional Horticulturalist, the Swanley Police, etc. until full information was obtained concerning the formal permission to trample on the verges. The response to our enquiries was very encouraging. Everyone we contacted showed considerable interest in the Project. The Regional Horticulturalist was particularly keen and suggested further possible sites and requested that a copy of the Project Report should be sent to him at regular intervals. We were instructed that fluorescent safety jackets would have to be worn by each member of the fieldwork team.

Steve and Barbara spent some time outlining the Project to their 'A' level students and, once again, encountered considerable enthusiasm. A kind of rota had to be established in order to involve all students who showed interest in the Project, and a team of six students was selected for the initial sampling work.

Last week of term — but, incredible though it seemed at the time, a date was found to set off for Junction 3 on the M25 to begin collecting the first set of data. It was like a summer outing — the sun shone down, everyone piled into the minibus which Steve had hired for the day and off they went, with poles, sextants and yellow fluorescent jackets in evidence!

Meanwhile, in order to be prepared to recommence activities in the Autumn, an order was placed for one of the latest AX1Z microcomputers. This was to be used as a station on the existing College network and was to be positioned in the Geography room for use as a class resource and as a workstation for the Project students to build up the storage and analysis of recorded data.

2 Take one printout.

3 Recall the text to your screen and make the following changes:

(a) Change the heading to 'STUDENTS SAMPLE THE M25 VERGES'.

(b) Paragraphs 4 and 5 are to be reversed.

(c) A *new* paragraph is to be inserted *before* the final paragraph, as follows:

The actual collection of the data took rather longer than expected. In places, the site was not just knee–deep but shoulder–high in stinging nettles! One student developed some kind of allergy to the grasses and her eyes began to stream and become sore. But, all in all, it was a successful day, and everyone returned home to begin their long–awaited summer break, knowing that a start had been made.

(d) Take a *new* printout — with the following changes to the layout:

i) Turn **off** the page numbering

ii) Set a Top Margin of 1½ inches

iii) Make a **Page Break** at paragraph 6

4 Introduction to spreadsheets

If your interests involve any type of numerical calculation, either simple or complex, then a spreadsheet package will be of great value to you. The word spreadsheet has its origins in the large sheets of paper used by accountants, over which they spread their figures and calculations in neat rows and columns. The little boxes made by the vertical and horizontal lines on the paper have their counterparts in the micro's spreadsheet and are called cells. The power of the spreadsheet is that each cell can carry out all the functions of a calculating machine. The cells can either act as simple calculating machines or can be linked together so that the calculations in one cell will be dependent on the results of the calculations in other cells. If your work is at all numeric then your appetite must be whetted by the potential of such a system.

The trouble is that you cannot really show the power of such a system in print. If you have to set up a sheet (or screenful) of figures and then make a small change in the data and recalculate the effect this will have on the rest of the data on the sheet, then the overall change occurs very quickly, virtually in an instant. All I can do here is to show you two, 'before and after' pictures, and assure you that the change did occur virtually instantaneously. Spreadsheet programs now are very comprehensive, fast and their effects dynamic, and it is very difficult to do justice to them in print, so get the ideas as quickly as possible from this chapter, and then obtain a spreadsheet package and get on with the worksheets, and then you will soon be convinced.

4.1 Finding your way about

Figure 4.1 shows the general appearance of the screen after a spreadsheet program has been loaded, and in this case four items of data entered into the first four cells of row 4. Each column is identified by a letter of the alphabet and the rows are numbered. To identify a cell you have to give its column–row reference: the first cell in the 'grid' is A1, the second cell in the third row will be C2, and the data occupies cells A4, B4, C4 and D4, and so on. The message on the screen in Figure 4.1 indicates the possible overall size of the spreadsheet, 64 columns with 256 rows which gives 16,384 cells

```
   :   A   ::   B   ::   C   ::   D   ::   E   :
 1:
 2:
 3:
 4:64*256    GIVES         16384CELLS      _________
 5:
 6:
 7:
 8:
 9:
10:
  .
  etc
  .
18:
19:
20:
```

Fig. 4.1 Screen display of a typical spreadsheet

in all. This would be the size of a very modest spreadsheet by current standards. If it has 64 columns the naming of the columns after the 26th, goes AA, AB, AC, to AZ, and then after the 52nd BA, BB, BC and on to BK. On this scheme the last cell would have reference BK256.

The spreadsheet cursor is shown resting at cell E4, and occupying the whole of the cell. Usually the arrowed or cursor control keys which you use for word processing can be used to move this larger cursor about the sheet. The cursor moves cell by cell, that is in units of one cell width, not character by character. Also, most packages use a special key to mean 'goto', so /E15, = E15 or &E15 could mean 'goto cell E15', which lets you move around the whole spreadsheet with great ease. The number of characters which you can enter into a cell varies with the type of spreadsheet, but in Supercalc3 which is used in the worksheet section you can use up to nine characters.

The spreadsheet is large but the screen is small, so you have to view the spreadsheet as if through a window. So when you enter 'goto M20' the whole window moves so that the top left cell becomes M20. Another analogy is that it is like a map where you find your way around by means of grid references, and you often need to have several sheets of maps to cover an area in the detail you want, and move from sheet to sheet.

4.2 Entering data

Usually the top or bottom few lines of the screen are made available for the user to enter data or instructions, and these are referred to as the status line. Imagine that I am just about to press the Enter key having just entered the data for cell A4; the status lines would give the following information and look something like:

```
Cell: A4>      Contents:
Prompt:        Data 9 chars width       ? for help
Entry:         8>"64*256_
```

The first line indicates that I am in cell A4, that the cursor is pointing to the right (>) across the row, and that so far the cell has no data in it, i.e. zero contents. The prompt line says that you are entering data into a cell width of nine characters, and if you want help to enter **?**. The entry line indicates that I have so far entered seven characters and that the cursor is waiting in the eighth position, and that those characters are "64*256 . Don't confuse the status line cursor with the cell cursor on the spreadsheet itself. On pressing the **Enter** key which as in many other software packages signals to the system that data or an instruction is now to be entered into memory, the string **64*256** appears in cell A4 on the spreadsheet, the status lines now look like:

Cell: B4>	Contents:	
Prompt:	Data 9 chars width	? for help
Entry:	1>	

Thus showing that I have moved to an empty cell, B4, still pointing right across the row, and that I'm entering data at the first position of the cell.

Now please don't get upset if the status lines on the first spreadsheet you look at in detail, even if it is a version of SuperCalc itself, do not look exactly like what I have shown above. The way that the status lines' information is displayed is the one thing that varies considerably even between versions of the same spreadsheet package, let alone between different packages. The details of the information given by these lines however remains fairly constant, so what I have shown is very close to what you will see.

The package sees the data in the two types which we have met before; strings and numbers. If you wish to enter just a string of characters, then this should be shown at the beginning of the entry with a quotation mark. The entry into A4 was "**64*256** , but only the string 64*256 appeared in the cell of the sheet. If the entry is not prefixed by " then it is interpreted as a number. The entry for B4 was "**GIVES** , and the string GIVES appeared in the cell of the sheet after **Return** had been pressed. The next cell introduces a new idea. I do not wish to enter a string so I do not start with " , and I could have reached for my calculating machine and worked out that 64*256 is 16,384 and then entered this value, but the whole purpose of the sheet is to calculate, so at the point of pressing Return the entry would be:

Cell: C4>	Contents:	
Prompt:	Data 9 chars width	? for help
Entry:	7>64*256_	

On pressing **Return** the result of the calculation 64*256 , the actual product **16,384** , appears in the cell C4, so the spreadsheet has not only responded to numeric data but also to a simple arithmetic formula. To finish off Figure 1.1, I entered the string **CELLS** into D4.

Here again, newer versions of spreadsheets including SuperCalc, do not require you to preface string entry with a " , they have been programmed to distinguish in most cases between numbers, strings and formulae. However, using the " will remind you of the differences between the types of spreadsheet entry, and you will not be in error if you do use the " .

Notice that the package puts the types of data into the sheet in slightly different ways. The strings go into the cells left–justified and the numbers go in right–justified. Obviously the whole question of data format is important and will have to be considered again later.

Although the objective is to get data or formulae into the spreadsheet itself, usually your attention is fixed almost totally on the status lines. It is with these three lines that you interact almost exclusively. Here you can see what has previously been put into the cell, how much data it will hold, what is currently being entered, and so on. It is from this point that you can also interact with the program itself, because in addition to entering data and formulae you can enter commands which give you additional programming functions. A few simple examples will show both the arithmetic potential of the package and the use of its commands.

```
   |    A    ||    B    ||    C    ||    D    ||    E    |
 1|
 2|
 3|DAY
 4|
 5|MON              412
 6|TUES             576
 7|WED              215
 8|THURS            244
 9|FRI              398
10|
11|TOTAL           1845
12|
13|COMM'N       138.375
```

Fig. 4.2 A weeks sales figures

4.3 Sums and some commands

We will use a specific example to illustrate the general principles, and the arithmetic potential of the spreadsheet, and hope that you can project from this to an application that is useful to you. Imagine that you are a salesperson or representative who, in addition to basic salary, receives a percentage commission on your sales, and decide to keep track of this part of your income by using a micro spreadsheet.

Figure 4.2 shows a week's sales, day by day in column B5 to B9 inclusive, with the week's total in shown in B11, and the commission at 7.5% of sales shown in B13. The strings of characters for the days of the week, the total and the commission (COMM'N) were entered in the corresponding positions in the A column.

If you start the entry line with the appropriate special symbol, the package knows that you wish to enter a command, as opposed to data or a formula. As soon as you enter the special symbol the prompt line offers you a list of possible commands. We shall look at these in more detail later, but one which will help you at the moment lets you look at all the formulae of the spreadsheet. So having entered this command the sheet will now look like Figure 4.3

```
  !   A    !!   B    !!   C    !!   D    !!   E   !
 1!
 2!
 3!DAY
 4!
 5!MON          412
 6!TUES         576
 7!WED          215
 8!THURS        244
 9!FRI          398
10!
11!TOTAL        SUM(B5:B9)
12!
13!COMM'N       0.075*B11
```

Fig. 4.3 How TOTAL and COMM'N are calculated

This shows the cells with data roughly as before, but also shows how the values in B11 and B13 were calculated. For B11 this was by taking the sum of the numbers in the B column from B5 to B9. A range of cells is expressed as B5:B9, so the sum of the values in these cells is given by SUM (B5:B9) . To find the commission you must take 7.5% of the value B11, and this is done by the formula 0.075*B11 , as shown in B13.

Column B does not look quite right. It involves money values in pounds and pence, and so should have a decimal point in the correct place. So another command which is very helpful here is the format command which when entered gives another menu of options on the prompt line. If you choose the decimal or money option then the spreadsheet will appear as shown in Figure 4.4

```
  !   A    !!   B    !!   C    !!   D    !!   E   !
 1!
 2!
 3!DAY
 4!
 5!MON             412.00
 6!TUES            576.00
 7!WED             215.00
 8!THURS           244.00
 9!FRI             398.00
10!
11!TOTAL          1845.00
12!
13!COMM'N          138.38
14!
```

Fig. 4.4 Display using decimal or money option

As an aside for those who may wish to use the mathematical or statistical facilities offered by a spreadsheet, Figure 4.5 shows that I have added four more functions in B15 to B18; to find the average of the five values in B5 to B9; count the number of non–zero values in this list; and to pick out the maximum and minimum values. These values would form the start of most statistical surveys. Figure 4.6 shows the formulae used.

```
   :   A    ::    B    ::    C    ::    D    ::    E    :
 1:
 2:
 3:DAY
 4:
 5:MON            412.00
 6:TUES           576.00
 7:WED            215.00
 8:THURS          244.00
 9:FRI            398.00
10:
11:TOTAL         1845.00
12:
13:COMM'N         138.38
14:
15:AVERAGE        369.00
16:COUNT            5.00
17:MAX            576.00
18:MIN            215.00
```

Fig. 4.5 Four statistical functions

```
   :   A    ::    B    ::    C    ::    D    ::    E    :
 1:
 2:
 3:DAY
 4:
 5:MON         412
 6:TUES        576
 7:WED         215
 8:THURS       244
 9:FRI         398
10:
11:TOTAL       SUM(B5:B9)
12:
13:COMM'N      0.075*B11
14:
15:AVERAGE     AVERAGE(B5:B9)
16:COUNT       COUNT(B5:B9)
17:MAX         MAX(B5:B9)
18:MIN         MIN(B5:B9)
```

Fig. 4.6 Formulae for statistical functions

From this point on spreadsheets come into their own. As pointed out earlier, the following recalculation of the table is best seen as a demonstration rather than described in a book. Imagine there was an error in the original data; the value of 576 at B6 was found to be wishful thinking and was really 476. If you now go to B6 and change the entry to 476, you will find that the whole column readjusts itself, as far as is practicable, instantaneously. So, Figure 4.7 could be produced in the time it takes to change B6 and press Return.

	A	B	C	D	E
1					
2					
3	DAY				
4					
5	MON	412.00			
6	TUES	476.00			
7	WED	215.00			
8	THURS	244.00			
9	FRI	398.00			
10					
11	TOTAL	1745.00			
12					
13	COMM'N	130.88			
14					
15	AVERAGE	349.00			
16	COUNT	5.00			
17	MAX	476.00			
18	MIN	215.00			

Fig. 4.7 Changing Tuesday's figures

4.4 Tables of data

Most accounting applications involve organising data in the form of tables. You can imagine the power of the system if it is possible to do calculations on rows and columns simultaneously. We will carry on with the example started above, to show the general principle. Imagine now the salesperson had three product lines, shown in figure 4.8 in columns B, C and D. The daily total would now be found by summing the values in the rows. Monday's total was found by adding the values in B5, C5 and D5, and this sum is stored in cell E5, and so on for all the days in the week. The sales of each product for the whole week are summed and stored in the cells B11 to D11. As a check on the procedures I have given the total of the day totals in E10, and the total of the product totals in E11. These two values must of course tally.

	A	B	C	D	E
1					
2					
3	DAY	PROD1	PROD2	PROD3	TOTAL
4					
5	MON	412.00	254.00	49.00	715.00
6	TUES	476.00	197.00	28.00	701.00
7	WED	215.00	305.00	27.00	547.00
8	THURS	244.00	119.00	19.00	382.00
9	FRI	398.00	154.00	43.00	595.00
10					2940.00
11	TOTAL	1745.00	1029.00	166.00	2940.00
12					
13	COMM'N	130.88	51.45	16.60	198.93
14					

Fig. 4.8 Calculations with three different products

An added complication is that each product has a different rate of commission; product 1 has 7.5%, product 2 has 5%, and product 3 has 10%. The commissions are calculated in cells B13 to D13, and then the overall weekly value summed into cell E13. The data shown in Figure 4.8 and the corresponding formulae in Figure 4.9.

	A	B	C	D	E
1					
2					
3	DAY	PROD1	PROD2	PROD3	TOTAL
4					
5	MON	412	254	49	SUM(B5:D
6	TUES	476	197	28	SUM(B6:D
7	WED	215	305	27	SUM(B7:D
8	THURS	244	119	19	SUM(B8:D
9	FRI	398	154	43	SUM(B9:D
10					SUM(E5:E
11	TOTAL	SUM(B5:B	SUM(C5:C	SUM(D5:D	SUM(B11:
12					
13	COMM'N	0.075*B1	0.05*C11	0.1*D11	SUM(B13:

Fig. 4.9 Formulae used

There is a small format problem in row 11 of Figure 4.9, because the length of the formula is greater than nine characters. Rather than adjust the width of the columns of the table you should by now be willing to accept that these sums have ranges B5:B9, C5:C9 and D5:D9.

Figure 4.8 was the salesperson's first attempt at getting the week's commission correct, but in the final analysis it was found that there were four errors: B9 was really 388, C6 was really 179 and D8 was 39. Further, the commission for that week on product 3 was not 10 but 15%. Figure 4.8 can be transformed into Figure 4.10 in the time it takes to make these four changes in data. All of the table readjusts itself automatically, virtually in a flash as each change is made: the column sums, row sums and commission sum. If you are interested in numbers, how can you resist a spreadsheet?

8

	A	B	C	D	E
1					
2					
3	DAY	PROD1	PROD2	PROD3	TOTAL
4					
5	MON	412.00	254.00	49.00	715.00
6	TUES	476.00	179.00	28.00	683.00
7	WED	215.00	305.00	27.00	547.00
8	THURS	244.00	119.00	39.00	402.00
9	FRI	388.00	154.00	43.00	585.00
10					2932.00
11	TOTAL	1735.00	1011.00	186.00	2932.00
12					
13	COMM'N	130.13	50.55	27.90	208.58
14					

Fig. 4.10 Changing data in Figure 4.8

4.5 Commands

You met the idea of commands in a previous section, but more detail about these will show you how useful a spreadsheet package can be. Most spreadsheets let you perform the above functions, but the feature which distinguishes a good spreadsheet is the range of functions given to you by the commands which are associated with it. If you have been entering data and formulae into a sheet and have returned to base, i.e. cell A1, and then entered the special command symbol (/ in this example) then the status lines will look something like:

Cell: A1>	Contents:	
Prompt	B/C/D/E/F/G/I/L/M/N/O/P/Q/R/S/U/Z	? for help
Entry:		

I have assumed that there was neither data nor formulae in cell A1, as no contents are shown. After entering **/** the prompt line fills up with a list of the commands which are available to you. It isn't really a menu, because there isn't room in just one line for any explanation of what the letters mean, so you either have to know what they stand for, or look them up in the handbook which comes with the package, or you can enter **?** and the screen will fill with explanations of the options which are available.

Most are similar to commands which you have met in other software, and are concerned with the general housekeeping of the spreadsheet on which you are currently working. The actual keys to press and the commands will vary between systems and even in SuperCalc will probably not be the same as those shown here. You can edit (**E**) the data or formula which you have entered on the entry line, similarly you can delete (**D**) or insert (**I**) individual cells, whole rows or columns, or even whole areas of the sheet. You mark out areas by giving the diagonal cell references, for example A1:E10 would indicate the whole areas bounded by the two columns: A1:A10 and E1:E10.

You can also blank off (**B**) individual cells, whole rows, columns or areas, i.e. make all entries equal zero. Some systems have a zap command (**Z**) which lets you blank off the whole of the spreadsheet, so that you can completely clear the decks and start again. Some programs also have a protect (**P**) function, which allows you to protect area of the sheet so that the data which you have entered into those cells cannot be accidentally over–written or changed. Quit (**Q**) lets you leave the spreadsheet without saving it. The whole sheet, formulae, format and data can be saved (**S**), and then at a later time loaded (**L**) from backing store.

You have seen how the format (**F**) of a sheet can be altered. The number of characters per cell may be changed for the whole sheet, and some packages allow for columns to have different widths to suit the application to which you are putting the sheet. Within the format command itself there are often several options: to have an integer, decimal, money or exponential layout for numbers, and there is usually the choice of having both numbers and strings left–or right–hand justified in the cell. You will obviously need to the sheet to the printer at some time, and here you usually have several options two of which are whether you want just the data output, or the data with the grid as shown in the figures in this book.

4.6 Copy and replicate

These are probably the two commands which are most useful when entering data. Figure 4.11 shows a spreadsheet being used to record transactions which occur in a typical home budget. Rows 4 to 8 inclusive show the regular monthly payments which will recur for the whole of the financial year. Having set up the headings for the sheet in rows 1 and 3, and down the A column, you then enter your figures for April in the B column, with the total in B17. When faced with entering the figures for May in the C column, you could start off by using the copy (**C**) command, and copy the range of B4 to B8 into C4 to C8, i.e. copy over the standing payment as a job lot. In the cell B17 is the formula SUM(B4:B15). The cells in the column which are empty count as zero when added up, and this sum lets you enter miscellaneous amounts into rows 14 and 16 if you wish. Now, if you copy cell B17 into C17, you will find that its sense has also been adjusted, so C17 reads SUM(C4:C15). You can now carry on with the task of entering the remaining payments in rows C10 to C15.

By the time you come to entering the data for June, you may decide to use the fact that the standing charges are likely to apply for the whole of the year. Here the replicate command (**R**) comes into its own because its function is to make repeat copies.

	A	B	C	D	E	F
1				HOME	BUDGET	
2						
3		APR	MAY	JUN	JUL	AUG
4	MORTGAGE	172.94	172.94	172.94	172.94	172.94
5	CAR LOAN	156.90	156.90	156.90	156.90	156.90
6	RATES	52.20	52.20	52.20	52.20	52.20
7	LIFE INS	48.60	48.60	48.60	48.60	48.60
8	MED INS	13.39	13.39	13.39	13.39	13.39
9						
10	TELE	49.23	.00	.00	52.09	.00
11	ELEC	.00	62.80	.00	.00	41.56
12	GAS	.00	.00	78.31	.00	.00
13	WATER	35.75	.00	.00	.00	.00
14						
15	CASH	150.00	200.00	175.00	205.00	200.00
16						
17	TOTALS	679.01	706.83	697.34	701.12	685.59
18						
19	SALARY	704.73	704.73	704.73	704.73	704.73
20						

Fig. 4.11 A home budget — Copy or Replicate function

With this command you can take B4 to B8 and repeat its contents over the range of columns D to M, to accommodate the remaining ten months of the year. If you do this for cell B17 you will find that the formula is also repeated and readjusted for each column, as in column C above. Copy is a one to one copy operation, but replicate is a one to many copy function. Both copy and replicate operations can be set up so that if a change is made to the data in the original cell, row or column, this change is automatically transmitted to all of the copied or replicated areas.

4.7 What if?

The speed with which changes can be made to the whole spreadsheet lets you indulge in some simple speculations. In the home budget example you may wish to try and predict what might happen to your expenditure next year. What if the mortgage rate went up by 2% and the rates by 4%? These changes could be made to this year's figures in a matter of seconds, and the whole set of projected figures would appear almost instantaneously. If in the case of the salesperson in the earlier example, product 1 would sell better against a competitor if its price were dropped by 5%, but because there is no real competitor for product 3 you could afford to increase its price by 5%, what would the commission be if you assumed the sales of product 1 increased by 10%, and the sales of product 3 stayed the same? The adjustments to the spreadsheet needed to answer such speculations would take only a little while, and could be very useful to a business person. You would be much less likely to try such 'What if?' exercises if you had to resort to pencil, paper and calculating machine.

4.8 Final words

I hope that by now you are convinced of the usefulness of spreadsheets for the type of simple numeric operations of the balance sheet type, which I have described here. I hope that the Worksheets will help you become adept in the practicalities of their use.

5 SuperCalc3

5.1 Getting in and out and moving round the sheet

1 **To get into SuperCalc3** — 'Boot up' your micro system and get to the A–prompt. Put your SuperCalc3 program disk in the A–drive and proceed:
A>SC3(Enter)
i.e. after the A–prompt, shown **A>**, enter **SC3** and strike the **Enter** or **Return** key. A 'title' page will appear on the screen with Version and Copyright details, followed by a prompt line which says:

Enter "**?**" for help or "**Return**" to start.
F1 = Help; **F2** = Erase Line/Return to Spreadsheet; etc.

Later you can enter **?** or press **F1** for help to see what happens; but for now you should strike the **Enter** key and you will be faced with a blank spreadsheet roughly as shown below.

```
      |    A    ||    B    ||    C    ||    D    ||    E    ||    F    ||
    1|_________
    2|
    3|
    4|
    5|
     .
     .
     .
   19|
   20|
 > A1
Width: 9 Memory:297 Last Col/Row:A1      ? for Help
    1>
```

On your screen the sheet will extend to column H, but for convenience on the page of the book, I have shown it extending only to column F.

You will see that the spreadsheet cursor is a blinking rectangle which covers the whole nine spaces of the cell where it is hovering. I have shown it above as nine spaces underlined at A1 — the Home cell.

If your micro has been configured for full MS–DOS then you will find that the arrowed keys will move this cursor round the sheet. Otherwise you will have to use the **Ctrl/E Ctrl/S Ctrl/D Ctrl/X** as you would in WordStar.

Try moving the cursor round and off the screen and watch how the column/row names change, and return to **A1** by pressing the Home key, just to get the feel of the sheet.

Cells are named by their column/row coordinates like reading a map. The top left cell shown above is **A1**, top right F1, bottom right F20, and bottom left A20. Remember that I am not showing the whole screen full, which would extend to column H.

You can 'goto' a cell directly by giving the '=' symbol.

Enter =**C9(Enter)**, =**A56(Enter)** and =**Z99(Enter)** and so on, to see what happens, and then return to **A1** with **Home**.

Cursor across the sheet to find out what happens after you reach column Z. You will see that the column names continue AA, AB, AC and so on. If you carry on across and down as far as possible you will find that the last cell is BK254.

3 **To understand the use of the three 'control' lines**

```
>A1                                                      .... status
Width:  9 Memory: 297 Last Col/Row:A1    ?for Help       .... prompt
   1>                                                    .... entry
```

The three lines at the bottom of the screen tell you what is happening on the sheet. The '**status**' line tells you what cell you are at, and what data is in there: A1 and 'none' at present. The > shows you which way your cursor is directed.

The **prompt** line says that your current cell width is nine spaces, that you have 297k of memory available to you, that your data extends as far as A1, and that you can enter **?** for Help.

The last or 'entry' line is where data and commands are entered, as you noticed when you entered the 'goto' instructions '=C9', '=A56' and so on above.

You will find as you become familiar with using SuperCalc3 that your attention is focussed on these control lines more than on what is actually happening on the sheet itself.

4 **To get out of the spreadsheet** — you have to give the command '**Quit**' to get out of the SuperCalc3. To summon a command you enter **/**, which appears on the data entry line, followed by **Q** for **Quit**. Then you will be asked '**Y**(es) or **N**(o)**?**', and on responding**Y** for YES you will find yourself back at the A–prompt.

Exercise

Take the disks out, switch off and then go through all the procedure again until you are quite familiar with it.

5.2 Introduction

The table of values on the spreadsheet show the approximate costs of feeding a champion dog for 1 week and 1 year. The columns A and B from rows 7 to 12 show the type of food, column C shows the quantity of food units and the column D the price per unit.

The weekly costs in column E are found by multiplying Quantity by Unit Cost, and the Yearly cost by multiplying this value in column E by 52. So column E = column C × column D and column F = 52 × column E.

The weekly and yearly Costs for each food item can be added up to get the total costs, weekly and yearly, for all of the food.

	A	B	C	D	E	F
1	FEEDING A CHAMPION ROTTWEILLER					
2						
3					COSTS	
4						
5	ITEM		QUANTITY	UNIT	WEEK	YEAR
6						
7	FROZEN PETMEAT		4	.52	2.08	108.16
8	CANNED DOGMEAT		3	.43	1.29	67.08
9	DOGMEAL		1	.98	.98	50.96
10	FRESH FISH		2	.45	.9	46.8
11	CEREAL		1	.36	.36	18.72
12	MILK		3	.22	.66	34.32
13						
14	TOTAL COSTS				6.27	326.04

Entering, saving and printing data

1 To enter the data shown below onto the spreadsheet

	A	B	C	D	E	F
1	FEEDING A CHAMPION ROTTWEILLER					
2						
3						
4						
5						
6						
7	FROZEN PETMEAT		4	.52		
8	CANNED DOGMEAT		3	.43		
9	DOGMEAL		1	.98		
10	FRESH FISH		2	.45		
11	CEREAL		1	.36		
12	MILK		3	.22		
13						
14	TOTAL COSTS					

The aim of this unit is to enter the text and numeric data shown above onto the spreadsheet, to print it out and save it on disk.

2 **To enter text** load SuperCalc3 into the micro as you did in worksheet 5.1, and get the blank sheet onto the screen with the cursor at A1. You wish to enter the heading to the sheet at this point, so in capital letters (**Caps Lock On**) start typing. You will see what you type appearing at the Enter line after 1>: >**1 FEEDING A CHAMPION ROTTWEILLER (Enter).**

After pressing Enter the whole phrase will appear along row 1 starting at the most left space of cell A1. Note that the signal to enter the data onto the sheet was striking the Enter key. I have shown it as (**Enter**) this once, but will not in future. Note also that you could continue typing the phrase, and the characters automatically just spilled over into the neighbouring cells. You did not have to begin the entry with " to indicate that it was text you wished to enter. Note that the status line now says
Text=FEEDING A CHAMPION ROTTWEILLER

The cursor is still at A1, so continue by cursoring down to A7, and note that the status line says vA7, showing that you are at A7 with the cursor direction downwards (v). Now continue

1>FROZEN PETMEAT	
1>CANNED DOGMEAT	and so on down to
1>TOTAL COSTS	at cell A14

3 **To correct errors** — if you notice an error in your entry before you have pressed Enter, then press the **F2** key on the left keypad and begin again.

If you notice an error later, then you can return to the cell and simply enter the new correct data at the entry line. You could alternatively use the Blank command **/B** to blank out the cell, if you did not want data in the cell at all.

4 **To enter numbers continue** 1>=C6 to go to cell C6 Now cursor down to C7 and your cursor is pointing down the column, and continue

1>4	
1>3	and so on down to
1>3	at cell C12

You will notice that the numbers have gone into the most right places in the cells.

To enter the D column of data

1>.D6	and cursor down to D7, and continue
1>.52	
1>.43	and so on down to
1>.22	at cell D12

Check with the previous spreadsheet that the data is correct and in the correct cells on the sheet.

5 **To save this data on disk** — check that you have a work disk in the B–drive.

```
1>/S            to call up the Save command
   B:FACR1,     to give the filename as prompted
         A      to say All of the sheet
```

6 **To print out the sheet** — check that the printer is connected, switched on and ready, then

```
1>/O              to call up the Output command
   D              for the whole Display
    A             to say All of the sheet
     P            to the Printer
```

Exercise

Enter onto a spreadsheet the data shown in Figure 4.8 of the Spreadsheets chapter. So far enter just the headings column A and row 3, and the data B to D rows 5 to 9.

5.3 Preview of commands

I have summarised the commands which are used in these worksheets on a spreadsheet — would you believe!

```
   :      A     ::     B     ::     C     ::     D     ::     E     :
  1:            SLASH (/)     COMMANDS
  2:
  3:/B(lank)    range
  4:            Enter for current cell
  5:
  6:/D(elete)   R(ow)        range
  7:            C(olumn)     range
  8:            F(ile)       filename
  9:
 10:/F(ormat)   G(lobal)                   $ for money
 11:            C(olumn)     range         TR text rt
 12:            R(ow)        range         width
 13:                                       ..10 other
 14:                                       possibilities
 15:/G(lobal)   F(ormula) ON/OFF
 16:            B(order) ON/OFF
 17:
 18:/I(nsert)   R(ow)        range
 19:            C(olumn)     range
 20:
 21:/L(oad)     filename     A(11)
 22:            Enter for directory(B22)
 23:            Esc for current filename(B23)
 24:
```

Cont'd

```
25¦/O(utput)    D(isplay)    range        P(rinter)
26¦                                       D(isk)       filename
27¦                                                    Enter(B22)
28¦                                                    Esc(B23)
29¦/Q(uit)      Y(es)
30¦             N(o)
31¦
32¦/R(eplicate)FROM,         TO(Enter)
33¦             cell         cell
34¦             cell         row  (or  part)
35¦             cell         col  (or  part)
36¦             part col     top part row (Worksheet 5 section 3)
37¦             part row     left part col
38¦
39¦/S(ave)      filename     A(11)
40¦             Enter(B22)
41¦             Esc(B23)
42¦
43¦/Z(ap)       Y(es)        clear sheet without save
44¦             N(o)         cancels command
45¦
```

When you wish to issue a command you enter **/** on the entry line, and the prompt line fills with the command key letters: /A/B/C/D/E/F . . . . /Z.

The list I have given is not complete. You should refer to your manual for a complete list. Read the sheet given in following way.

Issue the command from column A, e.g. **/F** for Format, without pressing Enter, the entry line looks like: **1>/Format**, the word Format is completed for you and the comma is inserted too.

The prompt line has changed to give you another set of options, these are shown in column B of the table: **G**(lobal), **C**(olumn) or **R**(ow) . . etc..

Again you respond with the key letter, let's say **R** for row. The entry line now looks like: **1/>/Format, Row**, the word Row is completed for you and the comma inserted too.

The prompt line now asks for a range to be given, as shown in column C of the sheet above. If it is row 4 you simply enter **4**: **1>/Format,Row,4,** you enter the comma this time.

You are now faced with 13 possibilities of which I have shown three in column **D10:D12** :– **$, TR and width**. If in row 4 you want the text right justified you would complete the entry: **1>/Format,Row,4,TR(Enter)**

Each successive column above gives you the next set of prompts; column A the slash command, column B the next set of prompts, and then after response column C the next prompts and so on, until your particular sequence of commands is complete.

To save a file named FACR1 on the disk in the B–drive enter:

```
1>/S                to summon up Save
    B:FACR1,        respond to 'filename' prompt
             A      to reply to A(ll),V(alues),P(art)
```

Ranges may be a letter for a whole column, or a number for a whole row. A part row is shown: A25:D25. A part column as D10:D14.

The range of an area of sheet is given by the top left–hand corner cell to bottom right–hand corner cell, e.g. for the above sheet A1:E45.

Formulae and replicate

To appreciate the importance of the Formula/Replicate combination — cells may contain text, numbers or formulae with the latter being the most powerful form of entry, and most characteristic of spreadsheets. The Replicate command allows you to repeat data or formulae of areas of cells containing formulae which are connected, such that a change in one can affect the contents of another, is the most powerful provision of a spreadsheet.

1 Load the sheet which you saved as B:FACR1 in worksheet 5.2.

2 **To enter the formula for a product** — the C column represents the number of units of food given to the dog per week, and column D represents the price per unit in pounds. So to get the amount spent per week on each item we need a column E which contains the products 4 × .52, 3 × .43, 1 × .98 and so on down the column. The entry in E7 would be the product C7 × D7, or with the SuperCalc3 symbol for multiplication C7*D7. Now enter:

```
1>=E7               to go to E7
1>C7*D7
```

and note what appears in cell E7 — the actual product 2.08, and what appears in status line below — the formula.

3 **To use Replicate to copy this formula down the column** — you could cursor down the E column and enter C8*D8, and then C9*D9 and so on entering in each cell until C12*D12.

```
1>=E8               go to E8
1>/R                to call up the Replicate command
    E7,             reply to the range from? prompt
       E8:E12(Enter)  to complete the command sequence
```

You will see that a column of values has appeared in the E column, but if you cursor down the column you see that the formulae are shown in the status line.

4 **To enter formula and Replicate for the F column** — in the F column I want the yearly costs, so to get these you must multiply each value in the E column by 52. So, continue:

1>=F7	to go to cell F7
1>52*E7	to enter the formula
1>/R	to call up the Replicate command
F7,F8:F12	to answer the range prompts

You should now see the column of values in the F column.

5 **To enter the formula for sum and Replicate it** — at A14 we have entered TOTAL COSTS and so under the Week and Year columns at E14 and F14 you want the sum of the six values in that column. Continue by entering

1>=E14	to go to cell E14
1>SUM(E7:E12)	to sum the range of cells E7 to E14
1>/R	to call up the Replicate command
E14,F14	to answer the range prompts indicating a one to one copy

The required sums will appear in cells E14 and F14. If you cursor to them you will see the formulae on the status line.

6 Save this version of the sheet as **B:FACR2**.

7 **To display the sheet with formulae** — if you wish to look at all of the values on the sheet, you are taking a global view of it, so it may seem reasonable to use the Global command to turn all the values into formulae. Enter

1>/G	to call up the Global command
F	to answer the prompts for Formulae

You will see the values of the sheet which are not raw data, but which were derived from formulae, change into their respective formulae. You can print and save the sheet in this form.

Exercise

Complete the data entry for the Sales and Commission values described in Figure 4.8 of the Spreadsheets chapter. Enter the formulae for the totals in row 11 and column E using the Replicate command, and the commission in row 13. Save the sheet and print it out, with data and then with the formulae.

5.4 Tidying up with format

1 **To enter the column headings** — if you compare the sheet which you saved after worksheet 5.2 with the target sheet shown in the Introduction to worksheet 5.2, you will see that there are a few additions and adjustments to be made. The main difference is the omission of column headings.

Boot up system, load SuperCalc3 and then load in the sheet from file **B:FACR2**, and continue

1>=E3	go to cell E3
1>COSTS	to enter that heading
1>=A5	go to cell A5
1>ITEM	to enter that heading

Cursor back to A5 and then cursor along to C5, and complete the row **1>QUANTITY** **1>UNIT** **1>WEEK** **1>YEAR.**

You remember that numbers go into cells right justified and text left justified. These headings are left justified and look very different from those in the target sheet.

2 **To right justify text using the format command** — the Format command lets you change the default left justification for text. To do so continue:

1>/F	to summon the Format command
R	for Row
3	for Row 3
TR	for Text Right

F, R, 3 and TR are made as responses to prompts which appear on the prompt line. On completing the input but before striking the Enter key, the entry line would look like: **1>/Format,Row,3,TextRight** because when you enter **F** the word Format is finished for you by the program, and for **R** Row and **TR** elicits **TextRight**. You will see that COSTS has become right justified at E3.

Now do the same for row 5 with **1>/Format,Row,5,TextRight** and the five headings have taken up right justified positions, over the values in the columns giving a better display.

3 **To underline the headings** — you could go to D4 and enter '–' nine times, and then on to E4 and enter nine more and on to F4, but there is a shorter way.

1>=D4	go to cell D4
1>'_	after Enter the underline stretches from D4 right across the sheet
1>=G4	go to cell G4
1>"	the " cuts off the line at G4

4 **To display money values as pounds and pence** — one niggling detail is the money values in the 10th row. 2*.45=.9 and 52*.9=46.8 and these results are not displayed as 0.90 for 90p or 46.80 for 46 pounds and 80p. The Format command comes to our rescue again. Continue

```
1>/F                        to summon the Format command
   E                        for Entry to enter a range
    D7:F14                  the range for money values
          $                 for 2 DP format
```

You will see that the values in the range specified have all changed to two decimal places, which is the money format in pounds or dollars.

5 Save and print out this final form of the FACR sheet. We are going to do some work with this sheet in the next worksheet, but it is as well to record it in its final form and note the file name carefully. Subsequent modified versions should be saved under different names so that this version remains as a standard. So print out the sheet and save it as **B:FACR3.**

Exercises

Return to the data in the sheet in Figure 4.8 of the chapter. Give the numerical values a money Format, and right justify the row 3 headings as appropriate.

5.5 Consolidation

The screen has two sections:
1 the cells which hold data
2 the three control lines at the bottom of the screen.

```
> A1                                                   .... status
Width: 9 Memory:297 Last Col/Row:A1    ? for Help      .... prompt
  1>                                                   .... entry
```

The **status line** tells you where you are and what's in that cell. The **prompt line** holds any necessary prompts. After **1**> on the entry line you enter data.

Data comprises: numbers, text and formulae.
Formulae involve cell names, arithmetic operators + − * /,
brackets (and), numbers and mathematical functions.
You enter commands on the entry line starting with a / (slash).

A cell reference or name consists of a column letter followed by a row number. Columns extend from A to BK, and rows from 1 to 254.

The cursor keys move the sheet cursor round the sheet. A quick way to move the cursor is to enter = followed by the cell name after **1>** on the entry line, e.g.

1>=B13	means 'go to cell B13'
1>=M22	means 'go to cell M22'

The **Home** key takes you back to A1. Key **F2** will cancel anything you have entered on the entry line. **?** will give you on–screen help.

Commands used so far

/S	S(ave)	to Save a sheet on disk
/L	L(oad)	to Load a sheet from disk
/Q	Q(uit)	to Quit from the Supercalc package
/O	O(utput)	to Output a copy of a sheet to disk or printer
/F	F(ormat)	to change the layout (Format) of a range of cells
/G	G(lobal)	to switch Formulae or Border On/Off
/R	R(eplicate)	to copy formulae from one range of cells to another range. When replicated, if the formulae involve cell references, then these references are automatically adjusted for their new positions on the sheet. Replicate can therefore be thought of as 'relative copy'.

I showed part of the Home Budget spreadsheet in Figure 4.11 of the Spreadsheets chapter.

	A	B	C	D	E	F	G
1			HOME	BUDGET			
2							
3		APR	MAY	JUN	JUL	AUG	SEP
4	MORTGAGE	172.94	172.94	172.94	172.94	172.94	172.94
5	CAR LOAN	156.90	156.90	156.90	156.90	156.90	156.90
6	RATES	52.20	52.20	52.20	52.20	52.20	52.20
7	LIFE INS	48.60	48.60	48.60	48.60	48.60	48.60
8	MED INS	13.39	13.39	13.39	13.39	13.39	13.39
9							
10	TELE	49.23	.00	.00	52.09	.00	.00
11	ELEC	.00	62.80	.00	.00	41.56	.00
12	GAS	.00	.00	78.31	.00	.00	49.35
13	WATER	35.75	.00	.00	.00	.00	.00
14							
15	CASH	150.00	200.00	175.00	205.00	200.00	250.00
16							
17	TOTALS	679.01	706.83	697.34	701.12	685.59	743.38
18							
19	SALARY	704.73	704.73	704.73	704.73	704.73	704.73

The data which was entered into the sheet is shown next. You will fill the appropriate blank cells with formulae using the Replicate command.

	A	B	C	D	E	F	G
1				HOME	BUDGET		
2							
3		APR	MAY	JUN	JUL	AUG	SEP
4	MORTGAGE	172.94					
5	CAR LOAN	156.90					
6	RATES	52.20					
7	LIFE INS	48.60					
8	MED INS	13.39					
9							
10	TELE	49.23	.00	.00	52.09	.00	.00
11	ELEC	.00	62.80	.00	.00	41.56	.00
12	GAS	.00	.00	78.31	.00	.00	49.35
13	WATER	35.75	.00	.00	.00	.00	.00
14							
15	CASH	150.00	200.00	175.00	205.00	200.00	250.00
16							
17	TOTALS						
18							
19	SALARY	704.73					

Exercises

1 Enter the heading HOME BUDGET left–justified into D1 and E1 respectively.

Enter the months' headings from B3 to G3 right–justified as shown.

Enter the headings in the A column from MORTGAGE in A4 down to SALARY in A19.

2 Enter the numeric data down column B from **172.94** in **B4** to **704.73** in B19.

Enter the numeric data in the rows 10 to 13, and row 15 from column C to G – you had already entered column B!

3 Use the Replicate command to copy the repeated payments and salary.

Enter the formula B4 in cell C4.

Replicate from C4 to C5:C8.

Now replicate the whole column C4:C8 across the table D4:G4.

Use the Global command to ensure that the block on sheet C4:G8 consists only of formulae which are cell names. Return to spreadsheet mode.

Enter the formula B19 in cell C19, and replicate C19 to D19:G19.

4 Enter a formula for the column total B4:B15 in B17. Now replicate this formula along row 17 from B17 to the range C17:G17.

Enter TOTALS in H3.

In H4 enter a formula for the sum across row 4 from B4 to G4. Replicate this sum from H4 to the range H5:H19. H17 will now show the total expenditure for the 6–month period, and H19 the total income.

5 Compare your spreadsheet with that shown in the commentary to this worksheet to check the data. Use the Global command to check the formulae which you entered.

6 Print out the sheet with data and with formulae.

7 Save the results of this exercise for future use, I wi l refer to the file as B:HOMBUG .

Commentary on consolidating exercise

Below is a printout of the sheet which resulted from the instructions given in the exercise. I have widened the columns so that you can see all of the formulae.

	A	B	C	D
1				HOME
2				
3		APR	MAY	JUN
4	MORTGAGE	172.94	B4	C4
5	CAR LOAN	156.90	B5	C5
6	RATES	52.20	B6	C6
7	LIFE INS	48.60	B7	C7
8	MED INS	13.39	B8	C8
9				
10	TELE	49.23	.0	0
11	ELEC	.0	62.80	0
12	GAS	.0	.0	78.31
13	WATER	35.75	.0	0
14				
15	CASH	150	200	175
16				
17	TOTALS	SUM(B4:B15)	SUM(C4:C15)	SUM(D4:D15)
18				
19	SALARY	704.73	B19	C19
20				

	E	F	G	H
1	BUDGET			
2				
3	JUL	AUG	SEP	TOTALS
4	D4	E4	F4	SUM(B4:G4)
5	D5	E5	F5	SUM(B5:G5)
6	D6	E6	F6	SUM(B6:G6)
7	D7	E7	F7	SUM(B7:G7)
8	D8	E8	F8	SUM(B8:G8)
9				
10	52.09	0	0	SUM(B10:G10)
11	0	41.56	0	SUM(B11:G11)
12	0	0	49.35	SUM(B12:G12)
13	0	0	0	SUM(B13:G13)
14				
15	205	200	250	SUM(E15:G15)
16				
17	SUM(E4:E15)	SUM(F4:F15)	SUM(G4:G15)	SUM(H4:H15)
18				
19	D19	E19	F19	SUM(E19:G19)
20				

5.6 Editing the sheet

There is a cell edit command in SuperCalc3 (**/E**) which allows you to change the details of the data or formula in a cell, using a simple line editor. As data and formulae in our examples are short and simple there is no need for us to use this facility. Changes to individual cells will be made by going to the cell and over–writing its contents. I will concentrate on the Insert and Delete commands in this worksheet.

1 Load the file **B:FACR3** onto the sheet.

2 **To change the contents of a cell** — the owner has found canned dogmeat of equal quality at 39p per can rather than 43, so change this value:

1>=D8	go to cell D8
1>.39	enter .39 for 39p

Note that the two cells to the right in 8th row (E8 and F8) change automatically, and that the Total at F14 also adjusts. If it all happens too quickly, then take a printout and compare with your original hard copy of FACR1.

3 **To insert a row** — a vet is not satisfied with the champion's diet and recommends a number of changes, the first being to include some vitamins. So continue:

1>/I	to call up the Insert command
R	response to 'R(ow) or C(olumn)' prompt
11	response to 'Range' prompt

The sheet divides with the CEREAL row 11 moving down to row 12 leaving a blank row at 11.

Now go to A11 and enter **VITAMINS (PER BOX)** across A11 and B11. At C11 enter 1 and at D11 enter **.48**'.

But, you still have E11 and F11 blank, which you are going to fill by replicating from E10 and F10 respectively. Continue

1>=E10	
1>/R	
E10,	response to 'From, Enter Range' prompt
E11	response to 'To, Enter Range' prompt

Repeat this sequence for F10 and F11, and you will find that all of the data on the sheet automatically readjusts.

4 **To delete a row** — the vet recommends further that the dog eats too much meat and cereal, so to get a better balance suggests that the DOGMEAL is taken out of the diet. So, to record this continue:

1>/D	to call up the Delete command
R	response to 'R(ow), C(olumn) or F(ile)'
9	to take out the 9th row

You will see that the values have all adjusted themselves automatically. Use the Global command and look at the formulae to convince yourself that the correct adjustment has occurred with them. Compare what is on the screen with the printouts from the original version of FACR1.

5 **To delete an 'edge' row** — if the vet had said that at his age the dog did not need milk in his diet, then you would proceed as before but now to take out the last row — still row 12 because we have made one insertion and one deletion so far. **1>/D(elete),R(ow),12** would bring about the deletion.

Now you will see that automatic ajdustment has not occurred all through the sheet, because at E13 and F13 on the data sheet you will see ERROR instead of the expected sum. If you use the Global command and look at the Formulae you will see in E13 you have SUM(E7:ERROR) and at F13 you have SUM(F7:ERROR) . This should give you a clue. By taking out the last row you have destroyed the limit of the range of values which was set in the SUM expression, and the program is unsure about what that limit now is!

The rule is that automatic adjustment occurs after a deletion in a replicated area of the sheet, provided that the deletion is neither of the top and bottom rows, nor extreme left and right columns. In other words — be careful when changing the limits of the ranges of a formula or replication!

In this case you have to go to E13 and redefine the SUM range to **SUM(E7:E11)** , and then you can Replicate this formula to F13.

6 Save as **B:FACR4** and print out the final sheet of values and then using the global command change to Formulae and print out this sheet, and compare your sheets with those given in the commentary to this worksheet.

Exercise

Return to Figure 4.8 of the Spreadsheet chapter and make an appropriate insertion of data between columns B and C, and at the new column F position.

Commentary

Here are the two sheets resulting from the inserting and deleting activities in the worksheet, one with the data and the other with the formulae.

	A	B	C	D	E	F
1	FEEDING A CHAMPION ROTTWEILLER					
2						
3					COSTS	
4						
5	ITEM		QUANTITY	UNIT	WEEK	YEAR
6						
7	FROZEN PETMEAT		4	.52	2.08	108.16
8	CANNED DOGMEAT		3	.39	1.17	60.84
9	FRESH FISH		2	.45	.9	46.8
10	VITAMINS (PER BOX)		1	.48	.48	24.96
11	CEREAL		1	.36	.36	18.72
12						
13	TOTAL COSTS				4.99	259.48

	A	B	C	D	E	F
1	FEEDING A CHAMPION ROTTWEILLER					
2						
3					COSTS	
4						
5	ITEM		QUANTITY	UNIT	WEEK	YEAR
6						
7	FROZEN PETMEAT		4	.52	C7*D7	52*E7
8	CANNED DOGMEAT		3	.39	C8*D8	52*E8
9	FRESH FISH		2	.45	C9*D9	52*E9
10	VITAMINS (PER BOX)		1	.48	C10*D10	52*E10
11	CEREAL		1	.36	C11*D11	52*E11
12						
13	TOTAL COSTS				SUM(E7:E	SUM(F7:F

```
These 2 last formulae are                SUM(E7:E11)
                          and                      SUM(F7:F11)
```

These two last formulae are SUM(E7:E11) and SUM(F7:F11)

5.7 A 'WHAT IF?' demonstration

You have already seen the power of the combination of Formulae and Replication, when a change in one data value can be replicated across the whole sheet. If you have appreciated this point already then this demonstration is superfluous, but it is at the heart of 'what if?' exercises to which spreadsheets are ideally suited.

Return to the Home Budget data in worksheet 5.5 and ask the following simple questions. What if the mortgage payments next year increased by 10%, and the rates by 5% and there was a salary increase of 2%, would this home owner be able to cope?

Load the file **HOMBUG** into the spreadsheet, and enter:

1>=B4	
1>172.94%110	to increase the mortgage by 10%
1>=B6	
1>52.20%105	to increase the rates by 5%
1>=B19	
1>704.73%102	to increase the salary by 2%

The sheet will change instantaneously to that shown below.

	B	C	D	E	F	G	H
3	APR	MAY	JUN	JUL	AUG	SEP	TOTALS
4	190.23	190.23	190.23	190.23	190.23	190.23	1141.40
5	156.90	156.90	156.90	156.90	156.90	156.90	941.40
6	54.81	54.81	54.81	54.81	54.81	54.81	328.86
7	48.60	48.60	48.60	48.60	48.60	48.60	291.60
8	13.39	13.39	13.39	13.39	13.39	13.39	80.34
9							
10	49.23	.00	.00	52.09	.00	.00	101.32
11	.00	62.80	.00	.00	41.56	.00	104.36
12	.00	.00	78.31	.00	.00	49.35	127.66
13	35.75	.00	.00	.00	.00	.00	35.75
14							
15	150.00	200.00	175.00	205.00	200.00	250.00	1180.00
16							
17	698.91	726.73	717.24	721.02	705.49	763.28	4332.69
18							
19	718.82	718.82	718.82	718.82	718.82	718.82	4312.95

Salary Total now 4312.95, expenditure 4332,69, and the answer to the above question is: No he/she could not quite cope!

If you are not convinced of the power of spreadsheets at this point, then you never will be! Imagine trying the above exercise with pencil, paper and calculation machine! You could now zap the screen, load HOMBUG again and try different percentages.

More format and filing

You have met the most potent features of SuperCalc3 so the rest of the worksheets tend to do essential tidying up with a bit of gilding the lily. This unit looks at new features of Format and how to prepare spreadsheet data for inclusion in a text document.

Let's have a new sheet of data to ring the changes. The data is the end of year balance sheet for a small pet shop business.

	A	B	C	D	E
1		OAKWOOD	PET	STORES	
2					
3		YEAR 1		1984	
4					
5	INCOME			EXPENDITURE	
6					
7	CASH IN HAND	10000.00		STOCK PURCHASED	17400.00
8	LIVESTOCK	1200.00		RENT OF PREMISES	6000.00
9	DRY FOODSTUFFS	8500.00		STAFF SALARIES	8500.00
.0	FROZEN MEAT	7800.00		PART-TIME WAGES	250.00
.1	TINNED GOODS	5600.00		SERVICES	1200.00
.2	ACCESSORIES	3200.00		ADVERTISING	800.00
3				PETTY CASH	250.00
4					
5	TOTAL INCOME	36300.00		TOTAL OUTGOINGS	34400.00
6					
7	------------------------	------------	------------	------------------------	------------
8					
9	CASH BALANCE				
0	AT YEAR END	1900.00			

1 **To change column width with Format** — columns B, C and E are normal widths (9 characters), but columns A and D are 16 characters wide. Start from a blank sheet and

1>/F	to call up Format
C	to repond to Global, Column, Row, etc
A	to respond to range
16	to enter column width

You will see that column A has widened relatively to the other columns, including the size of the cursor of course.

Repeat the above sequence of instructions but when prompted for the column range enter **D**, and that column will widen also.

2 **To enter data and formulae on the sheet** — now enter the data on to the sheet. Do not try to enter the numbers with the two decimal places yet.

Total Income and Total Outgoings should be entered as SUM formulae at B15 and E15 respectively.

The Cash Balance at Year End at B20 will be given by the formula B15–E15.

3 **To change the numbers to money format** — the sequence of commands **1>/F(ormat),G(lobal),$** will change all values on the sheet to $ or 2 DP format. You could have been more precise and named the columns B and E separately, but as all of the numbers on the sheet are in this form, Global's brute force is good enough.

4 Save the sheet as **B:PETSH84** .

5 Delete the border with Global. If you wish to include the information on the sheet in a report or letter or other document, it is unlikely that you will want the row/column borders to the sheet. The instructions: **1>G(lobal),B(order)** will do this deletion.

B for Border is a toggle command, if you now go back through Global and Border you will 'toggle' the border back on to the display.

6 **To prepare the sheet as a text file** — now without the border the sheet is in a suitable form for inclusion in a document. Use the Output command

1>/O	
D	displays as on the sheet
A1:E20	range of the display
D	disk output
B:PETSH84	after filename prompt

Now Quit from SuperCalc3 and look at the directory on your work disk.

You will see two files PETSH84.CAL and PETSH84.PRN resulting from the work you have just done. If at the MS–DOS A–prompt you say
A>TYPE B:PETSH84.PRN the file will be displayed on the screen.

If you are in a document file in WordStar you can read this sheet in by the **Ctrl/KR** command with filename **B:PETSH84.PRN**.

6 Data types

6.1 Introduction

The phrase 'data processing' often may conjure up ideas of highly theoretical texts in computing science. This chapter certainly does not come into that category, but it will encourage you to take a careful, tidy and even thoughtful approach to the data that you will use.

You have already started to do this in the earlier chapter on word processing. The text which you enter into a word processing package forms data for that software; the words are but groups or 'strings' of characters which are handled by the program. While you are entering text you are aware of the information given in the status line: what line you are on, your position in numbers of characters across the line, how many words you have entered, how much memory your text is taking up, etc. You will soon learn what line width best suits certain documents, and how many lines you can get on different sizes of paper. You will soon find yourself taking a much more analytical approach to your text and its overall layout, than you would do if you just used a typewriter.

So far in the book I have used the terms 'data' and 'information' as if they are interchangeable. They are not necessarily so. Imagine a wartime situation, where a radio operator detected and noted down an enemy message. On his pad the message may consist of groups of characters, which are meaningless to him because they are coded. Nonetheless the group of characters are items of data. It is only when the code has been cracked, and the groups of characters become words, that the data is decoded into meaningful message. Data has to have meaning to become information.

6.2 Numbers and strings

You will appreciate more clearly how a computer can be programmed to handle different types of data from the following example. You have received a bill from your garage for a service and repair work that it has carried out. Because the bill is rather excessive, the manager has sent it to you with a polite letter to soften the blow.

Dear Mr Ewing-Jones,

I enclose our detailed account, No MV58632/PHH, totalling £172.38 for the 12,000 mile service and repairs carried out on your Iberia Coupé Reg No CAP 123B.

An early settlement of this account would be appreciated.

Yours sincerely,

The letter is somewhat contrived, but it will suffice if we just concentrate on the items of data which have been underlined. The name of the person to whom the letter is addressed ('Mr Ewing-Jones') and the name of car ('Iberia Coupé) are items of data comprising groups of characters, in this case letters of the alphabet and a hyphen. Generally the term 'character' refers to letters both lower and upper case, the numerals (or digits) 0,1,2,3,4,5,6,7,8,9, punctuation marks, and any special symbols found on the keyboard of the computer. As far as the machine is concerned a name is just a string of these characters, including any spaces which occur in the name, and such items of data are often referred to as 'strings'.

The other items of data in the letter would be loosely referred to as 'numbers': the account number MN58632/PHH, the total cost £172.38, the service point 12,000 miles, and the vehicle registration number CAP 123B. Only the two numbers 172.38 and 12,000 are likely to be used in any sort of calculation. The cost may include tax, or a percentage discount, and will have been arrived at after a simple calculation of the next service point, perhaps by adding 6,000 to that figure. The other two 'numbers', however, would not be used in any sort of calculation, and are viewed by the machine as just groups of characters which happen to include some digits, and the special character / in one case.

Most software packages make this distinction between two types of data; numbers which are used in calculations, and the rest which are usually referred to as 'characters' or 'strings'. The distinction is fundamental because the two types of data are stored in different ways in the machine.

Numbers

Computers are often thought of as number crunching devices. I hope that this book will show, among other things, that they have much wider applications than just doing lots of arithmetic very quickly. We do need to take a brief closer look at numbers, even if it is for no other reason than for the preparation of the chapter on spreadsheets. If the next page or so looks a bit too fierce for you then you will not lose very much by moving on to the next section entitled 'Characters and the ASCII code'. If you wish to look at numbers even more closely, then Appendix 2 shows how spreadsheets functions can be used to illustrate some of their properties.

6.3 Large numbers

Let's say that the mileometer of your car records up to 99999 miles, then if the vehicle is driven this far and beyond, after the next mile the reading will be 00000, and then 00001 and so on, thus giving an inaccurate but easily understood reading. The mileometer is a number register of a fixed size. With a precision of five digits in the case described. Numbers in computers are held in registers too, and their representation leads to similar problems.

Imagine that the register in your micro has a precision of six decimal digits, that the number stored in it is 999999, and then 1 is added to this number. Two possibilities jump to mind. Firstly, if the machine is so clever why cannot another register be provided to cope with the overflow? This would give a number with double precision, i.e. two, six digit registers. In cases where great accuracy is required, double precision arithmetic is provided by some languages and packages. The difficulty here would be that you would have to go on providing additional registers to accommodate numbers of different magnitudes, and would not know how many registers would be needed until a calculation is in progress — a very unsatisfactory state of affairs!

The second possibility is that an approximation for the new number is given. So the number which results from the sum 999999+1 may appear on your screen as the two–part number 1.00000E+06, standing for 1.00000× 1,000,000. The symbol **E** stands for 'multiply by 10 raised to the power of', so **E**+06 means 'multiply by 10 raised to the power of 6' and is used to give the magnitude of the whole number. The precision is kept at six figures, but the magnitude is adjusted by changing the power of 10 of the second half of the number.

If a calculation should have given rise to the number 149,723,554 then in the machine the number would be expressed in the E-form as 1.49724**E**+08. The parts of the composite number are 1.49724, the precision given by the size of the register, and **E**+08 giving the magnitude of the number in this case standing for ×100,000,000.

The precision part has been 'rounded' and there is a loss of accuracy here. Whether this loss of accuracy is important will depend on the nature of the calculation in the application with which you are concerned. The precision part of the number is always expressed with one digit in front of the decimal point and of course to six figure precision for the register size I have chosen as an example. So, 57,492,837,293 would become 5.74928**E**+10. Different machines do offer different levels of precision, and most machines do allow double precision if your application needs it.

6.4 Small numbers

If you imagine large numbers overflowing out of the left–hand end of the register, then you must stretch your imagination and think of very small numbers being squeezed out the right–hand end, after division, or lots of subtractions. If for some reason your machine was involved in the following sum 1/147,723,554 then the result would be 6.67897**E**–08, where **E**–08 is 1/100,000,000. In the same way 0.0000013798254 would become 1.37983–06.

As far as the machine is concerned zero is just a very small number, whose representation is not precise. Calculations which may possibly involve division by zero should be handled with great care, because some very strange results may occur. This phenomenon is shown quite clearly in Appendix 2. Most machines do these days give error messages when 'division by zero' has occurred.

You should also remember that the numbers in the machine are all represented in binary form, even though they appear on the screen in decimal form. In the same way as some decimal numbers cannot be represented exactly, for example 1/3=0.33333..., some binary numbers are not exact. In decimal 1/5=0.2 is exact; but in binary it becomes a recurring bicimal and not exact — not a lot of people know that!

I won't go on any more about numbers; but you should always be mindful of the points I have made here, and treat all numbers with a great deal of care. Numbers only concern us in this book when we are using spreadsheets. Appendix 2 gives some insight into how SuperCalc deals with large and small numbers.

6.5 Characters and the ASCII code

All of the characters entered at the keyboard are represented inside the machine as numbers. Remember that the numbers to be used in calculations are stored in a different way from strings or groups of characters, and furthermore that numbers which are used just for counting purposes (integers) are stored differently from decimal numbers.

The ASCII code is an internationally standard way of representing characters inside the machine by numbers. ASCII stands for the American Standard Code for Information Interchange. A complete version of the code is given in Appendix 3, and a snippet of the whole code is shown in Figure 6.2 so that you can see the binary basis of the code.

First let's make the machine speak for itself, by looking at the following dBASE II program which prints out some sections of the ASCII code.

```
line
1 ? 'ASCII CHARACTER SET '
2 ?
3 STORE 40 TO COUNT
4 DO WHILE COUNT < 51
5 ? STR(COUNT,3),'---',CHR(COUNT)
6 STORE COUNT+1 TO COUNT
7 ENDDO
```

```
ASCII CHARACTER SET

 40 --- (
 41 --- )
 42 --- *
 43 --- +
 44 --- ,
 45 --- -
 46 --- .
 47 --- /
 48 --- 0
 49 --- 1
 50 --- 2
```

Fig 6.1 The ASCII code generated by a dBASEII program

The line numbers on the right–hand side of the program are not part of the program itself. I have added them so that I can talk about how the program works.

The **?** is the symbol which says print on the screen or page, so Line 1 says 'print the message ASCII CHARACTER SET', and Line 2 just says 'print' which has the effect of printing a blank line. Line 3 says store the number 40 in the memory location called COUNT. Now the DO command in Line 4 and the ENDDO command in line 7 form a repetitive loop. Line 4 says 'do the following commands while the value found in the store location called COUNT is less than 51'. Line 6 adds 1 to the number in COUNT. The loop will end at Line 7, but only if the condition set down in Line 4 applies, i.e. that the number in COUNT is not less than 51. So the effect then is that the command in Line 5 is repeated 11 times while COUNT increases from 40 to 50 inclusive.

Line 5 prints out the value of COUNT as a string of length 3 characters **[STR(COUNT,3)]** followed by --- , and then the ASCII value of COUNT by the command [CHR(COUNT)] . The net effect is that the value of COUNT and the character which has this ASCII value are printed side by side on separate lines, as seen in the printout.

If the start value of the loop is changed to 60 and the ending value to < 71, then the following section of the ASCII code will be seen.

```
ASCII CHARACTER SET

 60 --- <
 61 --- =
 62 --- >
 63 --- ?
 64 --- @
 65 --- A
 66 --- B
 67 --- C
 68 --- D
 69 --- E
 70 --- F
```

If the limits to the DO-loop are 90 and while COUNT < 101 then the following section of the ASCII code appears.

```
ASCII CHARACTER SET

 90 --- Z
 91 --- [
 92 --- \
 93 --- ]
 94 --- ^
 95 --- _
 96 --- `
 97 --- a
 98 --- b
 99 --- c
100 --- d
```

Figure 6.2 shows a small section of the code, with the underlying number system shown in binary as well as decimal form.

```
         CODES                          Keyboard Character
Decimal         Binary
65              100 0001                       A
66              100 0010                       B
67              100 0011                       C
68              100 0100                       D
69              100 0101                       E
```

Fig. 6.2 The ASCII code, decimal and binary, for some characters

This figure shows how a code can be made up of patterns of 1s and 0s. You can easily imagine that these patterns represent electronic circuits inside the machine, which are either 'on' or 'off'. In this way it is possible to represent 128 ($=2\times2\times2\times2\times2\times2\times2$) different patterns, and thus 128 different characters in 8–bit form. But there are only 7 'bits' to each binary number above: the 8th bit is included as a 'check–bit', to check whether the code has been interpreted correctly, but does not affect the overall representation of the codes. The whole code in decimal form is shown in the Appendix 2.

6.6 True or false?

Computers are capable of making comparisons between items of data. For example: Is a number in one record greater than (>) a number in another record? Is the name just entered into the machine lower in alphabetical order (<) than the name in the record that the computer is currently scanning? Is the date on an invoice in the current financial year?

You can use symbols > 'greater than', < 'less than', and = 'equal to', and combinations of them to ask quite complicated questions about data, using a computer. You will soon appreciate this when you have read through the 'Logic and Data–bases' chapter and worked through the dBASE II worksheets later in the book. You can turn these questions into assertions, such as: This number is greater than that number. This name is lower than that in alphabetical order. The date is in this financial year. Thus the computer's electronic logic is concerned with whether such assertions are true or false, rather than answering questions with Yes or No.

Computers are very good at making simple comparisons very quickly, and if these simple comparisons are joined together in a sequence, the machine appears to be able to make quite complicated decisions at great speed. It is this feature of computers which makes them most useful, and apparently lifelike. You will remember that the assertions and the resultant actions must have been programmed into the machine in the first place by a human being.

As far as this chapter is concerned, for the correct operation of the system, we must see the TRUE and FALSE state of these assertions as important items of data.

6.7 Checklist

You may like to review some of the ideas introduced in this chapter by answering the following questions.

1 Can you specify clearly what is meant by the terms
   (a) strings (b) integers (c) decimal numbers?

2 Using the three categories set out in question 1, classify the following items of data:

   (a) National insurance number
   (b) Telephone number
   (c) Gross annual salary
   (d) Number of records in a file
   (e) Current base lending rate
   (f) Number of months in which to repay a loan
   (g) Library accession number
   (h) Price of a TV set
   (i) date of an invoice
   (j) Time of a train departure

3 Now take a look at some of the jobs that you may wish to carry out on the computer, and classify the items of data using these three categories.

4 Can you think up more examples where loops could be used for simple repetitive calculations? Appendix 2 may be of interest.

5 Write the following numbers in the standard 6–figure form used in the text.

(a) 0.000345497 (b) 78,965,300,000 (c) 236.857×10^{6}

and the following standard numbers in their natural form.

(d) 2.92384E+03 (e) 5.86321E–13 (f) 1.86439E+20

6 From the data given in Figure 6.2, work out the ASCII code for: F, P, U, J and S, and check your results with the given in the Appendix 2.

7 Say there are two memory locations called NUMBER1 and NUMBER2 in your micro.
If they hold the numbers: NUMBER1=11.7 and NUMBER2=2.3, are the following assertions TRUE or FALSE?

(a) NUMBER2 > NUMBER1
(b) NUMBER2 <= NUMBER1
(c) NUMBER2 < 0
(d) NUMBER1 > 6 × NUMBER2

8 Now look at some of the tasks you may wish to carry out on the machine and decide what questions and comparisons you may wish to make of the data.

7 Data processing

In the last chapter you were introduced to the different data types which you are likely to meet. Now we will look at some of the activities which are usually included under the general heading of 'data processing'.

In our everyday lives, data impinges on us in a wide variety of shapes and forms. The telephone directory is probably the most frequently used; then there are shopping lists and the resultant supermarket receipts; lists of football fixtures, results and league tables; racing results and stock market prices; bus and rail timetables; the menu at the local Chinese restaurant; and many more.

Different ways of presenting different types of data will appear throughout the rest of the book, not least the index of the book itself. The shapes and forms of data are referred to as data structures. If your choice of data structure is appropriate and your data coding accurate and complete, then your data processing problems are largely solved. And the decisions about structure and coding should be made before you sit down at your computer to enter the first item of data.

7.1 Lists and tables

Some data structures are very complicated, but the two examples which you will encounter most frequently are lists and tables. Figure 7.1 may be thought of as a simple list of names.

1	Parks
2	Stevens
3	Hughton
4	Roberts
5	Miller
6	Perryman
7	Ardiles
8	Archibald
9	Falco
10	Hoddle
11	Galvin

Fig. 7.1 A list of names

This list seems to have no particular order; it is certainly not in alphabetical order. The main feature of a list as a structure is that the position of each item of data is assumed to have a number associated with it, as shown in the left–hand column. This set of numbers is referred to as the index of the list. So instead of referring to the item of data (here a name) directly, it is possible to refer to it by means of its position in the list through its index. Although they are very important for programmers, lists of single items of data are not practically very useful in data processing. Usually there are associated items of data like an address, a telephone number, and so on; and the simple list grows into several associated lists, and such a collection of lists is called a table.

The structure of data is largely determined by the purpose for which the data has been collected. The list in Figure 7.1 seems to be simply a list of names, but to a Tottenham Hotspur football supporter this description gives the lie to the real structure. The index number here is the number on the shirt worn by the player, which is in turn related to his playing position on the field. So even this simple list has a hidden structure and meaning.

00001	WW14	WEST WICKHAM	D	3	2	0	L	55000
00002	CI23	CHISLEHURST	D	5	3	2	M	168000
00003	PW48	PETTS WOOD	D	3	1	1	M	69995
00004	OR09	ORPINGTON	T	3	1	0	S	28500
00005	BE73	BEXLEY	D	4	2	1	M	52750
00006	BI37	BICKLEY	F	1	1	0	N	22950
00007	PW19	PETTS WOOD	D	3	2	1	L	69950
00008	OR63	ORPINGTON	M	3	1	1	N	29950
00009	CI50	CHISLEHURST	D	5	3	2	M	95000
00010	BR82	BROMLEY	S	4	3	0	S	36250

Fig. 7.2 A table of data, the HOUSES file

Figure 7.2 shows a table of data. It can be seen as consisting of eight columns of data (as eight lists) or ten rows, but it is most meaningful to see it as a homogenous block of data, where each item can be picked out by referring to a row and column along that row. So to identify an item of data you must specify two numbers: one for the row, and the other for the column, hence the academic name of two–dimensional array. Such tables are often also referred to by mathematicians as matrices or arrays. You have already met a similar idea of using two numbers to specify the position of the cursor on the screen, when the function of the status line in word processing software was described.

7.2 Files, records and fields

Computer literature bristles with terms like lists, tables, arrays and matrices. They are part of the jargon of book, magazine articles and advertisements, software and hardware manuals, and in the specifications you will read when trying to decide whether to buy and item of software. The terms originate from the more academic programming sources, but the ideas of fields, records and files may be more useful when talking about data 'en bloc'.

So far we have used the word 'file' in word processing to mean quantity of textual data stored on disk. In data processing the term can be used in a more specific way, to refer to a set of data records which have been collected for a common purpose. This leaves us asking what is meant by the terms 'record' and 'field'. Let us approach these ideas through an example.

Figure 7.2 shows data which could be held on file by an estate agent. The agent has several different types of file, but the most important must be the one which contains the detailed features and measurements of individual properties. The file in Figure 7.2 gives a small section from a summary file of all the properties which are available at any time. When a customer seeks the services of the estate agent in the first instance, this summary file could be used to look for those properties which most closely match the customer's needs. Having thus found some suitable properties from this file, the customer could then pass on to the details of these individual properties.

Each row of the table in Figure 7.2 contains data which relates to a particular house, and the collection of data items for each house is referred to as a record. Each record consists of 8 separate units of data. This basic unit of data is called a field. So a record is a collection of fields, and a file is a collection of records.

In more complicated files there may not be the same number of fields in each record; but all of the data files in this book will have this regular structure. Only ten records are shown in the file in Figure 7.2, but obviously in reality there would likely be many more.

7.3 Coding the data

Remember that the purpose of the HOUSES file is to summarise all of the properties which the agent has available. So, some considerable thought must first be put into deciding which are the most critical features needed to summarise a customer's future home, and then how these features may be coded so that the data in each record may be as accurate and unambiguous as possible. The coding must take into account the different types of data which may be needed, as discussed in the last chapter.

This file takes seven features which are seen to be critical in choosing a property, and each record has coded versions of these features in fields 2–8.

Field 2 — this field holds the name of the geographical area where the property is situated. It is a character field, and for the purpose of uniform appearance on the screen when the file is displayed, should contain no more than 15 characters.

Field 3 — this gives the type of property as a single character: **D**(detached), **S**(semi-detached), **T**(terraced), **B**(bungalow), **F**(flat), and **M**(maisonette).

Fields 4–6 — these contain integers, whole numbers which give how many bedrooms, reception rooms and garages the property has.

Field 7 — this field contains one character which summarises the size of the garden: **L**(large), **M**(medium), **S**(small), **N**(none).

Field 8 — this gives the price of the property as a decimal number, because eventually certain calculations will have to be done using this number. Having picked out a likely property from this summary file the customer would then wish to pass on to the individual file for further details of it. 'I like the look of the semi–detached house in Petts Wood for £69,950' is rather an ambiguous piece of information with which to start the next stage of the search. This is where the Reference Number in **Field** 1 comes into its own, because this number is the link which leads you to the file where further details can be found. The field is a 4–character field; the first two characters give a cryptic for the geographical area of the house, and the last two are digits that identify which house in that area.

If the estate agent's office were completely computerised, this number could be input into the machine and a more detailed file could be called up from backing store, and viewed there and then by the customer. Similarly, this reference number could also lead the agent onto the file which summarises the details of the person who is selling the house, and eventually to the file which summarises the financial transactions which occur during the purchase, and so on.

7.4 File preparation

The purpose of setting up a file of data is to use it for reference, to ask questions of it, to look for relationships between the records, to keep the details accurate and up to date, and so on. The activity of asking questions of a data file is called interrogation. The estate agent may wish to interrogate the house data file to find all those houses with more than 4 bedrooms, or all those houses in Bromley with prices under £50,000, or all of the houses in Chelsfield or Chislehurst having a large garden, depending on the requirements of a particular customer. Before you reach the interrogation stage, however, there is a lot of routine but vital processing to be carried out.

It's all very well to see a file printed on a page, to imagine that it has 100 records rather than 10, but how do you get it into the machine in the first place? How do you save it, print it out in various different layouts (formats), change a field if it is incorrect or just needs modification, delete a record which is no longer needed in the file, add more records to the file, or sort the file into a particular order? These activities can be generally described as file preparation, and are carried out using a data–base package such as dBASE II, and will be worked through in detail in the Worksheet section using that package.

Imagine that you are now the Activities Secretary of a Ramblers Club. The club has more than a thousand members who come from a fairly widespread area. Once every half–year you mail all members with brief summaries of the main events for the next six months, together with routine documents relating to subscriptions and committee meetings. The club has decided that it is too expensive to mail all members with the details of each event. To help you make your mail shot more accurate i.e. to send details to those members who are most likely to take part in the event, you have devised and maintained the data file shown in Figure 7.3.

00001	BROADBENT D	M/2974	A	E	P
00002	EVANS D	Y/6281	C	N	O
00003	GEORGE B	J/2953	A	N	P
00004	HOWSON H	F/3453	A	S	O
00005	JACKSON H	M/8243	B	W	O
00006	LEMMING B	Y/9742	A	N	O
00007	MURDOCH K	M/7594	B	E	P
00008	PRINGLE S	Y/0944	C	S	O
00009	SMYTHE J	M/4688	A	S	O
00010	WILLIS B	F/7724	B	W	O

Fig. 7.3 Data file for the Ramblers' club

Imagine that this, your main or master file contains about 1000 records. You have four types of membership: male (M/), female (F/), joint (J/) and family (Y/), indicated by the first character of the membership in the second field. The third field gives the preferred distance each member likes to ramble: A for more than 10 miles in one day, B for medium distances of 5–10 miles, and C for less than 5 miles. Field 4 gives one of the four regions into which the area of membership is divided, N/S/E/W for the four points of the compass. Finally, Field 5 says whether the members have their own transport (O) or have to rely on public (P) transport.

You can now mail to members who will most likely be interested in certain types of short family outings, a ladies' evening walk for the Eastern region, a long all–male walk where own transport is required to get to the starting point, and so on. The membership number would lead on to other files for addresses, subscription details, and so on.

7.5 Creating and editing files

Entering data into a file for the first time is called creating a data file; editing occurs at some later stage when changes have to be made to the data. But we have already spent a lot of time talking about editing using a word processor so why can't we just use the word processing software to edit the file, or even to create it in the first place? The sad answer to this question is that most word processing packages do not readily allow you to create and edit data files, and conversely most data processing packages will not accept files which have been created or edited by a word processor. So you either have to write your own programs to perform these operations, or rely on prepared software to do them for you. This unsatisfactory situation is gradually improving.

Whether the software is home–grown or bought as a package it should let you define the number of fields in each record, and to name the fields. So, the task on running the software is to give names to the fields, the number of characters which are likely to be used in each field, and the data type. Having done this, the screen is given a set layout on which you can enter data which will look something like Figure 7.4, which is shown as if you had just completed entering data into the first record.

```
----------------------------------------------

Name             |Broadbent D          |
Membership No.   |M/2974|
Distance         |A|
Region           |E|
Transport        |P|
----------------------------------------------

Enter: to go to the next record
ESC: to return to the main menu
```

Fig. 7.4 Entering data into fields of a record

The structure of each record is displayed on the screen and you enter the data, between the markers, against the appropriate field name. Usually you are allowed to move around within the fields of each record using the cursor, over–writing characters where necessary; but once you have pressed the Enter key to pass on to the next record, then you cannot go back without going through the main menu, by pressing Escape (Esc). In your particular package the keys may be different from Enter and Esc, and usually the prompt line, which occurs in this example gives you the general idea.

If you press Esc and return to the main menu, you will be faced with a wide range of possible functions, similar to those described in the word processing chapter. These would include: to edit or delete old records, to continue entering new data, to load in data from another data file stored on disk (it would need to have the same record structure as the current file), to save the records created so far, to quit the current activities with or without saving the data entered so far.

Another very important option would be the print function. You can easily get a printout of the file record by record as shown in figure 7.4 but if you want the layout to be changed to show the data as displayed in Figure 7.3 then the print option will have to let you specify the format you require.

7.6 Sorting and merging files

If your master file holds as many as 1000 records, you may well make up to 50 changes to it per month. These changes will include deletions, changes of region within the club area and other minor changes, and will also involve adding new members to your files. The changes and additions will accumulate over a period of time, and it would be better to make the amendments periodically in batches, rather than continuously. In mainframe computer work, this 'batch processing' is the main method used.

The following method for dealing with new members to the club is a good general method to use for dealing with additions to large files. You collect the records for the new members in a small subsidiary file usually referred to as the 'work' file. A work file of new members to the club is shown in Figure 7.5.

00001	MORRIS J	M/8803	C	N	O
00002	ASHCROFT P	F/4239	A	N	O
00003	WILLIAMS A	Y/1146	C	E	O
00004	RICHARDS D	M/3219	B	S	P
00005	STANDEN D	Y/8318	A	W	O

Fig. 7.5 A work file of new members

The first thing you notice is that this file is not in any particular order, except probably in the order new applications were received. The master file is in alphabetical order of the surnames of the members. Most files have a dominant or key field, which tends to dictate the order of the records in the file, and it is often the first field of the record. In the case of the HOUSES file in the earlier example, the reference number (the first field) would be the key.

Many of the fairly rudimentary data–base packages which are available for micros will sort only on the first field of a record, but in the majority of applications this is all that is really needed, and usually you have the option to reorder the fields so that the desired field is in the first position. So you should sort the work file into the same order as the master file, which in this case would give the following file:

00001	ASHCROFT P	F/4239	A	N	O
00002	MORRIS J	M/8803	C	N	O
00003	RICHARDS D	M/3219	B	S	P
00004	STANDEN D	Y/8318	A	W	O
00005	WILLIAMS A	Y/1146	C	E	O

Fig. 7.6 The work file reordered

If you intended to work very carefully right from the start, which is the only sensible thing to do, then you should have saved the sorted version. You can now merge the sorted work file into the old master file to get a new master file, and this is what you would get:

00001	ASHCROFT P	F/4239	A	N	O
00002	BROADBENT D	M/2974	A	E	P
00003	EVANS D	Y/6281	C	N	O
00004	GEORGE B	J/2953	A	N	P
00005	HOWSON H	F/3453	A	S	O
00006	JACKSON H	M/8243	B	W	O
00007	LEMMING B	Y/9742	A	N	O
00008	MORRIS J	M/8803	C	N	O
00009	MURDOCH K	M/7594	B	E	P
00010	PRINGLE S	Y/0944	C	S	O
00011	RICHARDS D	M/3219	B	S	P
00012	SMYTHE J	M/4688	A	S	O
00013	STANDEN D	Y/8318	A	W	O
00014	WILLIAMS A	Y/1146	C	E	O
00015	WILLIS B	F/7724	B	W	O

Fig. 7.7 The 'merged' new master file

The records of the sorted work file have now been entered into their correct alphabetical positions in the master file. To do this merge operation, both files obviously have to be sorted on to the same key fields. You could just have added the unsorted work file record on to the end of the old master file, (append is the word used for this operation) and then sorted this rather large untidy collection, but the sort would probably take a long time and it is a rather inefficient approach to the problem. Having generated a new master file you should now save it. This is the best general routine: create a small work file and save it, sort it, then save again, merge it with the old master file to create a new one, and then save the result. If you keep to this routine, and create work files with only about ten records as one batch, you will save a lot of time and frustration in the long run.

You've now got the data coded and into a file with a particular record structure, and in a given order, ready to start the interrogation procedure, which is covered next.

7.7 Checklist

1 Check your understanding of the term 'data processing' by clarifying in your mind, or even jotting down on paper, the meanings of the following terms':

list, index, table (what do the indexes refer to in the tables?), array, matrix, field, record, file, (what is meant by the term 'structure'?), coding data, creating, editing, sorting, merging, key field (explain the relationship between merging and sorting), append (what is the difference between merge and append?) and interrogation.

2 Think of the ways in which data impinges on you, in your work or your hobbies, and all everyday activities. Think of your diet sheets, holiday brochures, mail order catalogues, knitting patterns, radio and television schedules. Have a 'data awareness' week and write down all of the occasions when you refer to data in some structured form.

3 Now take a look at some of the jobs which you are considering carrying out on a micro. Go back through the terms in question 1 above and decide whether they have any meaning for your task. Does your data have a natural, clearly defined structure? If it does, can you decide on the number and nature of the fields in each record, and the maximum number of records you are likely to want in the file? Can you see clearly the best way to code your data? Will this method of coding let you process the data without ambiguity? Do you know what questions you wish to ask of your data file? Have you allowed for questions which you don't wish to ask at the present time, but may wish to ask when the data is stored in a more accessible way?

8 Logic and data-bases

8.1 Introduction

In the previous chapter you saw how data was collected, coded and organised into files. The reason for doing this is to let you use the data in a file as a source of information. To do this you have to learn how to ask questions of the data, to look for new relationships which are not easily picked out from a casual visual scan of the file on the screen or from a printout. The process of asking questions of a data–base is called interrogation. Most data–base software packages let you interrogate the data using simple and fairly standard logical methods.

This chapter is largely concerned with the logic of asking questions of data–bases. The methods illustrated here are quite general, and would not be out of place in a mathematics lesson, with their relationship to Sets and Logic. Furthermore, if you accept that the next generation of micros will most likely be knowledge–based machines, and that the languages used to run them will be logic–based languages, then the material in this chapter does not merely form an introduction to the practical section of dBASE II worksheets, but has a general educational value in its own right.

Every business organisation from the smallest to the multinational company will entail the collection and storage of data in the form of a data–base, even though in the case of the small business the data may not be stored on a computer. Even the most rudimentary data–base — just a list of names, addresses and statements of accounts of even a small firm's customers, would be much too large and unweildy to be used in a book such as this. It is difficult to choose an example which will be readily understood and interesting to all readers. I have chosen a file of holiday options, and hope that it will be sufficiently familiar and interesting to most readers. You may now, or in the future, use your machine as a terminal to a Prestel or viewdata data–base to select a holiday. It is the underlying logical methods which are important, so to get the most out of the chapter, you should be reviewing your own particular applications to see how the methods could be applied in your case.

8.2 The holiday file

The time is mid June and the place a travel agent's office. Most of the holidays in the multitude of brochures are no longer available, so to save time for the travel agent and for the customers the travel company has compiled a file, which can be accessed through the agent's computer terminal, of those holidays which are still available for the four weeks in August later that summer.

It is a summary file and in reality would have hundreds of records, but we show only 20 of these in Figure 8.1. To simplify the file and its coding I have assumed that the file relates to holidays of the same type, beach holidays, and that all of the associated air flights are at the weekends of the four weeks. The reference number of each record would be used to direct you to another file, or to a brochure which contained further details of the holiday. This secondary file would have more details of the type of holiday, the resort, the type of accommodation available and the number of places still vacant, time of flight, and so on.

When the file was set up in the first place, the fields of each record were given the names shown above the columns in Figure 1. The field codes are largely self explanatory. The first column of numbers 1–20 are the record numbers given by dBASE II with which I produced the data–base for the book, and were not defined by me as an actual field, but I have left them in all printouts in this chapter because I felt that it might help you identify the records when they are selected.

	Refno	Country	Type	Weeks	Airport	Price
00001	FR072	FRANCE	FULL	OBCD	GAT	195
00002	FR211	FRANCE	HALF	OBCD	GAT	225
00003	FR382	FRANCE	APT	OOCD	MAN	255
00004	IT229	ITALY	FULL	ABCD	LUT	210
00005	IT365	ITALY	HALF	OBCD	GAT	205
00006	IT509	ITALY	HALF	OOCD	GLAS	215
00007	IT882	ITALY	FULL	ABCD	GAT	265
00008	MA078	MAJORCA	HALF	OOCD	BIRM	185
00009	MA147	MAJORCA	FULL	OBCD	GAT	205
00010	MA364	MAJORCA	FULL	OOCO	GAT	175
00011	MA662	MAJORCA	APT	ABOD	MAN	190
00012	MA771	MAJORCA	HALF	ABCD	GAT	215
00013	PO339	PORTUGAL	HALF	OBOD	GAT	265
00014	PO887	PORTUGAL	HALF	OBCO	BIRM	245
00015	SP137	SPAIN	FULL	ABOD	GLAS	190
00016	SP258	SPAIN	FULL	ABOO	LUT	205
00017	SP481	SPAIN	HALF	ABCO	GAT	170
00018	SP551	SPAIN	FULL	OBCO	BIRM	195
00019	SP722	SPAIN	APT	OBCD	GAT	190
00020	SP901	SPAIN	HALF	ABCD	GLAS	210

Fig. 8.1 The HOLIDAY file

The accommodation in the type field can be FULL for full-board, HALF for half-board, or APT for apartment. The airport field contains shortened versions of the names GATwick, LUTon, BIRMingham, MANchester and GLASgow. The price field gives the cost per person for a one week unit of holiday. You would be passed on to another file to find out the costs for two or three week holidays, and special prices for children, and all of the other mysterious price factors which occur when you go into the details of the costings. The common link between a record and other files giving more details would be the reference number in the refno field. This is meant to be a simple summary file where you make your initial enquiries to find a holiday which is possibly suitable. The price field is the only field in each record which is numerical in nature.

In the weeks field, the four weeks in this hypothetical August have been named A, B, C and D. If the holiday is available in any week the letter is given, but if it is not then an O occurs. So, OOCO would indicate a holiday which is available only in the third week, whereas OBCO is available for the whole period. The code OBCD would not only indicate that there are three one–week holidays available, but also that there are two possible two–week holidays OBCO and OOCD, as well as the one three–week holiday OBCD. Once again, in reality it is all more complicated than this, but this will give us enough scope for our interrogation process.

8.3 True or false?

Remember that in actual use the file would have 200 or 2,000 records rather than 20, and that when it is called up on to the travel agent's screen you will want to select certain holidays which seem suitable for you and your family. Your first criterion for selecting a holiday may be very simple; you may want to go to Spain. It would be relatively easy just to look through all of the Spain records in this case, because they have been collected all together, and the file has been sorted into alphabetical order by country. In fact it was sorted on the reference number field, but that is incidental to the story. It may be a simple process just to pass your finger down over all the Spain records on the screen, but if there were 60 or 600 rather than 6 it would be tedious, and you would be likely to miss some. Furthermore, your criterion for selecting a holiday may not just be on country, e.g. 'I want an apartment holiday', or 'I don't mind where I go, but I must fly from Gatwick', or 'I can't afford more than £200 per person'.

All data–base packages let you ask such questions of the data in a fairly standard way. They can be seen as saying:

> pass through the file record by record
> and if a given condition is true for a record
> then print it on the screen and/or save it in a file
> otherwise ignore the record.

Or, more simply:

IF the condition is true **THEN** select the record.

If we apply this idea to the selection of all the apartment holidays from the holiday file, then the critical statement would become:
IF Type=APT **THEN** select the record.
The records selected would be:

00003	FR382	FRANCE	APT	OOCD	MAN	255
00011	MA662	MAJORCA	APT	ABOD	MAN	190
00019	SP722	SPAIN	APT	OBCD	GAT	190

Note that 'Type=APT' is the condition by which these records are selected.

To select those holidays which fly from Gatwick airport the selecting statement would be:
IF Airport=GAT **THEN** select the record
and the resulting file would be:

00001	FR072	FRANCE	FULL	OBCD	GAT	195
00002	FR211	FRANCE	HALF	OBCD	GAT	225
00005	IT365	ITALY	HALF	OBCD	GAT	205
00007	IT882	ITALY	FULL	ABCD	GAT	265
00009	MA147	MAJORCA	FULL	OBCD	GAT	205
00010	MA364	MAJORCA	FULL	OOCO	GAT	175
00012	MA771	MAJORCA	HALF	ABCD	GAT	215
00013	PO339	PORTUGAL	HALF	OBOD	GAT	265
00017	SP481	SPAIN	HALF	ABCO	GAT	170
00019	SP722	SPAIN	APT	OBCD	GAT	190

In the same way, to find those holidays which cost less than £200 the selection statement would be

IF Price>200 THEN select the record:

00001	FR072	FRANCE	FULL	OBCD	GAT	195
00008	MA078	MAJORCA	HALF	OOCD	BIRM	185
00010	MA364	MAJORCA	FULL	OOCO	GAT	175
00011	MA662	MAJORCA	APT	ABOD	MAN	190
00015	SP137	SPAIN	FULL	ABOD	GLAS	190
00017	SP481	SPAIN	HALF	ABCO	GAT	170
00018	SP551	SPAIN	FULL	OBCO	BIRM	195
00019	SP722	SPAIN	APT	OBCD	GAT	190

The sense of logic is:
IF (condition is true) **THEN** select the record.
If the condition is not true then the record is not selected, and the process passes on to the next record. If you have done some BASIC programming then you will recognise the form of this statement. It uses the usual mathematical symbols:

>	for 'less than'
<	for 'greater than'
=	for 'equal to' as you would expect.

The statements also rely on the TRUE or FALSE judgement about an expression, which is the third type of data used in computing, together with numbers and strings.

8.4 The AND function

Usually you want to ask more complicated questions than these. What about the customer who requests a holiday which is less than £200 but which also departs from Gatwick airport? Here there are two restrictions which have to be obeyed, and the 'AND' operator is used to compose this type of statement. In this case the conditional statement would be:

```
IF Airport=GAT AND Price<200 THEN select the record:

00001  FR072 FRANCE     FULL  OBCD  GAT     195
00010  MA364 MAJORCA    FULL  OOCO  GAT     175
00017  SP481 SPAIN      HALF  ABCO  GAT     170
00019  SP722 SPAIN      APT   OBCD  GAT     190
```

You could have achieved the same result by passing through the first to form a second file: the first pass to find all of those holidays flying from Gatwick and store them in a file, and then a pass through this second file to find all those whose price is less than £200. Or conversely, to find all those holidays which are less than £200, and through that file those flying from Gatwick. The AND operator puts a double restriction on the data making a much more restrictive condition, as you will see from the following if you ask for a holiday which is full board and less than £200. The condition:

```
IF Type=FULL AND Price<200 THEN select the record:

00001  FR072 FRANCE     FULL  OBCD  GAT     195
00010  MA364 MAJORCA    FULL  OOCO  GAT     175
00015  SP137 SPAIN      FULL  ABOD  GLAS    190
00018  SP551 SPAIN      FULL  OBCO  BIRM    195
```

The form of the selecting crtierion using the AND operator is:
IF (condition 1 **AND** condition 2 are true) **THEN** select the record.

8.5 The OR operator

This is a less selective operator, for it allows a selection to be made if either condition 1 or condition 2 applies. The form of the criterion now is:
IF (condition 1 **OR** condition 2 is true) **THEN** select.

The crux of the difference between AND and OR is seen in the phrases 'are true' and 'is true'. With the AND operator selection is made only when both are true, but with the OR operator selection occurs when either one or the other is true. 'I would like to go to Spain or Majorca' would be expressed:

```
IF Country=SPAIN OR Country=MAJORCA THEN select the record:

00008  MA078 MAJORCA    HALF  OOCD  BIRM    185
00009  MA147 MAJORCA    FULL  OBCD  GAT     205
00010  MA364 MAJORCA    FULL  OOCO  GAT     175
00011  MA662 MAJORCA    APT   ABOD  MAN     190
00012  MA771 MAJORCA    HALF  ABCD  GAT     215
00015  SP137 SPAIN      FULL  ABOD  GLAS    190
00016  SP258 SPAIN      FULL  ABOO  LUT     205
00017  SP481 SPAIN      HALF  ABCO  GAT     170
00018  SP551 SPAIN      FULL  OBCO  BIRM    195
00019  SP722 SPAIN      APT   OBCD  GAT     190
00020  SP901 SPAIN      HALF  ABCD  GLAS    210
```

This request involved scanning the second column, or looking at the second field in each record and selecting the record if the data in that field was either SPAIN or MAJORCA. So the OR function can operate on the same field, but in different records. It can apply simultaneously to two fields in the same record. If a customer is concerned about the cost especially of eating out when on holiday, especially if there with family, he may consider a holiday which is either full board or priced at under £200. The selecting statement now becomes:

```
IF Type=FULL OR Price <200 THEN select the record:

00001   FR072 FRANCE        FULL  OBCD  GAT      195
00004   IT229 ITALY         FULL  ABCD  LUT      210
00007   IT882 ITALY         FULL  ABCD  GAT      265
00008   MA078 MAJORCA       HALF  OOCD  BIRM     185
00009   MA147 MAJORCA       FULL  OBCD  GAT      205
00010   MA364 MAJORCA       FULL  OOCO  GAT      175
00011   MA662 MAJORCA       APT   ABOD  MAN      190
00015   SP137 SPAIN         FULL  ABOD  GLAS     190
00016   SP258 SPAIN         FULL  ABOO  LUT      205
00017   SP481 SPAIN         HALF  ABCO  GAT      170
00018   SP551 SPAIN         FULL  O3CO  BIRM     195
00019   SP722 SPAIN         APT   OBCD  GAT      190
```

The OR operator has in this case applied to the type field or to the price field in a given record, and sometimes simultaneously, as this file includes those records for which both criteria apply. You will have noticed that, the data derived from the use of the OR function, includes the data which was derived from the use of the AND function, i.e. the data from the criterion (Type=FULL AND Price <200) are included in the above file.

8.6 The NOT operator

The third and last operator which is needed to interrogate databases is the NOT operator, which simply negates the conditions on which it operates. To form the more loosely worded request 'I don't mind where I go as long as it is not Spain or Majorca', you ask for those holidays in Spain or Majorca and then negate the statement. The condition to ask for Spain or Majorca would be

IF Country=SPAIN **OR** Country=MAJORCA **THEN** select. The negated condition would be expressed:

```
IF NOT(Country=SPAIN OR Country=MAJORCA) THEN select.

00001   FR072 FRANCE        FULL  OBCD  GAT      195
00002   FR211 FRANCE        HALF  OBCD  GAT      225
00003   FR382 FRANCE        APT   OOCD  MAN      255
00004   IT229 ITALY         FULL  ABCD  LUT      210
00005   IT365 ITALY         HALF  OBCD  GAT      205
00006   IT509 ITALY         HALF  OOCD  GLAS     215
00007   IT882 ITALY         FULL  ABCD  GAT      265
00013   PO339 PORTUGAL      HALF  OBOD  GAT      265
00014   PO887 PORTUGAL      HALF  OBCO  BIRM     245
```

Note how the first positive expression is contained in brackets before it is negated, to avoid possible ambiguity.

This would have been a fairly easy request to answer by the finger–down–the–screen technique, even if there had been 200 rather than 20 records, mainly because the file is sorted conveniently for this question into blocks of countries. Also because there are only five countries involved in the whole file, it might be thought easier to ask the more direct question 'I want to go France, Italy or Portugal'. A more suitable circumstance perhaps, in which to use the NOT operator, would be by someone living in the Midlands, who doesn't wish to travel through London to get to the airport, nor indeed to travel as far as Glasgow, but could travel to the other airports relatively easily. The question in this case could be expressed as:

```
IF NOT(Airport=GAT OR Airport=GLAS) THEN select:

00003  FR382 FRANCE     APT   OOCD  MAN    255
00004  IT229 ITALY      FULL  ABCD  LUT    210
00008  MA078 MAJORCA    HALF  OOCD  BIRM   185
00011  MA662 MAJORCA    APT   ABOD  MAN    190
00014  PO887 PORTUGAL   HALF  OBCO  BIRM   245
00016  SP258 SPAIN      FULL  ABOO  LUT    205
00018  SP551 SPAIN      FULL  OBCO  BIRM   195
```

8.7 The 'Joker' or 'Wild Card'

We haven't yet used the Weeks field in the record to make any selections. This field was simplified considerably by considering only four weeks in the hypothetical August, and units of seven days only. You may have noticed that there is only one one–week holiday in the whole list, namely MA364 whose week field is OOCO, which indicates that the only week available is the third week of August. But if someone wanted a one–week holiday in the third week, they would not just be offered this one possibility, because any code which includes the C in the third column would give a one–week holiday at that time. You could decide to get at this information by brute force by writing down all the possible codes which include C in the third column: OOCO, OOCD, OBCD, AOCO, and so on, and use the OR operator. However, the condition in the selection expression would become very complicated.
IF Weeks=OOCO **OR** Weeks=OBCD . . . etc.

What you need to get round this problem is a way of saying 'any combination of characters which includes C in the third column', and this may be expressed as **C*, where * is that 'joker' or 'wild card' character. You read **C* as 'any character in positions 1 and 2, with C in position 3, and any character in position 4'. It is like holding a hand of four cards in which you have three jokers, which can stand for any other card, and a C card. So the statement which you would now have to enter to answer the query 'I would like a one–week holiday in the third week of August', would be:
IF Weeks=**C* **THEN** select the record
and you would get all of the file except for five records. So, to save a very long printout, look for one–week holiday starting in the first week of August, with the statement:

```
IF Weeks=A*** THEN select the record:

00004  IT229 ITALY      FULL  ABCD  LUT    210
00007  IT882 ITALY      FULL  ABCD  GAT    265
00011  MA662 MAJORCA    APT   ABOD  MAN    190
00012  MA771 MAJORCA    HALF  ABCD  GAT    215
00015  SP137 SPAIN      FULL  ABOD  GLAS   190
00016  SP258 SPAIN      FULL  ABOO  LUT    205
00017  SP481 SPAIN      HALF  ABCO  GAT    170
00020  SP901 SPAIN      HALF  ABCD  GLAS   210
```

All data–base packages of any real worth provide this 'wild card' facility in some form or other. We have expressed the weeks field in this form in order to demonstrate the 'wild card' function. We could have taken more care over how this information should be coded. We could even have had separate fields for each of the four weeks, with another code in the field to say what length holidays are available starting at that week. There are many ways in which this information could be coded and organized. You could usefully spend some time trying to code and express the data in different ways, and consider carefully the advantages of each method. The point is that in this case, having to resort to the 'wild card' approach is largely a result of the simplistic way we have presented the data.

The method hasn't answered all of the questions yet, however; it isn't the universal answer by any means. It lets us ask specific questions, like 'I want a two week holiday starting in the second week of August', for which the code would be ***BC*** , and the condition **Week=*BC*** . But it isn't so convenient for the more general question 'I don't mind which weeks I go, but I want a two–week holiday in August'. This selection statement would be:
IF Weeks=AB** **OR** Weeks=*BC* **OR** Weeks=**CD **THEN** select ,
and most of the file would be selected. So we will look for a three–week holiday in August starting either in the first or second week, with the expression:
IF Weeks=ABC* **OR** Weeks=*BCD **THEN** select the record
which would give the smaller file:

```
IF Weeks=ABC* OR Weeks=*BCD THEN select the record

which would give the smaller file:

00001  FR072 FRANCE     FULL  OBCD  GAT    195
00002  FR211 FRANCE     HALF  OBCD  GAT    225
00004  IT229 ITALY      FULL  ABCD  LUT    210
00005  IT365 ITALY      HALF  OBCD  GAT    205
00007  IT882 ITALY      FULL  ABCD  GAT    265
00009  MA147 MAJORCA    FULL  OBCD  GAT    205
00012  MA771 MAJORCA    HALF  ABCD  GAT    215
00017  SP481 SPAIN      HALF  ABCO  GAT    170
00019  SP722 SPAIN      APT   OBCD  GAT    190
00020  SP901 SPAIN      HALF  ABCD  GLAS   210
```

The Weeks field in the file contains one or other of the three–week combination of holidays.

8.8 More complicated questions

You could pick out the records for this file easily by looking at the last file above and picking out those records for which the number in the Price field is less than £200. There will be only three records in this file. You could ask the question 'I want a half board holiday, flying from Gatwick for less than £200 per head', with the expression
IF Type=HALF AND Airport=GAT AND Price <200 **THEN**
select: 00017 SP481 SPAIN HALF ABC0 GAT 170

As you would expect, the more conditions you put in the statement, the fewer will be the holidays which satisfy these conditions. An even more complicated question could be: 'I would like to go to Spain or Majorca, for one week in either the first or second week in August, fly from Gatwick, and it must be full board'. The statement would be
IF (Country=SPAIN **OR** Country=MAJORCA) **AND** Type=FULL AND (Weeks=A*** **OR** Weeks=*B**) **AND** Airport=GAT **THEN**
select: 00009 MA147 MAJORCA FULL 0BCD GAT 205

This is another one–record file because the restrictions on choice of holiday have become so severe.

8.9 Summary

The methods which have been used in this chapter are generally applicable to any information which is amenable to this sort of classification. Searching for data, recognising it according to different criteria, and looking for new relationships, are activities which form the basis of much administrative work. The classification of data and information and the adducing of new relationships from them should be activities which form the basis of much of the process of education system.

There is usually more to data–base software than just the sorting of data and interrogating it on demand, in what is often referred to as 'immediate mode', as we have done above. Most professional packages let you write routines or procedures using commands which are very similar to those used by the most high–level programming languages, to handle the files, do the interrogation and control the printing and writing of new information to new files quite automatically, without the user having to sit at the machine issuing the commands one by one. In dBASE II this function is carried out by its Command Language.

8.10 Checklist

1 If you found the terms slightly unfamiliar in earlier chapters, you should now refresh your ideas by considering the meaning of the terms: field, record, file, data structure, coding of data, key field.

2 What is the main purpose of the reference number field in the holiday example used in this chapter?

3 What is the meaning of the new terms which you have met in this chapter, namely: data–base, interrogation, logic, AND, OR, NOT, 'wild card'

How would you explain the fact that the AND function is included as a special case of the OR function?

4 Think about the Holiday, Estate Agent or Ramblers files, or better still, a data file which is of interest or of use to you directly. Code the information in what seems to be the fairly formal way which you have seen throughout the chapter — the key to all data processing is appropriate and accurate coding of the data, as you will have realised by now.

5 The future of microcomputing is in the area of 'knowledge processing', using languages which have their foundation in logic. Be constantly aware of how you use knowledge and information in your everyday work, hobby or studies; of its underlying logic and the logic of the questions you ask it. Try and write down the processes which you use, and in doing so you will be preparing yourself for the next generation of software, as well as making yourself more efficient at your current activities. You will be developing 'information mentality' to match the new 'information technology'.

9 dBASE II worksheets

9.1 Introduction

I have presented these worksheets assuming the classroom situation where the data files HOUSES and HOLIDAY have already been entered and exist as write protected files on the disk in the A–drive of the system. The reason for this approach is that I have found that students find the introduction to data–bases tedious and uninteresting if they have to start by struggling to create the files they are going to use. It is more encouraging if the student can get on with interrogation as quickly as possible, where he/she will see the usefulness of the package in action. If this approach is not possible then I have given a summary of the required commands as a revision at the start of worksheet 9.5, so the student without the files already created may start at that point to create them for him/herself, and then return to follow the intended path back at worksheet 9.2.

9.2 Inspecting a data file

Introduction

Techniques

How you get into dBASE II will depend on your particular system. If you have the computer's system on a separate disk then you will need to put this systems disk into the A–drive and press the appropriate key. When you get the A–prompt, shown on the screen as A>, and the drive light has gone out, meaning that the disk is not rotating in the drive, then you replace this systems disk with the dBASE II program disk and enter **'DBASE'** and press the **Enter** key (sometimes referred to as the **Return** key or perhaps just marked as ↵ on the keyboard). From now on when I say that data or an instruction or command is 'entered' I will mean you to enter the characters shown and end the line by pressing the **Enter** key.

The capacity of floppy disks has increased so much over recent years, that it is quite easy to get all of the systems files and dBASE II onto the same disk, together with several standard data files such as the HOUSES and HOLIDAY files which I use as examples. It is very convenient in the classroom situation to have standard data files safely stored away on the 'write protected' program disk, for obvious reasons. The following worksheets assume that the standard data files referred to are on the protected disk in the A–drive.

You can use upper or lower case symbols when entering data and instructions in dBASEII, but flipping between the two often causes unnecessary problems for the beginner, so I use upper case throughout the worksheets.

The symbol which dBASE II gives you to tell you that it has obeyed your instructions and all is well is a '.' on the left side of the screen, referred to as the 'dot–prompt'. It does often seem rather insignificant to the beginner, but the dot–prompt and A–prompt are important reference points to which you will frequently return during the exercises in these worksheets.

Holding down the **Ctrl** key and then striking **S**, shown as **Ctrl/S** lets you control the screen scrolling function, and in the same way **Ctrl/P** switches the printer on and off.

Revision: file structure and data types

Before starting the worksheets you should refresh your memory about the meaning of the terms 'file', 'record' and 'field', and the idea of the structure of a file as outlined in Chapter 7. In the same way you should be clear as to the differences between types of data: numbers, strings of characters, and the logic states of 'true' and 'false'. Recall the context in which the HOUSES file may be used by our imaginary Estate Agent.

1 Switch on the computer and 'boot up' the system to get an A–prompt.

2 **To load the dBASE II package into the computer** having got as far as the A–prompt you proceed:
A>DBASE

Remember that a command is not entered into the machine until you have pressed the **Enter** or **Return** key. After some disk drive whirrings you will be asked to enter the date, and when you have done this you will see the dot–prompt on the left side of the screen.

3 **To use a data file** You wish to use the data file named 'HOUSES' which has been stored on the disk in the A–drive, so continue
.USE A:HOUSES

4 **To see the data in the file** One way to see the data is to issue the LIST command;
.LIST

5 **To see the structure of a record**:
.LIST STRUCTURE
You will now have on the screen the tail end of the data in the file, and the details of the structure of a record. Stop at this point and make sure

that you understand the details of the structure file, and can relate the data on the screen to this structure.

6 **To control 'scrolling' and use the DISPLAY command** If the file had had many records then the listing would roll down (up) the screen and you would have to use the **Ctrl/S** command to control this 'scrolling'. You can get round this by using the DISPLAY command:
.DISPLAY
This shows the current record, which as your last data command was LIST turns out to be the last record of the file (No 24).

7 **To browse through the data with GOTO and DISPLAY commands** Go to the top of the file and try the following sequence:

```
.GO TOP
.DISPLAY
.DISPLAY NEXT 5
.GOTO 7
.DISPLAY
.DISPLAY NEXT 4
```

So, you see that you can control how many records appear.

8 **To use DISPLAY ALL** The command **DISPLAY ALL** gives you 15 records at a time, try it and see! At the **WAITING** prompt you only have to touch any key for the next 15 to appear.

9 **To print out the results of commands** To get what you have seen on the screen onto paper, make sure the printer connected to your computer is available, give the **Ctrl/P** command, and then continue with the **LIST** and **DISPLAY** commands as above.

10 **To get out of dBASE II to end a session**
.QUIT
After some more disk whirrings the A–prompt will appear. When the disks have stopped rotating and the drive lights have gone out, it is safe to take out the disks and then switch off the machine.

Exercise

Start with your machine switched off, load the system and dBASE II, and then get into the HOLIDAY file which should be on the A disk. Go through the same sequence of commands as for the HOUSES file above, make sure that you can relate the data to the details of the structure file, and finally take a printout of these activities.

Commentary

```
WORKSHEET 1   COMMENTARY

 .USE A:HOUSES
 .LIST
00001  WW14  WEST WICKHAM      D   3   2   0 L    55000
00002  CI23  CHISLEHURST       D   5   3   2 M   168000
00003  PW48  PETTS WOOD        D   3   1   1 M    69995
00004  OR09  ORPINGTON         T   3   1   0 S    28500
00005  BE73  BEXLEY            D   4   2   1 M    52750
```

```
00006  BI37  BICKLEY            F   1   1   0 N    22950
00007  PW19  PETTS WOOD         D   3   2   1 L    69950
00008  OR63  ORPINGTON          M   3   1   1 N    29950
00009  CI50  CHISLEHURST        D   5   3   2 M    95000
00010  BR82  BROMLEY            S   4   3   0 S    36250
00011  OR57  ORPINGTON          S   4   1   1 L    50000
00012  SE72  SEVENOAKS          B   2   1   1 L    35000
00013  BR29  BROMLEY            D   3   2   1 L    75000
00014  CE05  CHELSFIELD         B   3   2   2 L    75000
00015  BE79  BEXLEY             S   3   1   2 L    51000
00016  FA32  FARNBOROUGH        D   6   2   3 L   200000
00017  OR35  ORPINGTON          M   2   1   1 N    31000
00018  BE88  BEXLEY             S   2   1   1 L    33500
00019  OR40  ORPINGTON          B   2   1   1 M    64500
00020  SI24  SIDCUP             F   2   1   1 N    32500
00021  SI30  SIDCUP             S   4   2   2 M    55000
00022  BR62  BROMLEY            D   4   2   0 M    69995
00023  BR12  BROMLEY            T   3   1   1 S    42000
00024  WW43  WEST WICKHAM       S   3   2   1 M    49750
 .LIST STRUCTURE
STRUCTURE FOR FILE:  A:HOUSES  .DBF
NUMBER OF RECORDS:   00024
DATE OF LAST UPDATE: 09/27/87
PRIMARY USE DATABASE
FLD       NAME       TYPE WIDTH   DEC
001      REFNO        C    005
002      AREA         C    018
003      TYPE         C    002
004      BEDROOMS     N    002
005      RECROOMS     N    002
006      GARAGES      N    002
007      GARDEN       C    002
008      PRICE        N    006
** TOTAL **              00040
 .DISPLAY
00024  WW43  WEST WICKHAM       S   3   2   1 M    49750
 .GO TOP
 .DISPLAY
00001  WW14  WEST WICKHAM       D   3   2   0 L    55000
 .DISPLAY NEXT 5
00001  WW14  WEST WICKHAM       D   3   2   0 L    55000
00002  CI23  CHISLEHURST        D   5   3   2 M   168000
00003  PW48  PETTS WOOD         D   3   1   1 M    69995
00004  OR09  ORPINGTON          T   3   1   0 S    28500
00005  BE73  BEXLEY             D   4   2   1 M    52750
 .GOTO 7
 .DISPLAY
00007  PW19  PETTS WOOD         D   3   2   1 L    69950
 .DISPLAY NEXT 4
00007  PW19  PETTS WOOD         D   3   2   1 L    69950
00008  OR63  ORPINGTON          M   3   1   1 N    29950
00009  CI50  CHISLEHURST        D   5   3   2 M    95000
00010  BR82  BROMLEY            S   4   3   0 S    36250
 .DISPLAY ALL
00001  WW14  WEST WICKHAM       D   3   2   0 L    55000
00002  CI23  CHISLEHURST        D   5   3   2 M   168000
00003  PW48  PETTS WOOD         D   3   1   1 M    69995
00004  OR09  ORPINGTON          T   3   1   0 S    28500
00005  BE73  BEXLEY             D   4   2   1 M    52750
00006  BI37  BICKLEY            F   1   1   0 N    22950
00007  PW19  PETTS WOOD         D   3   2   1 L    69950
00008  OR63  ORPINGTON          M   3   1   1 N    29950
00009  CI50  CHISLEHURST        D   5   3   2 M    95000
00010  BR82  BROMLEY            S   4   3   0 S    36250
00011  OR57  ORPINGTON          S   4   1   1 L    50000
00012  SE72  SEVENOAKS          B   2   1   1 L    35000
00013  BR29  BROMLEY            D   3   2   1 L    75000
```

Cont'd

```
00014  CE05  CHELSFIELD       B   3  2  2 L    75000
00015  BE79  BEXLEY           S   3  1  2 L    51000
WAITING
00016  FA32  FARNBOROUGH      D   6  2  3 L   200000
00017  OR35  ORPINGTON        M   2  1  1 N    31000
00018  BE88  BEXLEY           S   2  1  1 L    33500
00019  OR40  ORPINGTON        B   2  1  1 M    64500
00020  SI24  SIDCUP           F   2  1  1 N    32500
00021  SI30  SIDCUP           S   4  2  2 M    55000
00022  BR62  BROMLEY          D   4  2  0 M    69995
00023  BR12  BROMLEY          T   3  1  1 S    42000
00024  WW43  WEST WICKHAM     S   3  2  1 M    49750
 . QUIT
*** END RUN      dBASE II     ***
```

9.3 Interrogating a data file

Introduction

Revision

Refresh your memory about how to switch on, 'boot up' the system to get to the A–prompt, and then load in the dBASE II program and get to the dot–prompt. To end a session in dBASE II and get back to the system's A–prompt you use the **QUIT** command.

You can look at a file of records using the **LIST** command, and move round the file using **GOTO** and **GO TOP** commands to look at individual or smaller blocks of records using **DISPLAY** and **DISPLAY NEXT** .

Preview

Remember the difference between the two data types: numbers and strings of characters. The equal symbol = has its usual arithmetic meaning with numbers. The > symbol as in 'a > b' means 'a is greater than b', or 'left is greater than right'. In the same way < means 'less than', so 'a < b' means 'a is less than b'.

These symbols are easy to understand when used with numbers, but with strings of characters it is not quite so straightforward. Here the = sign signifies that one string of characters is exactly matched to another. If a and b now represent strings of characters, then 'a < b' means that a is lower in alphabetical order than b; lower meaning nearer the front (a, b, c, . .) end of the alphabet.

The symbol for 'not equal to' is <>, so 'a <> b' is seen to mean 'a is either less than or greater than b', which implies that a is not equal to b.

Remember how it is imagined that an estate agent would use this file. It is a summary file which the agent would use when a customer makes his/her enquiry about a house. 'I wish to live in Bromley', or 'It must cost less than £50,000', or 'It must have at least 4 bedrooms' — are the types of first statements which a potential customer may make.

To interrogate someone means to ask them questions, so to interrogate a data–base means to ask questions of it.

1 Load the HOUSES file from the A disk, remind yourself of the structure and data in the file with the sequence:

```
.USE A:HOUSES
.LIST STRUCTURE
.LIST
```

2 **To use LIST FOR with a numeric expression** The BEDROOMS, PRICE and GARAGES fields are all number fields so you can ask questions like: 'Which houses have 4 bedrooms?'
.LIST FOR BEDROOMS = 4
'Which houses cost less than £40,000?'
.LIST FOR PRICE < 40000
Note that there is neither £ nor , in the number representing the price.

It is not likely that anyone would go into an estate agent and ask for a house which only had exactly 4 bedrooms, which the first question implied. It is more likely that the request would be 'We must have at least 4 bedrooms!'
.LIST FOR BEDROOMS > = 4 In the same way: 'Which houses have at least 2 garages?' becomes
.LIST FOR GARAGES > = 2

3 **To use LIST FOR with a 'string' expression** — Switching attention to the character fields you can pick out houses which are detached with
.LIST FOR TYPE = 'D'
Note in this case that the value in the field, D in this case, must be enclosed in quotes. So, the request 'I would like a house with a large garden!' would be posed:
.LIST FOR GARDEN = 'L' Or, 'I do not want a large garden!' becomes
.LIST FOR GARDEN <> 'L'

A silly question gets a silly yet logical answer:
.LIST FOR AREA < 'ORP' Your screen shows all those houses in areas whose name is lower than ORP in alphabetical order, which is not the sort of thing that either estate agent or customer needs to know, but it stands up logically and does say something about the data. 'I wish to live in Chislehurst!' becomes
.LIST FOR AREA = 'CHISLEHURST'

4 **To use the 'in string' or 'contains' operator $** .
The above query can be simplified by using the $ operator:
.LIST FOR 'CHIS' $ AREA

The $ can be read as 'contained in', so the query reads 'find the records for which the string of 4 characters CHIS is contained in the data in the AREA field.
.LIST FOR 'ORP' $ AREA
would give you the houses in ORPINGTON, which could also have been found from the reference number field REFNO
.LIST FOR 'OR' $ REFNO

5 **To step through the file using LOCATE and DISPLAY** – If the file is large and the **LIST** command inconvenient, then you can step through record by record with the **LOCATE**, **DISPLAY** and **CONTINUE** sequence:

```
.LOCATE FOR PRICE < 40000
.DISPLAY            will show just the one record
.CONTINUE           passes on to the next record
                    with price < #40,000
.DISPLAY            and so on.
```

6 **To COUNT the records which obey an expression.** If you just wish to count the records which fit a particular description then

```
.COUNT FOR PRICE < 40000      will do, or
.COUNT FOR GARDEN = 'L'       and so on.
```

Exercise

Load the HOLIDAY file from the A disk and find the answers to the following queries.

Which holidays involve flying from Gatwick airport?

List the holidays in Spain!

Which holidays cost less than £200?

Which holidays do not include full board?

I wish to go for the first 2 weeks in August!

How many holidays start from Gatwick?

How many holidays cost less than £200?

Commentary

```
WORKSHEET 2     COMMENTARY

 .USE A:HOUSES
 .LIST FOR BEDROOMS = 4
00005  BE73  BEXLEY               D    4    2    1 M     52750
00010  BR82  BROMLEY              S    4    3    0 S     36250
00011  OR57  ORPINGTON            S    4    1    1 L     50000
00021  SI30  SIDCUP               S    4    2    2 M     55000
00022  BR62  BROMLEY              D    4    2    0 M     69995
```

```
 .LIST FOR PRICE < 40000
00004  OR09  ORPINGTON        T   3   1   0 S    28500
00006  BI37  BICKLEY          F   1   1   0 N    22950
00008  OR63  ORPINGTON        M   3   1   1 N    29950
00010  BR82  BROMLEY          S   4   3   0 S    36250
00012  SE72  SEVENOAKS        B   2   1   1 L    35000
00017  OR35  ORPINGTON        M   2   1   1 N    31000
00018  BE88  BEXLEY           S   2   1   1 L    33500
00020  SI24  SIDCUP           F   2   1   1 N    32500
 .LIST FOR BEDROOMS >= 4
00002  CI23  CHISLEHURST      D   5   3   2 M   168000
00005  BE73  BEXLEY           D   4   2   1 M    52750
00009  CI50  CHISLEHURST      D   5   3   2 M    95000
00010  BR82  BROMLEY          S   4   3   0 S    36250
00011  OR57  ORPINGTON        S   4   1   1 L    50000
00016  FA32  FARNBOROUGH      D   6   2   3 L   200000
00021  SI30  SIDCUP           S   4   2   2 M    55000
00022  BR62  BROMLEY          D   4   2   0 M    69995
 .LIST FOR GARAGES >= 2
00002  CI23  CHISLEHURST      D   5   3   2 M   168000
00009  CI50  CHISLEHURST      D   5   3   2 M    95000
00014  CE05  CHELSFIELD       B   3   2   2 L    75000
00015  BE79  BEXLEY           S   3   1   2 L    51000
00016  FA32  FARNBOROUGH      D   6   2   3 L   200000
00021  SI30  SIDCUP           S   4   2   2 M    55000
 .LIST FOR TYPE = 'D'
00001  WW14  WEST WICKHAM     D   3   2   0 L    55000
00002  CI23  CHISLEHURST      D   5   3   2 M   168000
00003  PW48  PETTS WOOD       D   3   1   1 M    69995
00005  BE73  BEXLEY           D   4   2   1 M    52750
00007  PW19  PETTS WOOD       D   3   2   1 L    69950
00009  CI50  CHISLEHURST      D   5   3   2 M    95000
00013  BR29  BROMLEY          D   3   2   1 L    75000
00016  FA32  FARNBOROUGH      D   6   2   3 L   200000
00022  BR62  BROMLEY          D   4   2   0 M    69995
 .LIST FOR GARDEN = 'L'
00001  WW14  WEST WICKHAM     D   3   2   0 L    55000
00007  PW19  PETTS WOOD       D   3   2   1 L    69950
00011  OR57  ORPINGTON        S   4   1   1 L    50000
00012  SE72  SEVENOAKS        B   2   1   1 L    35000
00013  BR29  BROMLEY          D   3   2   1 L    75000
00014  CE05  CHELSFIELD       B   3   2   2 L    75000
00015  BE79  BEXLEY           S   3   1   2 L    51000
00016  FA32  FARNBOROUGH      D   6   2   3 L   200000
00018  BE88  BEXLEY           S   2   1   1 L    33500
 .LIST FOR GARDEN <> 'L'
00002  CI23  CHISLEHURST      D   5   3   2 M   168000
00003  PW48  PETTS WOOD       D   3   1   1 M    69995
00004  OR09  ORPINGTON        T   3   1   0 S    28500
00005  BE73  BEXLEY           D   4   2   1 M    52750
00006  BI37  BICKLEY          F   1   1   0 N    22950
00008  OR63  ORPINGTON        M   3   1   1 N    29950
00009  CI50  CHISLEHURST      D   5   3   2 M    95000
00010  BR82  BROMLEY          S   4   3   0 S    36250
00017  OR35  ORPINGTON        M   2   1   1 N    31000
00019  OR40  ORPINGTON        B   2   1   1 M    64500
00020  SI24  SIDCUP           F   2   1   1 N    32500
00021  SI30  SIDCUP           S   4   2   2 M    55000
00022  BR62  BROMLEY          D   4   2   0 M    69995
00023  BR12  BROMLEY          T   3   1   1 S    42000
00024  WW43  WEST WICKHAM     S   3   2   1 M    49750
 .LIST FOR AREA < 'ORP'
00002  CI23  CHISLEHURST      D   5   3   2 M   168000
00005  BE73  BEXLEY           D   4   2   1 M    52750
00006  BI37  BICKLEY          F   1   1   0 N    22950
00009  CI50  CHISLEHURST      D   5   3   2 M    95000
00010  BR82  BROMLEY          S   4   3   0 S    36250
```

Cont'd

```
00013  BR29  BROMLEY          D   3   2   1 L    75000
00014  CE05  CHELSFIELD       B   3   2   2 L    75000
00015  BE79  BEXLEY           S   3   1   2 L    51000
00016  FA32  FARNBOROUGH      D   6   2   3 L   200000
00018  BE88  BEXLEY           S   2   1   1 L    33500
00022  BR62  BROMLEY          D   4   2   0 M    69995
00023  BR12  BROMLEY          T   3   1   1 S    42000
 .LIST FOR AREA = 'CHISLEHURST'
00002  CI23  CHISLEHURST      D   5   3   2 M   168000
00009  CI50  CHISLEHURST      D   5   3   2 M    95000
 .LIST FOR 'CHIS' $ AREA
00002  CI23  CHISLEHURST      D   5   3   2 M   168000
00009  CI50  CHISLEHURST      D   5   3   2 M    95000
 .LIST FOR 'ORP' $ AREA
00004  OR09  ORPINGTON        T   3   1   0 S    28500
00008  OR63  ORPINGTON        M   3   1   1 N    29950
00011  OR57  ORPINGTON        S   4   1   1 L    50000
00017  OR35  ORPINGTON        M   2   1   1 N    31000
00019  OR40  ORPINGTON        B   2   1   1 M    64500
 .LIST FOR 'OR' $ REFNO
00004  OR09  ORPINGTON        T   3   1   0 S    28500
00008  OR63  ORPINGTON        M   3   1   1 N    29950
00011  OR57  ORPINGTON        S   4   1   1 L    50000
00017  OR35  ORPINGTON        M   2   1   1 N    31000
00019  OR40  ORPINGTON        B   2   1   1 M    64500
 .LOCATE FOR PRICE < 40000
RECORD: 00004
 .DISPLAY
00004  OR09  ORPINGTON        T   3   1   0 S    28500
 .CONTINUE
RECORD: 00006
 .DISPLAY
00006  BI37  BICKLEY          F   1   1   0 N    22950
 .CONTINUE
RECORD: 00008
 .DISPLAY
00008  OR63  ORPINGTON        M   3   1   1 N    29950
 .COUNT FOR PRICE < 40000
COUNT = 00008
 .COUNT FOR GARDEN = 'L'
COUNT = 00009
 . QUIT

*** END RUN      dBASE II      ***
```

9.4 Logic and interrogation

1 **To use the .AND. operator in LIST expressions** To say that you want a holiday in Majorca puts one restriction on your choice of holidays from the data file. To say that you must fly from Gatwick airport is another restriction. To request a holiday in Majorca which starts at Gatwick puts two restrictions on the data. In this case you would expect to get only those holidays which satisfy both of these criteria. The query may be asked in dBASE II as:
.LIST FOR COUNTRY = 'MAJORCA' .AND. AIRPORT = 'GAT'

As you see from the output, this query selects only the 3 records which satisfy both criteria. When you join 2 expressions by the .AND. operator in a query, the resultant output consists of records which satisfy the requirements of both of the expressions. Those who have met Set theory will see the similarities between .AND. and intersection.

If a customer insisted on a full board holiday in Spain then the query would be:
.LIST FOR COUNTRY = 'SPAIN' .AND. TYPE = 'FULL'
This gives us only 3 records. In the same way a holiday to anywhere but flying from Gatwick and under £200 in price could be found by:
.LIST FOR AIRPORT = 'GAT' .AND. PRICE < 200

A range of cheap full-board holidays could be found by:
.LIST FOR TYPE = 'FULL' .AND. PRICE < 200

2 **To use the .OR. operator in LIST expressions** Compare the effect of the .AND. operator in the last expression with that of the .OR. operator, using the same two criteria:
.LIST FOR TYPE = 'FULL' .OR. PRICE < 200

You see that you select a record if it obeys the criteria TYPE = 'FULL' or if it satisfies PRICE < 200, so you can now get records which obey either one of these conditions or both. You get many more records in the output for this operator, because it is less restrictive in its requirements.

If you did not live in the London area but in the Midlands, your main requirement may be that you start your holiday by flying from either Luton or Birmingham airport, so would ask:
.LIST FOR AIRPORT = 'BIRM' .OR. AIRPORT = 'LUT'

You remember that in the weeks field A000 means that the holiday is available in the first week in August, while AB0D means that it is available in the first 2 weeks and the 4th. So if a customer does not mind which resort he/she goes to but must go for 2 weeks somewhere in the first 3 weeks in August, then the query would be:
.LIST FOR 'AB' $ WEEKS .OR. 'BC' $ WEEKS

But if the customer wished to go for all of the first 3 weeks in the month, then the following query would do:
.LIST FOR 'ABC' $ WEEKS

3 **To use the .NOT. operator in LIST expressions** This operator negates the expression which follows it, so if you do not want a holiday with full-board then
.LIST FOR .NOT. (TYPE = 'FULL')

Someone who has been to Spain and Majorca several times before and wants a change, may say please not Spain or Majorca:
.LIST FOR .NOT. (COUNTRY = 'SPAIN' .OR. COUNTRY = 'MAJ')

If you want a cheap holiday and to be well fed then
.LIST FOR .NOT. (TYPE = 'FULL' .OR. PRICE > 200)

You can see that by using a combination of .AND., .OR. and .NOT. operators that you can ask quite complicated and meaningful questions of a data–base.

Exercise

Load the HOUSES file from the A disk and form queries in dBASE II which ask the following questions of the data–base.

1 Find all those houses which:
   - a are in the Bromley area and have a large garden
   - b are detached and have at least 4 bedrooms
   - c have a large garden and a price less than £75,000

2 Find all those houses which:
   - a are either in the Orpington or Petts Wood areas
   - b have at least 4 bedrooms or at least 2 reception rooms
   - c are detached or have a large garden

3 Find all those houses which
   - a do not have a large garden
   - b do not have more than 3 bedrooms or more than 1 reception room
   - c do not have a large garden and price greater than £75,000

Commentary

```
 .USE A:HOLIDAY
 .LIST FOR COUNTRY = 'MAJORCA' .AND. AIRPORT = 'GAT'
00009  MA147 MAJORCA     FULL  OBCD  GAT       205
00010  MA364 MAJORCA     FULL  OOCO  GAT       175
00012  MA771 MAJORCA     HALF  ABCD  GAT       215
 .LIST FOR COUNTRY = 'SPAIN' .AND. TYPE = 'FULL'
00015  SP137 SPAIN       FULL  ABOD  GLAS      190
00016  SP258 SPAIN       FULL  ABOO  LUT       205
00018  SP551 SPAIN       FULL  OBCO  BIRM      195
 .LIST FOR AIRPORT= 'GAT' .AND. PRICE < 200
00001  FR072 FRANCE      FULL  OBCD  GAT       195
00010  MA364 MAJORCA     FULL  OOCO  GAT       175
00017  SP481 SPAIN       HALF  ABCO  GAT       170
00019  SP722 SPAIN       APT   OBCD  GAT       190
 .LIST FOR TYPE = 'FULL' .AND. PRICE < 200
00001  FR072 FRANCE      FULL  OBCD  GAT       195
00010  MA364 MAJORCA     FULL  OOCO  GAT       175
00015  SP137 SPAIN       FULL  ABOD  GLAS      190
00018  SP551 SPAIN       FULL  OBCO  BIRM      195
 .LIST FOR TYPE = 'FULL' .OR. PRICE < 200
00001  FR072 FRANCE      FULL  OBCD  GAT       195
00004  IT229 ITALY       FULL  ABCD  LUT       210
00007  IT882 ITALY       FULL  ABCD  GAT       265
00008  MA078 MAJORCA     HALF  OOCD  BIRM      185
00009  MA147 MAJORCA     FULL  OBCD  GAT       205
00010  MA364 MAJORCA     FULL  OOCO  GAT       175
00011  MA662 MAJORCA     APT   ABOD  MAN       190
00015  SP137 SPAIN       FULL  ABOD  GLAS      190
00016  SP258 SPAIN       FULL  ABOO  LUT       205
00017  SP481 SPAIN       HALF  ABCO  GAT       170
00018  SP551 SPAIN       FULL  OBCO  BIRM      195
00019  SP722 SPAIN       APT   OBCD  GAT       190
 .LIST FOR AIRPORT = 'BIRM' .OR. AIRPORT = 'LUT'
00004  IT229 ITALY       FULL  ABCD  LUT       210
00008  MA078 MAJORCA     HALF  OOCD  BIRM      185
00014  PO887 PORTUGAL    HALF  OBCO  BIRM      245
00016  SP258 SPAIN       FULL  ABOO  LUT       205
```

```
00018  SP551 SPAIN       FULL  OBCO  BIRM    195
 .LIST FOR 'AB' $ WEEKS .OR. 'BC' $ WEEKS
00001  FR072 FRANCE      FULL  OBCD  GAT     195
00002  FR211 FRANCE      HALF  OBCD  GAT     225
00004  IT229 ITALY       FULL  ABCD  LUT     210
00005  IT365 ITALY       HALF  OBCD  GAT     205
00007  IT882 ITALY       FULL  ABCD  GAT     265
00009  MA147 MAJORCA     FULL  OBCD  GAT     205
00011  MA662 MAJORCA     APT   ABOD  MAN     190
00012  MA771 MAJORCA     HALF  ABCD  GAT     215
00014  PO887 PORTUGAL    HALF  OBCO  BIRM    245
00015  SP137 SPAIN       FULL  ABOD  GLAS    190
00016  SP258 SPAIN       FULL  ABOO  LUT     205
00017  SP481 SPAIN       HALF  ABCO  GAT     170
00018  SP551 SPAIN       FULL  OBCO  BIRM    195
00019  SP722 SPAIN       APT   OBCD  GAT     190
00020  SP901 SPAIN       HALF  ABCD  GLAS    210
 .LIST FOR 'ABC' $ WEEKS
00004  IT229 ITALY       FULL  ABCD  LUT     210
00007  IT882 ITALY       FULL  ABCD  GAT     265
00012  MA771 MAJORCA     HALF  ABCD  GAT     215
00017  SP481 SPAIN       HALF  ABCO  GAT     170
00020  SP901 SPAIN       HALF  ABCD  GLAS    210
 .LIST FOR .NOT.(TYPE = 'FULL')
00002  FR211 FRANCE      HALF  OBCD  GAT     225
00003  FR382 FRANCE      APT   OOCD  MAN     255
00005  IT365 ITALY       HALF  OBCD  GAT     205
00006  IT509 ITALY       HALF  OOCD  GLAS    215
00008  MA078 MAJORCA     HALF  OOCD  BIRM    185
00011  MA662 MAJORCA     APT   ABOD  MAN     190
00012  MA771 MAJORCA     HALF  ABCD  GAT     215
00013  PO339 PORTUGAL    HALF  OBOD  GAT     265
00014  PO887 PORTUGAL    HALF  OBCO  BIRM    245
00017  SP481 SPAIN       HALF  ABCO  GAT     170
00019  SP722 SPAIN       APT   OBCD  GAT     190
00020  SP901 SPAIN       HALF  ABCD  GLAS    210
 .LIST FOR .NOT.(COUNTRY = 'SPAIN' .OR. COUNTRY = 'MAJ'
00001  FR072 FRANCE      FULL  OBCD  GAT     195
00002  FR211 FRANCE      HALF  OBCD  GAT     225
00003  FR382 FRANCE      APT   OOCD  MAN     255
00004  IT229 ITALY       FULL  ABCD  LUT     210
00005  IT365 ITALY       HALF  OBCD  GAT     205
00006  IT509 ITALY       HALF  OOCD  GLAS    215
00007  IT882 ITALY       FULL  ABCD  GAT     265
00013  PO339 PORTUGAL    HALF  OBOD  GAT     265
00014  PO887 PORTUGAL    HALF  OBCO  BIRM    245
 .LIST FOR .NOT.(TYPE = 'FULL' .OR. PRICE > 200)
00008  MA078 MAJORCA     HALF  OOCD  BIRM    185
00011  MA662 MAJORCA     APT   ABOD  MAN     190
00017  SP481 SPAIN       HALF  ABCO  GAT     170
00019  SP722 SPAIN       APT   OBCD  GAT     190
 . QUIT
*** END RUN     dBASE II     ***
```

9.5 Creating a data file

Introduction

Revision

You just need to remind yourself about the details of data file structure: file, records and fields; and the differences between the 2 main types of data: numbers and strings.

In particular remember that a data–base in dBASE II has two files associated with it: one containing details of the structure of the records of the file, and the other the actual data itself. It is self–evident then that you have to start by deciding on and entering the details of the structure of a file, before you can enter any data into it.

Techniques

Entering the structure one line at a time When entering details of the structure of a record you are restricted by dBASE II to working on one line only. You enter strings of characters in the normal way as prompted. You can move about in that line by using the WordStar **Ctrl/S** and **Ctrl/D** for left and right movements respectively, or if the software has been configured for your machine then the <– and –> keys may be used, and so may **Ctrl/Del**. The usual mode is Overwrite, so you can go back over incorrect characters and overwrite them, or you can usually toggle on the Insert mode with **Ctrl/V** and insert characters which you have omitted. **Ctrl/G** can be used to delete incorrect entries.

So, you have flexibility to edit the line where you are working, but after you have pressed **Enter** at the end of the line, you cannot get back to that line to change it. The only remedy is to go back to the beginning and start entering the structure for a new file with a different name. The message then is to make sure that the details of each line is correct *before you press the Enter key*.

In APPEND you are restricted to the Record. When in APPEND mode and are entering data into the file, you are restricted to the particular record where you are working. You can enter data and move around in each line to edit the details as described above. You can also move from line to line (i.e. between fields) within the record using **Ctrl/E** for **UP**, and **Ctrl/X** for **DOWN**, or the arrow keys if your machine has them and the software has been configured for their use; but you cannot pass from one record to another. So, make sure your data is accurate before pressing Enter at the end of the last field. If you make a mistake, then leave it until you can return to tidy up the file using the **EDIT** operator, which is described in the next worksheet.

So far you have used data–bases which have already been created. Now you will go through the process of creating a data–base from scratch. The data is given below in the STAFF file. The 7 fields are Surname (or Second Name), First Name, Date of Birth (DOB in the form YYMMDD), Employee Number, Salary, Region and Office.

SMITH	CHARLOTTE	450620	F174	5800	S	BRISTOL
JONES	DORIS	380801	F263	6500	N	LEEDS
HOBBINS	HAROLD	390722	M622	6800	C	BIRMINGHAM
JOHNSON	BERT	330705	M441	9400	N	MANCHESTER
BURTON	CHARLES	661124	M235	8200	S	LOND(EUS RD)
APRON	JOHN	320930	M886	12300	N	LEEDS
BULL	JOAN	410525	F074	13000	S	CROYDON
LISTER	JUDY	560311	F993	11600	S	BRISTOL
GREEN	JAMES	541010	M758	12200	S	CROYDON

```
ALBERT       JENNIFER     480606 F547  10500 S LOND(WAR ST)
SAMSON       ROGER        440916 M356  11250 S LOND(EUS RD)
JANES        CLIVE        530422 M525  10900 S BRISTOL
SMALES       KATIE        400228 F803  14200 N LEEDS
SMALL        SUSAN        360418 F476  15000 C BIRMINGHAM
JAMES        JIM          440101 M365  12800 N MANCHESTER
ROLLS        RAY          670726 M256   7650 S LOND(EUS RD)
BONEFIELD    WILLIAM      600325 M154   8700 N LEEDS
ADAMS        BILL         491208 M367  14200 C BIRMINGHAM
BATTEN       DEAN         500420 M652  12000 N LEEDS
MUNN         KURT         631011 M092  13500 S BRISTOL
```

You will recall that in dBASE II a data–base consists of 2 files, one containing the structure of each record, and the other holding the actual data. So, when you issue the CREATE command you are first expected to specify the structure of a record.

1 **To enter the details of the structure of a file** Load dBASE II and at the dot prompt say:

```
 .CREATE B:STAFF
ENTER RECORD STRUCTURE AS FOLLOWS:
 FIELD    NAME,TYPE,WIDTH,DECIMAL PLACES
 001
```

After having entered the name of the file you want to create, B:STAFF, and pressed Return, the next two lines appear on the screen and after 001 on the third line, you are expected to enter details of the structure of the first record. So continue to enter the details as I have shown underlined in what follows:

```
001       SNAME,C,12
```

the name of the field is **SNAME**, a character field so enter **C** with width of 12 spaces, after pressing **Return** after the 12, 002 appears on the next line inviting you to continue with record 2, so continue:

```
002       FNAME,C,12
003       DOB,N,6,0
```

Here the field name is **DOB**, it is a number so **N**, of six digits and zero decimal places. After **Return** continue

```
004       EMPNO,N,4,0
005       SALARY,N,5,0
006       REGION,C,1
007       OFFICE,C,12
008
```

There are only seven fields in a record, so at the 008 prompt just press **Enter** and the structure will be saved, and you are asked
INPUT DATA NOW?N
to which you answer **N** for No! If you answer **Y** for Yes here and make an error later while entering data, you will lose not only your data but the structure as well — so say No!

2 **To enter data into this structure** you issue the command: **.APPEND** and at the top of a new screen will appear

```
RECORD # 00001
SNAME       :            :
FNAME       :            :
DOB         :      :
EMPNO       :    :
SALARY      :      :
REGION      : :
OFFICE      :            :
```

You now have to enter the data, field by field into the spaces provided next to the field name. There are twelve spaces between the colons for both the **SNAME** and **FNAME** fields, and six for **DOB** and so on, because that is what you allowed for when you set up the structure file.

When you enter data, if you do not fill the available space, SMITH will not fill the 12 spaces in the first **SNAME** field, then you end that entry by pressing the **Enter** key. You will notice that when you fill the space, as when entering the six digits for the **DOB** field, the machine 'beeps' and automatically goes on to the next field.

When you have entered the first record your screen will look like

```
RECORD # 00001
SNAME       :SMITH       :
FNAME       :CHARLOTTE   :
DOB         :450620:
EMPNO       :1174:
SALARY      :5800  :
REGION      :S:
OFFICE      :BRISTOL     :
```

As soon as you press **Enter** after BRISTOL, you find yourself with a new blank 'form' headed **RECORD # 00002** waiting for you to start entering the 2nd record. Remember that you cannot now go back to the 1st record. You should now carry on and enter the data for the rest of the STAFF file as given above.

Exercise

Choose either the HOUSES or HOLIDAY data files and create your own version of the file on the B disk of your system, even if these files are already on the A–disk.

9.6 Editing a data file

Introduction

Revision

Data processing is a dynamic activity. You do not just have to edit a data file because the data was entered inaccurately in the first place. When a data–

base is being used, in practice the data is changing constantly. In the Estate Agent's file the price of the houses may change, or properties may be sold or taken off the market. In the use of the HOLIDAY file likewise, customers may come and book up quickly if the holidays are late bargains, and so on.

Data processing is about creating files of data, editing the data, deleting records or inserting new ones, interrogating the base to select particular records, sorting the records into different orders for a new purpose, and so on. In addition to some of these functions you have already met, others will be introduced in this worksheet.

Techniques

Be clear about the use of the field and record editing features which you met in the last worksheet when appending new data into a data–base, for they are the same when in EDIT mode. Now you wish to move from record to record at will to make the changes needed.

After you have issued the command **EDIT** at the dot–prompt you get the prompt **ENTER RECORD #** : which is an invitation to enter the number of the record which you wish to change.

When you have made the necessary changes to a record and wish to move on, you have several options.

Ctrl/R writes the changes you have made to disk, and moves you back to the previous record.

Ctrl/C writes the changes and moves you to on to the next record.

Ctrl/W writes the changes to disk and returns you to the Enter Record prompt, where you can enter the number of the next record you wish to edit.

Ctrl/Q quits the record you are working on without writing the changes you made in that record, but changes you may have made in other records will have been written. **Ctrl/Q** returns you to the dot–prompt.

If you press the **Enter** key at the **ENTER RECORD** prompt then you will be returned to the dot–prompt.

1 **To use COPY to back up a data file** Before you edit a file you must make sure that the original data is safely stored away, i.e. that you have a back–up copy. You are going to change the HOLIDAY data which is in a file on the A–disk which is write–protected and quite safe; but to drive the above point home, I suggest that you copy the data from the original file into a temporary file (TEMP) and use that TEMP file.

```
.USE A:HOLIDAY
.COPY TO B:TEMP
.USE B:TEMP
```

2 **To use the EDIT command to change the details of a record** There has been a financial crisis in Italy, and the result has been an increase of £10 on airport taxes, so the price of all the holidays has to be increased by that amount. You can change data in a file by means of the **EDIT** facilities, so

.EDIT give you the **ENTER RECORD** prompt
ENTER RECORD # :

The # : is asking you to give the number of the record which you wish to change. So, as the first holiday in Italy occurs at record 4, complete the prompt with 4 and **Enter**. **ENTER RECORD** # **:4**

The screen clears and then record 4 is displayed as it was when you were entering data into it in APPEND mode in the last worksheet.

3 **To use the Ctrl/ . . functions in EDIT** You move the cursor around in **EDIT** mode in the same way as in **APPEND**. The overwriting, inserting and deleting functions also work in exactly the same way. So, cursor down to the 6th field and change the price from 210 to 220.

Ctrl/C writes this change and moves you on to the next record.
Ctrl/R would write the change and go to the previous record.
Ctrl/W writes any changes and returns to the **ENTER RECORD** prompt.
Ctrl/Q quits the record you are in, without making any changes, and returns you to the dot–prompt.

At the **ENTER RECORD** prompt press the **Enter** key to get back to the dot–prompt.

4 **To INSERT a record into the data file**
To insert the following record at position 11 in the file

MA552 MAJORCA HALF 0B0D BIRM 205 enter

.GOTO 11
.INSERT BEFORE

On the screen will appear a blank record form into which you enter the data as before with **Enter** or **Ctrl/W** after the last field entry. The new record will be in position 11 and the file now has 21 records. List the file to see what has happened.

Insert the following two records at the positions given:

```
IT601  ITALY  FULL  OBOD  GLAS  210    before record 7
SP628  SPAIN  HALF  ASCO  GAT   195    before record 21
```

5 **To DELETE records from a data file** To delete record number 2 you say
.DELETE RECORD 2.

Now list the file to see what has happened. You will see that the record has not disappeared but has an * against the first field. If you had tried to delete the wrong record all is not lost for you can remove the delete marker (the *) with

.RECALL ALL

List the file again and you will see that the * has gone. To complete the deletion process say:

```
.DELETE RECORD 2
.PACK
```

You will see that the record has been deleted this time.

To delete the 2 PORTUGAL records with one command say:

```
.GOTO 15
.DELETE NEXT 2
.PACK
```

To see what is happening you could list the file before and after the last PACK command.

Exercise

Load the HOUSES file from the A–disk and copy its contents into a temporary file. Add £2000 to the price of every Orpington house in the file. Delete all of the houses in the Bexley and Sidcup areas. Insert the following records into the relative positions occupied by the two Sidcup houses in the original file.

```
BR77 BROMLEY        D 5 2 1 S   57900
WW27 WEST WICKHAM   S 4 2 2 L   67500
```

Commentary

```
.USE A:HOLIDAY
.COPY TO B:TEMP
00020 RECORDS COPIED
.USE B:TEMP
.EDIT
ENTER RECORD # :4
```

The data entered is not shown here, but in the LIST below.

```
.GOTO 11
.INSERT BEFORE

Data entry here.

.GOTO 7
.INSERT BEFORE

Data entry here.

.GOTO 21
.INSERT BEFORE
```

Cont'd

Data entry here.

```
 .LIST
00001  FR072 FRANCE     FULL  OBCD  GAT     195
00002  FR211 FRANCE     HALF  OBCD  GAT     225
00003  FR382 FRANCE     APT   OOCD  MAN     255
00004  IT229 ITALY      FULL  ABCD  LUT     220
00005  IT365 ITALY      HALF  OBCD  GAT     215
00006  IT509 ITALY      HALF  OOCD  GLAS    225
00007  IT601 ITALY      FULL  OBOD  GLAS    210
00008  IT882 ITALY      FULL  ABCD  GAT     275
00009  MA078 MAJORCA    HALF  OOCD  BIRM    185
00010  MA147 MAJORCA    FULL  OBCD  GAT     205
00011  MA364 MAJORCA    FULL  OOCO  GAT     175
00012  MA552 MAJORCA    HALF  OBOD  BIRM    205
00013  MA662 MAJORCA    APT   ABOD  MAN     190
00014  MA771 MAJORCA    HALF  ABCD  GAT     215
00015  PO339 PORTUGAL   HALF  OBOD  GAT     265
00016  PO887 PORTUGAL   HALF  OBCO  BIRM    245
00017  SP137 SPAIN      FULL  ABOD  GLAS    190
00018  SP258 SPAIN      FULL  ABOO  LUT     205
00019  SP481 SPAIN      HALF  ABCO  GAT     170
00020  SP551 SPAIN      FULL  OBCO  BIRM    195
00021  SP628 SPAIN      HALF  ABCO  GAT     195
00022  SP722 SPAIN      APT   OBCD  GAT     190
00023  SP901 SPAIN      HALF  ABCD  GLAS    210
 .DELETE RECORD 2
 00001 DELETION(S)
 .GO TOP
 .DISPLAY NEXT 5
00001  FR072 FRANCE     FULL  OBCD  GAT     195
00002 *FR211 FRANCE     HALF  OBCD  GAT     225
00003  FR382 FRANCE     APT   OOCD  MAN     255
00004  IT229 ITALY      FULL  ABCD  LUT     220
00005  IT365 ITALY      HALF  OBCD  GAT     215
 .RECALL ALL
00001 RECALL(S)
 .GO TOP
 .DISPLAY NEXT 5
00001  FR072 FRANCE     FULL  OBCD  GAT     195
00002  FR211 FRANCE     HALF  OBCD  GAT     225
00003  FR382 FRANCE     APT   OOCD  MAN     255
00004  IT229 ITALY      FULL  ABCD  LUT     220
00005  IT365 ITALY      HALF  OBCD  GAT     215
 .DELETE RECORD 2
00001 DELETION(S)
 .PACK
PACK COMPLETE, 00022 RECORDS COPIED
 .GO TOP
 .DISPLAY NEXT 5
00001  FR072 FRANCE     FULL  OBCD  GAT     195
00002  FR382 FRANCE     APT   OOCD  MAN     255
00003  IT229 ITALY      FULL  ABCD  LUT     220
00004  IT365 ITALY      HALF  OBCD  GAT     215
00005  IT509 ITALY      HALF  OOCD  GLAS    225
 .GOTO 14
 .DELETE NEXT 2
00002 DELETION(S)
 .PACK
PACK COMPLETE, 00020 RECORDS COPIED
 .LIST
00001  FR072 FRANCE     FULL  OBCD  GAT     195
00002  FR382 FRANCE     APT   OOCD  MAN     255
00003  IT229 ITALY      FULL  ABCD  LUT     220
00004  IT365 ITALY      HALF  OBCD  GAT     215
00005  IT509 ITALY      HALF  OOCD  GLAS    225
00006  IT601 ITALY      FULL  OBOD  GLAS    210
00007  IT882 ITALY      FULL  ABCD  GAT     275
```

```
00008  MA078 MAJORCA      HALF   OOCD   BIRM      185
00009  MA147 MAJORCA      FULL   OBCD   GAT       205
00010  MA364 MAJORCA      FULL   OOCO   GAT       175
00011  MA552 MAJORCA      HALF   OBOD   BIRM      205
00012  MA662 MAJORCA      APT    ABOD   MAN       190
00013  MA771 MAJORCA      HALF   ABCD   GAT       215
00014  SP137 SPAIN        FULL   ABOD   GLAS      190
00015  SP258 SPAIN        FULL   ABOO   LUT       205
00016  SP481 SPAIN        HALF   ABCO   GAT       170
00017  SP551 SPAIN        FULL   OBCO   BIRM      195
00018  SP628 SPAIN        HALF   ABCO   GAT       195
00019  SP722 SPAIN        APT    OBCD   GAT       190
00020  SP901 SPAIN        HALF   ABCD   GLAS      210
 .QUIT
```

9.7 Sorting and indexing

Introduction

You will already have realised how much more useful data becomes when it is sorted into an appropriate order. Start with why you sort a hand of playing cards into order, think of school registers and electoral registers, telephone directories etc., and imagine how difficult it would be to use the data if it were left in random order.

1 **To use the SORT command on the data in a file** dBASE II lets you sort the records of a file into either alphabetic or numerical orders. Before you start sorting you should make sure that your file has been stored away safely in its original order. So, start off with

```
.USE A:HOLIDAY
.COPY TO B:HOLTEMP
00020 RECORDS COPIED
```

and then continue

```
 .USE B:HOLTEMP
 .SORT ON PRICE TO B:HOLPRI
 SORT COMPLETE
 .USE B:HOLPRI
 .GO TOP
 .DISPLAY NEXT 7
00001  SP481 SPAIN        HALF   ABCO   GAT       170
00002  MA364 MAJORCA      FULL   OOCO   GAT       175
00003  MA078 MAJORCA      HALF   OOCD   BIRM      185
00004  MA662 MAJORCA      APT    ABOD   MAN       190
00005  SP137 SPAIN        FULL   ABOD   GLAS      190
00006  SP722 SPAIN        APT    OBCD   GAT       190
00007  FR072 FRANCE       FULL   OBCD   GAT       195
```

You will readily see what has happened, the SORT ON PRICE command has reordered the file, with the record with the lowest price first and then on upwards to the holiday with the highest price last. It has stored this new file on the B disk with name HOLPRI. I have shown only the first 7 records of the file which should be enough for you to see what is happening. Load the original file B:HOLTEMP to see that it is unchanged by this sorting operation.

2 **To use the INDEX command to 'sort' a file** The SORT command sorts the file in USE according to the conditions stated in the command, and stores the whole file away in its new sorted form in the new file. This means that all of the data is duplicated in a different file on the disk. This method of sorting a file in several ways could lead to a lot of wasted storage space on a disk, and could slow down processing accordingly. The **INDEX** command comes to our rescue.

Try sorting the file with the following command

```
 .INDEX ON PRICE TO B:PRIND
 00020 RECORDS INDEXED

 .GO TOP
 .DISPLAY NEXT 7
00017  SP481 SPAIN        HALF   ABCD   GAT       170
00010  MA364 MAJORCA      FULL   OOCD   GAT       175
00008  MA078 MAJORCA      HALF   OOCD   BIRM      185
00011  MA662 MAJORCA      APT    ABOD   MAN       190
00015  SP137 SPAIN        FULL   ABOD   GLAS      190
00019  SP722 SPAIN        APT    OBCD   GAT       190
00001  FR072 FRANCE       FULL   OBCD   GAT       195
```

The effect of indexing is almost the same as sorting, except that, although the positions of the records in the file are correctly in Price order, the record numbers are those which the records had in the original file. The index file contains just this list of numbers, often called pointers, because they point to the positions which the records had in the original file, HOLTEMP or HOLIDAY in this particular example. So the index file would have:

> 17 as record 1, 10 as record 2, 8 as record 3, 11 as record 4 and so on to the 20th record which holds 13.

but would contain no other data, just a list of the pointers.
To index in order of Airports say:
.INDEX ON AIRPORT TO B:AIRPIND

Indexing on the weeks field gives a list of the availability of holidays during the chosen month, to see this try
.INDEX ON WEEKS TO B:WEEKIND

3 **To INDEX on 2 string fields** You will appreciate the power of indexing when you see how you can index on more than one field. If you wanted to have the file arranged in order of countries, and then within that order the holidays were arranged in order of the airports from which the holiday starts:

```
 .INDEX ON COUNTRY + AIRPORT TO B:COUNTAIR          leads to
00020 RECORDS INDEXED
 .GO TOP
 .DISPLAY NEXT 7
00001  FR072 FRANCE       FULL   OBCD   GAT       195
00002  FR211 FRANCE       HALF   OBCD   GAT       225
00003  FR382 FRANCE       APT    OOCD   MAN       255
00005  IT365 ITALY        HALF   OBCD   GAT       205
00007  IT882 ITALY        FULL   ABCD   GAT       265
00006  IT509 ITALY        HALF   OOCD   GLAS      215
```

4 **To INDEX on a mixture of string and numeric fields** A more meaningful example is to arrange holidays according to their type, APT, FULL, and HALF, and then with these categories arrange again in order of PRICE, with the command as follows:

```
 .INDEX ON TYPE + STR(PRICE,4,0) TO B:TYPRI
00020 RECORDS INDEXED
 .GO TOP
 .DISPLAY NEXT 7
00011   MA662 MAJORCA     APT    ABOD   MAN      190
00019   SP722 SPAIN       APT    OBCD   GAT      190
00003   FR382 FRANCE      APT    OOCD   MAN      255
00010   MA364 MAJORCA     FULL   OOCO   GAT      175
00015   SP137 SPAIN       FULL   ABOD   GLAS     190
00001   FR072 FRANCE      FULL   OBCD   GAT      195
00018   SP551 SPAIN       FULL   OBCO   BIRM,    195
```

The reason for the STR(PRICE,4,0) is that you can index on either character fields or number fields but not a mixture of both, so the STR operator is used to change PRICE which is a number field into a character field, STR being short for 'string'. The '4,0' just specifies completely the number field which has to be changed, as defined in the STRUCTURE file, i.e. 4 digits with 0 decimal places.

You can see how useful indexing on more than one field could be if, for example, you had a large file of employees' names with several people with the same surname. You could do a second indexing on either first name or Works or Employee number.

Quit from your current use of dBASE II and then load HOLTEMP back into the machine and list the file. You will see that it has the original order of the HOLIDAY file. Now say:

```
 .USE B:HOLTEMP INDEX B:TYPRI
 .GO TOP
 .DISPLAY NEXT 7
00011   MA662 MAJORCA     APT    ABOD   MAN      190
00019   SP722 SPAIN       APT    OBCD   GAT      190
00003   FR382 FRANCE      APT    OOCD   MAN      255
00010   MA364 MAJORCA     FULL   OOCO   GAT      175
00015   SP137 SPAIN       FULL   ABOD   GLAS     190
00001   FR072 FRANCE      FULL   OBCD   GAT      195
00018   SP551 SPAIN       FULL   OBCO   BIRM     195
```

As the command indicates this loads HOLTEMP into the workspace indexed in the order of B:TYPRI. So, once indexed in a particular order the file may be called into use at any time in that order.

Exercise

Sort the HOUSES file on Price to B:HOUSPRI, and then use and list this new file. Index the HOUSES file on Price to B:PRINCIND, list it and compare with the sorted version B:HOUSPRI. Index HOUSES on Area, and then on Type. Index the HOUSES file on the following combined criteria: Area and Type, Number of Bedrooms and Price, Type and Price, Area and Price.

9.8 Assignment

1 **Introduction**
You should imagine that the STAFF file which you created in worksheet 9.5 is the summary file of the employees of a firm whose total number of staff is in reality about ten times the size of the STAFF file. The staff is distributed round several offices in the country. It is a summary file in that it gives very basic details about the employee, and the Employee Number (EMPNO) would be used to refer to a larger file which contains greater details of the employees' record of employment. The following activities are meant to represent the sort of processing which would be associated with such a file, although not necessarily in the order presented in the assignment.

2 Load the STAFF file from the A–disk and list the employees in the file who satisfy the following conditions:

a those who work in the Southern region
b those whose salary is greater than £12,000 per annum
c those who are female
d those who are over 45 years of age on 1st January 1988
e those who work in either the London or Croydon offices
f those women whose salary is greater than £12,000 per annum
g those men who are over 45 years of age on 1/1/89
h those women who do not work in the London office

3 Copy the file to a temporary file TEMP1 say, because you will now be making changes to the original, and may wish to keep the original for reference purposes.

4 Those employees in the two London offices have been awarded an increased allowance of £500 – make the appropriate changes to their records.

5 The Manchester branch has to be closed down, but the two members of staff accept relocation to the Croydon branch with an increase to their salary of £1,500 – make the necessary changes to the file.

6 The Birmingham branch is closed down and the staff not redeployed, so their names should be deleted from the file.

7 Sort the file in alphabetical order of surname to a new temporary file TEMP2.

8 Two new members of staff have been appointed to work at the Croydon office, insert their records into their appropriate alphabetical positions.

HOWTON	PAUL	560702	M783	9400	CROYDON
PRITCHARD	JEAN	550304	F527	10500	CROYDON

9 Copy this new file to a file called NEWSTAFF and then use it to carry out the following indexing operations. Print out enough of the resulting fi es to show the results of the indexing processes.

   a When looking at the possibility of early retirement or redundancy it would be useful to have a list of all employees in order of date of birth, index NEWSTAFF on date of birth.

   b There will be occasions when a list of names for each office in alphabetical order would be useful, so produce an index file which will produce this list.

   c It may be quite meaningful to look at the relative staff costs for the various regions, so produce an index file to help this enquiry.

   d Following on from above it might be helpful to look at the dates of birth of staff at the different offices — produce a suitable index file.

10 To clear your data disk of unwanted files delete the 2 temporary files which you created en route, TEMP1 and TEMP2.

Commentary

```
2
 .USE A:STAFF

2a
 .LIST FOR REGION = 'S'
00001  SMITH     CHARLOTTE    450620 F174   5800 S BRISTOL
00005  BURTON    CHARLES      661124 M235   8200 S LOND(EUS RD)
00007  BULL      JOAN         410525 F074  13000 S CROYDON
00008  LISTER    JUDY         560311 F993  11600 S BRISTOL
00009  GREEN     JAMES        541010 M758  12200 S CROYDON
00010  ALBERT    JENNIFER     480606 F547  10500 S LOND(WAR ST)
00011  SAMSON    ROGER        440916 M356  11250 S LOND(EUS RD)
00012  JANES     CLIVE        530422 M525  10900 S BRISTOL
00016  ROLLS     RAY          670726 M256   7650 S LOND(EUS RD)
00020  MUNN      KURT         631011 M092  13500 S BRISTOL

2b
 .LIST FOR SALARY > 12000
00006  AFRON     JOHN         320930 M886  12300 N LEEDS
00007  BULL      JOAN         410525 F074  13000 S CROYDON
00009  GREEN     JAMES        541010 M758  12200 S CROYDON
00013  SMALES    KATIE        400228 F803  14200 N LEEDS
00014  SMALL     SUSAN        360418 F476  15000 C BIRMINGHAM
00015  JAMES     JIM          440101 M365  12800 N MANCHESTER
00018  ADAMS     BILL         491208 M367  14200 C BIRMINGHAM
00020  MUNN      KURT         631011 M092  13500 S BRISTOL

2c
 .LIST FOR 'F' $ EMPNO
00001  SMITH     CHARLOTTE    450620 F174   5800 S BRISTOL
00002  JONES     DORIS        380801 F263   6500 N LEEDS
00007  BULL      JOAN         410525 F074  13000 S CROYDON
00008  LISTER    JUDY         560311 F993  11600 S BRISTOL
00010  ALBERT    JENNIFER     480606 F547  10500 S LOND(WAR ST)
00013  SMALES    KATIE        400228 F803  14200 N LEEDS
00014  SMALL     SUSAN        360418 F476  15000 C BIRMINGHAM

2d
 .LIST FOR DOB < 430101
00002  JONES     DORIS        380801 F263   6500 N LEEDS
00003  HOBBINS   HAROLD       390722 M622   6800 C BIRMINGHAM
```

Cont'd

```
00004  JOHNSON      BERT          330705 M441   9400 N MANCHESTER
00006  APRON        JOHN          320930 M886  12300 N LEEDS
00007  BULL         JOAN          410525 F074  13000 S CROYDON
00013  SMALES       KATIE         400228 F803  14200 N LEEDS
00014  SMALL        SUSAN         360418 F476  15000 C BIRMINGHAM
```

2e

```
.LIST FOR 'LOND' $ OFFICE .OR. 'CROY' $ OFFICE
00005  BURTON       CHARLES       661124 M235   8200 S LOND(EUS RD)
00007  BULL         JOAN          410525 F074  13000 S CROYDON
00009  GREEN        JAMES         541010 M758  12200 S CROYDON
00010  ALBERT       JENNIFER      480606 F547  10500 S LOND(WAR ST)
00011  SAMSON       ROGER         440916 M356  11250 S LOND(EUS RD)
00016  ROLLS        RAY           670726 M256   7650 S LOND(EUS RD)
```

2f

```
.LIST FOR 'F' $ EMPNO .AND. SALARY > 12000
00007  BULL         JOAN          410525 F074  13000 S CROYDON
00013  SMALES       KATIE         400228 F803  14200 N LEEDS
00014  SMALL        SUSAN         360418 F476  15000 C BIRMINGHAM
```

2g

```
.LIST FOR 'M' $ EMPNO .AND. DOB < 430101
00003  HOBBINS      HAROLD        390722 M622   6800 C BIRMINGHAM
00004  JOHNSON      BERT          330705 M441   9400 N MANCHESTER
00006  APRON        JOHN          320930 M886  12300 N LEEDS
```

2h

```
.LIST FOR 'F' $ EMPNO .AND. .NOT.('LOND' $ OFFICE)
00001  SMITH        CHARLOTTE     450620 F174   5800 S BRISTOL
00002  JONES        DORIS         380801 F263   6500 N LEEDS
00007  BULL         JOAN          410525 F074  13000 S CROYDON
00008  LISTER       JUDY          560311 F993  11600 S BRISTOL
00013  SMALES       KATIE         400228 F803  14200 N LEEDS
00014  SMALL        SUSAN         360418 F476  15000 C BIRMINGHAM
```

3

```
.COPY TO B:TEMP1
00020 RECORDS COPIED
```

4 and 5

```
.USE B:TEMP1
.EDIT
ENTER RECORD # 5
```

Here the changes to the London salaries are made, and to the 2 Manchester records as required in question 5.

6

```
.DELETE RECORD 3
00001 DELETION(S)
.DELETE RECORD 14
00001 DELETION(S)
.DELETE RECORD 18
00001 DELETION(S)
.PACK
PACK COMPLETE, 00017 RECORDS COPIED
```

7

```
.SORT ON SNAME TO B:TEMP2
SORT COMPLETE
```

8

```
.USE B:TEMP2
.GOTO 14
.INSERT BEFORE
```

```
RECORD # 00014
The 2nd of the 2 new records is inserted here.

 .GOTO 8
 .INSERT BEFORE
RECORD # 00008
The 1st of the 2 new records is inserted here.
```

9

```
 .COPY TO B:NEWSTAFF
00019 RECORDS COPIED
 .USE B:NEWSTAFF
 .LIST
00001  ALBERT      JENNIFER    480606 F547  11000 S LOND(WAR ST)
00002  APRON       JOHN        320930 M886  12300 N LEEDS
00003  BATTEN      DEAN        500420 M652  12000 N LEEDS
00004  BONEFIELD   WILLIAM     600325 M154   8700 N LEEDS
00005  BULL        JOAN        410525 F074  13000 S CROYDON
00006  BURTON      CHARLES     661124 M235   8700 S LOND(EUS RD)
00007  GREEN       JAMES       541010 M758  12200 S CROYDON
00008  HOWTON      PAUL        560702 M783   9400 S CROYDON
00009  JAMES       JIM         440101 M365  12800 N MANCHESTER
00010  JANES       CLIVE       530422 M525  10900 S BRISTOL
00011  JOHNSON     BERT        330705 M441   9400 N MANCHESTER
00012  JONES       DORIS       380801 F263   6500 N LEEDS
00013  LISTER      JUDY        560311 F993  11600 S BRISTOL
00014  MUNN        KURT        631011 M092  13500 S BRISTOL
00015  PRITCHARD   JEAN        550304 F527  10500 S CROYDON
00016  ROLLS       RAY         670726 M256   8150 S LOND(EUS RD)
00017  SAMSON      ROGER       440916 M356  11750 S LOND(EUS RD)
00018  SMALES      KATIE       400228 F803  14200 N LEEDS
00019  SMITH       CHARLOTTE   450620 F174   5800 S BRISTOL
```

9a

```
 .INDEX ON DOB TO B:DOBIND
00019 RECORDS INDEXED
 .GO TOP
 .DISPLAY NEXT 7
00002  APRON       JOHN        320930 M886  12300 N LEEDS
00011  JOHNSON     BERT        330705 M441   9400 N MANCHESTER
00012  JONES       DORIS       380801 F263   6500 N LEEDS
00018  SMALES      KATIE       400228 F803  14200 N LEEDS
00005  BULL        JOAN        410525 F074  13000 S CROYDON
00009  JAMES       JIM         440101 M365  12800 N MANCHESTER
00017  SAMSON      ROGER       440916 M356  11750 S LOND(EUS RD)
```

9b

```
 .INDEX ON OFFICE + SNAME TO B:OFFNAME
00019 RECORDS INDEXED
 .GO TOP
 .DISPLAY NEXT 7
00010  JANES       CLIVE       530422 M525  10900 S BRISTOL
00013  LISTER      JUDY        560311 F993  11600 S BRISTOL
00014  MUNN        KURT        631011 M092  13500 S BRISTOL
00019  SMITH       CHARLOTTE   450620 F174   5800 S BRISTOL
00005  BULL        JOAN        410525 F074  13000 S CROYDON
00007  GREEN       JAMES       541010 M758  12200 S CROYDON
00008  HOWTON      PAUL        560702 M783   9400 S CROYDON
```

9c

```
 .INDEX ON REGION + STR(SALARY,5,0) TO B:REGSAL
00019 RECORDS INDEXED
 .GO TOP
 .DISPLAY NEXT 7
00012  JONES       DORIS       380801 F263   6500 N LEEDS
00004  BONEFIELD   WILLIAM     600325 M154   8700 N LEEDS
```

Cont'd

```
00011   JOHNSON        BERT            330705 M441    9400 N MANCHESTER
00003   BATTEN         DEAN            500420 M652   12000 N LEEDS
00002   APRON          JOHN            320930 M886   12300 N LEEDS
00009   JAMES          JIM             440101 M365   12800 N MANCHESTER
00018   SMALES         KATIE           400228 F803   14200 N LEEDS

9d
 .INDEX ON OFFICE + STR(DOB,6,0) TO B:OFFDOB
00019 RECORDS INDEXED
 .GO TOP
 .DISPLAY NEXT 7
00019   SMITH          CHARLOTTE       450620 F174    5800 S BRISTOL
00010   JANES          CLIVE           530422 M525   10900 S BRISTOL
00013   LISTER         JUDY            560311 F993   11600 S BRISTOL
00014   MUNN           KURT            631011 M092   13500 S BRISTOL
00005   BULL           JOAN            410525 F074   13000 S CROYDON
00007   GREEN          JAMES           541010 M758   12200 S CROYDON
00015   PRITCHARD      JEAN            550304 F527   10500 S CROYDON

10
 .DELETE FILE B:TEMP1
FILE HAS BEEN DELETED
 .DELETE FILE B:TEMP2
FILE HAS BEEN DELETED
 . QUIT
*** END RUN      dBASE II      ***
```

9.9 List layouts and reports

Introduction

So far to display the output from an interrogation I have used the simplest and most general form of the LIST command. This command is more flexible than I have led you to believe, as you will soon see. The designers of dBASE II realised that the users of the package would wish to be able to display the results of their data processing activities in a variety of ways, and so they provided the REPORT command. The word 'report' is used widely in data processing as a general term to cover all forms of output from processing activities.

To use the LIST command more flexibly First of all 'boot up' the system and get into dBASE II. Then load in the STAFF file with **USE A:STAFF**, assuming that this file is on the A–drive. As a start try **.LIST OFF** instead of just **LIST** and you will see that the file is listed without the left–hand column of record numbers, so **OFF** switches off the record number facility.

You can also specify which fields you want displayed and in what order, rather than have all of the fields in the order specified by the file structure. Try:

```
.LIST OFF FNAME SNAME EMPNO OFFICE

CHARLOTTE     SMITH         F174 BRISTOL
DORIS         JONES         F263 LEEDS
HAROLD        HOBBINS       M622 BIRMINGHAM
BERT          JOHNSON       M441 MANCHESTER
CHARLES       BURTON        M235 LOND(EUS RD)
JOHN          APRON         M886 LEEDS
JOAN          BULL          F074 CROYDON
JUDY          LISTER        F993 BRISTOL
JAMES         GREEN         M758 CROYDON
JENNIFER      ALBERT        F547 LOND(WAR ST)
```

and so on for the rest of the file.

You can also use the more complicated form of
LIST OFF . . field names . . FOR . . condition . .

So, to get those members of staff who are over 45 years of age at the start of 1988, you could ask

```
.LIST OFF FNAME SNAME EMPNO DOB FOR DOB < 430101

DORIS         JONES         F263  380801
HAROLD        HOBBINS       M622  390722
BERT          JOHNSON       M441  330705
JOHN          APRON         M886  320930
JOAN          BULL          F074  410525
KATIE         SMALES        F803  400228
SUSAN         SMALL         F476  360418
```

Exercises

Instances where you could use this more flexible form of the LIST command will have already occurred to you, either for use with the files in this book or with other files which have more direct relevance for you. But, if you want more specific exercises for practice, try the following.

1 (a) output the Reference Number, Area, Type of property and Number of bedrooms for those records in the HOUSES files whose Price is less than £50,000,
  (b) for those properties in the Orpington Area list the Reference Number, Type of property, Number of bedrooms and Price.

2 In the HOLIDAY file list:
  (a) the Reference Number, Type of holiday, the Weeks when available and Price for those holidays whose Price is less than £200,
  (b) the Country, Type of holiday and Price for two–week holidays which are available in the first two weeks of August,
  (c) the Reference Number, Type of holiday, availability and Price for holidays which start from Gatwick airport.

2 **To use the REPORT facility to display data** — The details of the layout of the report is stored in a special file, called a FORM file. I am going to

produce staff lists as above using REPORT, and so will call the file STLIST and store it on the B–drive. If, after it is stored, you examine the directory of the B–disk you will find it stored with the full name STLIST.FRM, the file 'extension' .FRM shows that it is a FORM file created by the REPORT command.

The details of the layout or format of the FORM file are entered by responding to 'prompts' on the screen, in a very similar way to when you entered the structure of a data file when creating it. You will be able to follow the interaction between user and system from the following 'screen dump'. User responses are underlined, and I have included comments where necessary after the command. Strings are entered into the right–hand end of the allotted space, so to fit 'SURNAME' into the left–hand side of a column of 12 spaces you have to enter SURNAME + 5 spaces, or SURNAME   .

So, you get to **USE A:STAFF** and continue:

```
 .REPORT FORM B:STLIST2
ENTER OPTIONS, M=LEFT MARGIN, L=LINES/PAGE, W=PAGE WIDTHM=10,W=60
PAGE HEADING? (Y/N)Y
ENTER PAGE HEADING:STAFF LIST
DOUBLE SPACE REPORT? (Y/N) N
ARE TOTALS REQUIRED? (Y/N) N
 COL      WIDTH,CONTENTS
 001      12,SNAME
ENTER HEADING: SURNAME                   ** SURNAME + 5 spaces
 002      12,FNAME
ENTER HEADING: FIRST NAME                ** FIRST NAME + 2 spaces
 003      5,EMPNO
ENTER HEADING: EMPNO                     ** + 0 spaces
 004      6,REGION
ENTER HEADING: REGION                    ** + 0 spaces
 005      12,OFFICE
ENTER HEADING: OFFICE                    ** + 6 spaces
 006      hit the Enter key here
```

After hitting the **Enter** Key at column 6 to show that this is the end of the details of the Form, the display starts automatically showing first the Page No and the Date.

```
PAGE NO. 00001
12/17/87

                   STAFF LIST

SURNAME      FIRST NAME   EMPNO REGION OFFICE

SMITH        CHARLOTTE    F174  S      BRISTOL
JONES        DORIS        F263  N      LEEDS
HOBBINS      HAROLD       M622  C      BIRMINGHAM
JOHNSON      BERT         M441  N      MANCHESTER
BURTON       CHARLES      M235  S      LOND(EUS RD)
APRON        JOHN         M886  N      LEEDS
BULL         JOAN         F074  S      CROYDON
LISTER       JUDY         F993  S      BRISTOL
GREEN        JAMES        M758  S      CROYDON
ALBERT       JENNIFER     F547  S      LOND(WAR ST)
```

and so on for the rest of the STAFF file.

3 **To use REPORT with 'conditions'** — Assuming that you are still in **USE A:STAFF** you can continue:

```
.REPORT FORM B:STLIST FOR DOB < 430101

          PAGE NO. 00001
          12/17/87

                              STAFF LIST

          SURNAME       FIRST NAME    EMPNO REGION OFFICE

          JONES         DORIS         F263  N      LEEDS
          HOBBINS       HAROLD        M622  C      BIRMINGHAM
          JOHNSON       BERT          M441  N      MANCHESTER
          APRON         JOHN          M886  N      LEEDS
          BULL          JOAN          F074  S      CROYDON
          SMALES        KATIE         F803  N      LEEDS
          SMALL         SUSAN         F476  C      BIRMINGHAM
```

You will see that this has kept the display format of the STLIST.FRM file, and has picked out those under 45 years of age on the 1st January 1989.

4 **To use REPORT with an INDEXed file** — Assume that you are still in **USE A:STAFF**, you continue:

```
.INDEX ON OFFICE + SNAME TO B:STIND
00020 RECORDS INDEXED
.SET HEADING TO 1ST JANUARY 1988
.REPORT FORM B:STLIST

          PAGE NO. 00001       1ST JANUARY 1988
          12/17/87

                              STAFF LIST

          SURNAME       FIRST NAME    EMPNO REGION OFFICE

          ADAMS         BILL          M367  C      BIRMINGHAM
          HOBBINS       HAROLD        M622  C      BIRMINGHAM
          SMALL         SUSAN         F476  C      BIRMINGHAM
          JANES         CLIVE         M525  S      BRISTOL
          LISTER        JUDY          F993  S      BRISTOL
          MUNN          KURT          M092  S      BRISTOL
          SMITH         CHARLOTTE     F174  S      BRISTOL
          BULL          JOAN          F074  S      CROYDON
          GREEN         JAMES         M758  S      CROYDON
```

and so on for the rest of the file.

You will see that the output has now been 'sorted' into alphabetical order of Offices, and alphabetical order of Surnames within those offices, and output in the form of STLIST.FRM.

Exercise

You can now use the REPORT command to carry out the tasks set in Exercises 1 and 2. For instance (a) with the HOUSES file design a Report

Form with columns for just Type of property, Number of Bedrooms, Area, and Price, followed by the Reference Number, for properties costing less than £50,000, or (b) for the HOLIDAY file design a Report Form with columns for Country, Type, Price and Reference Number for those holidays which start from Gatwick airport. Having designed the Report output the data, and then output the same data indexed on Price of property or holiday.

10 Programming in dBASE II

10.1 Introduction

In the worksheets we used dBASE II 'immediate mode' by issuing commands at the keyboard and seeing an immediate response to them on the screen. We were able to do a lot of data processing in this mode — as you saw. Many data–base packages give you these facilities at a much lower price than dBASE II, and so why buy it in preference to others? dBASE II has become a standard for data–bases in the same way as WordStar has for word processing packages — but this is not the reason. The fact is that the cheaper data base packages only give you immediate mode processing, with about the range of facilities we have covered in the worksheets, and no more.

With dBASE II there is much more. In fact it is true to say that so far we have only barely used the true power of the package, which lies in its command language. This language lets you collect together in one file, a command file, sets of the commands which we have used singly in immediate mode, and later run the whole set of commands as a job lot automatically.

I suppose the reason why the command language is not used so readily is that it involves some programming skills. These need only be very modest, as I will demonstrate, to lead quickly to an increase in processing power. I think that you will easily see how the language works even if you have done no programming before, and if you have used BASIC you will soon see close similarities. The beauty of dBASE II is that it is as straightforward to program as BASIC, but because of the file based nature of the package all of the file handling techniques have been made easily available to you.

If you have done no programming before all you need to appreciate before you start is that there are only three essential elements to any programming language. Firstly it should allow you to give the machine a sequence of instructions. Next it should provide you with a decision making procedure, this is usually accomplished by dividing your instructions into two alternative sequences. When processing reaches a certain point in the program, the data provided will determine whether sequence 1 or sequence 2 is selected. The logic goes something like: 'If expression 1 is true then do sequence 1, else do sequence 2.' You have already met the 'If . . . then . . . else . . .' idea in the chapter Logic and Databases. The third essential facility is the repetitive loop, which will let you perform repeated operations.

So, in summary the three essential components of any programming language are sequences, selection and loops.

10.2 Sequences

If you return to your answers relating to the questions asked in the exercise of Worksheet 9.3, then you probably obtained as answers a set of instructions similar to the following sequence.

```
USE A:HOLIDAY
LIST FOR AIRPORT = 'GAT'
LIST FOR COUNTRY = 'SPAIN'
LIST FOR 'SP' $ COUNTRY
LIST FOR PRICE < 200
LIST FOR TYPE <> 'FULL'
LIST FOR 'AB' $ WEEKS
COUNT FOR 'GAT' $ AIRPORT
COUNT FOR PRICE < 200
```

Fig. 10.1 A sequence of instructions

These commands were entered in the sequence shown at the keyboard and the results shown on the screen immediately after each command, in what I described as 'immediate mode'. This is the first element of the programmer's toolkit – a sequence of instructions. If this sequence is entered into a command file and wrapped up a little, then when that file is activated the sequence of instructions will be carried out automatically. Assume that the file has the name B:DB2EX, after it had been typed in it would then have three additional instructions, and would look like:

```
**TO WRITE THE ANSWERS TO DB2EX**
SET ECHO ON
SET TALK ON
USE A:HOLIDAY
LIST FOR AIRPORT = 'GAT'
LIST FOR COUNTRY = 'SPAIN'
LIST FOR 'SP' $ COUNTRY
LIST FOR PRICE < 200
LIST FOR TYPE <> 'FULL'
LIST FOR 'AB' $ WEEKS
COUNT FOR 'GAT' $ AIRPORT
COUNT FOR PRICE < 200
RETURN
```

Fig. 10.2 The B:DB2EX.PRG command file

If at the dot–prompt you said **.DO B:DB2EX** then the answers as shown in the Answer section of the book would appear on the screen. **DO** is the command which activates the instructions in a command file. So, **DO:DB2EX** is just saying to the system, 'do the instructions found in file B:DB2EX'.

This command file has four additional lines to those shown in Figure 10.1, but only three of these are active. Any line which starts with a * acts as a comment line for the programmer to 'document' the program, i.e. add comments of explanation. This line is not 'executed' — it is ignored, when the program is run. I have used this first line just to give a heading to the program. Any line beginning with * or NOTE is ignored when the program is run.

SET ECHO ON is a command which ensures that all of the commands which are issued by a command file are 'echoed' out to the screen. If this command were not there the commands would still be obeyed and you would see the results of the commands on the screen, but you would not see the commands themselves. In immediate mode you see your commands and their results on the screen at all times, but you have to get used to the fact that in command mode dBASE II is quite happy to get on and carry out its commands without showing you on the screen every step of its working — unless you ask it to.

SET TALK ON acts in similar way in displaying the results from commands on the screen. The results would be displayed anyway for those explicit commands like LIST, but you will notice that the program does not ask explicitly for the results of the two COUNT commands, but they appear in the display with SET TALK ON.

If you do not specify it dBASE II leaves SET TALK ON and SET ECHO OFF, these are called the 'default' states.

The last command is **RETURN**, and this marks the end of the command file, and simply 'returns' you to immediate mode working.

You can do a lot of work with such single sequence command files. Following on from the work you did in the exercise for worksheet 9.7, imagine that the Estate agent wanted to prepare once a week for example, his properties in various orders to suit clients, who he/she knows from experience, will ask certain stereotypes questions. He/she will not wish to sit at the terminal and sort the files while the customer waits. The following command file would help:

```
**VARIOUS SORTS ON THE HOUSES FILE**
SET TALK ON
SET ECHO ON
USE A:HOUSES
INDEX ON PRICE TO B:PRICIND
INDEX ON AREA + TYPE TO B:ARTYP
INDEX ON BEDROOMS + PRICE TO B:BEDPRI
INDEX ON TYPE + STR(PRICE,6,0) TO B:TYPRI
INDEX ON AREA + STR(PRICE,6,0) TO B:ARPRI
RETURN
```

Fig. 10.3 House sort command file

So if the client wishes to examine the types of property which are available starting from the lowest price range and upwards, the agent could continue:

```
.USE A:HOUSES INDEX B:PRICIND
.LIST
```

If the client wants to live in a certain area and type of property, then:

```
.USE A:HOUSES INDEX B:ARTYP
.LIST
```

The estate agent could get to the essential data more quickly with these files having been created in the background and ready to be used, or even provide lists for the client to browse through.

10.3 Creating command files

dBASE II provides its own primitive little wordprocessing system, referred to as the editor, to let you create command files. You start at the dot–prompt with **.MODIFY COMMAND B:DB2EX**

This is a bit of a strange command but can be read as 'edit the command file DB2EX on the B–drive'. CREATE and EDIT cannot be used with command files, because they are themselves commands in dBASE II. If DB2EX were a new file it would seem strange to modify or edit a non–existent file, but you have to read it as modifying an empty file. If it is a new file then after issuing the command you are faced with a blank screen, with the cursor blinking in the top left–hand corner. You then proceed to enter the commands as seen in Figure 10.3 one by one down the screen.

In MODIFY COMMAND mode you only have very limited editing facilities available to you.

The line is ended with **Enter** key as usual.

If the package has been configured for your system you should be able to use the arrowed keys to go back and forth along the line, and between lines. If not then you will have to resort to:

Wordstar's:	**Ctrl/E**	**Ctrl/X**	**Ctrl/D**	**Ctrl/S**	
Wordstar's:	**Ctrl/G**	deletes at the cursor			
	Ctrl/V	toggles the Insert on and off			

As soon as you press **Enter** the Insert is toggled off.

Ctrl/T deletes a whole line. **Ctrl/N** inserts a blank line. So, to insert a new line you cursor to the line below where you wish to insert, then open up the text by inserting a blank line with **Ctrl/N**, then cursor back up into the blank line and key in the new set of instructions.

Ctrl/W writes the changes made to the named file, and then returns you to the dot–prompt in immediate mode and out of MODIFY COMMAND mode. This is the same as in EDIT mode and so as you would expect **Ctrl/Q** will quit the file without any changes being made.

Exercise

Write command file programs for Exercises 1 and 2 of Worksheet 9.9.

10.4 Output and interfacing with WordStar

Before looking at loops and decisions I want to look at two different ways of outputting the results of command files. If you wish to get a hard–copy of the results on paper then you could press **Ctrl/P** before entering the DO command and all of the results would appear at the printer. There is a more selective print command which you can use in command files. Let's look at my command file for Exercise 1 (a) of worksheet 9.9.

```
**WORKSHEET 9.9 EXERCISE 1A**
SET ECHO ON
USE A:HOUSES
SET PRINT ON
LIST OFF REFNO AREA TYPE BEDROOMS FOR PRICE < 50000
LIST OFF REFNO TYPE BEDROOMS PRICE FOR 'ORP' $ AREA
SET PRINT OFF
SET ECHO OFF
RETURN
```

Fig. 10.4 Use of the SET PRINT command

Had you used the **Ctrl/P** method every command would have been echoed out to the printer. Using the **SET PRINT ON/OFF** commands allows you to switch the printer on and off just before and after the listing section of the program, thus restricting your printout to that part of the activity which you wish to record.

Now imagine that you wished to include these two lists in a report or similar document which you are creating with WordStar. You could cut out and stick in the printout which you obtained from the above program, or photocopy it and insert it into the report as a separate page. The modification to the program shown in Figure 10.5 sets you on the road to a much more professional solution to this problem.

```
**WORKSHEET 9.9 EXERCISE 1A**
SET ECHO ON
USE A:HOUSES
SET ALTERNATE TO B:WKT9EX1A.TXT
SET ALTERNATE ON
LIST OFF REFNO AREA TYPE BEDROOMS FOR PRICE < 50000
LIST OFF REFNO TYPE BEDROOMS PRICE FOR 'ORP' $ AREA
SET ALTERNATE OFF
SET ECHO OFF
RETURN
```

Fig. 10.5 Output to a TEXT file

Comparing the two programs you will see that the only difference is the replacement of SET PRINT ON/OFF with 3 SET ALTERNATE statements. You may think of printing as the most frequently used form of output, but there must be provision for alternative forms of output, writing to disk for example. So, you can read these new lines as 'setting up an alternative form of output to disk'.

The first new line **SET ALTERNATE TO B:WKT9EX1A.TXT** instructs that output should be made to file name WKT9EX1A.TXT on the B–drive, WKT9EX1A standing for 'Worksheet 9.9 Exercise 1(a)' and the extension .TXT indicating that it should be a 'text' file. Having told the system where to make the output, SET ALTERNATE ON now just tells it to get on and do it, i.e. make the output to disk from that point on, and later SET ALTERNATE OFF switches off that mode of output.

The .TXT file may be read into a WordStar document with the usual **Ctrl/KR** instruction. If you had named your command file B:WKT9EX1A then after you had saved and run it, you would find two files on your disk WKT9EX1A.PRG and WKT9EX1A. The command or program file has the extension .PRG, and is also stored on the disk in ASCII form. So, to write about how these programs work I can use **Ctrl/KR** to read into my 'script' both WKT9EX1A.PRG and WKT9EX1A.TXT, to show the program and the effects of its execution.

Currently software manufacturers are concentrating on making their packages 'integrated' so that the results of data–base or spreadsheet processing may be used in wordprocessing or graphics modules; but the simple and very powerful reading of the results of data file processing into word processor as shown above, has always been available with even the earliest versions of dBASE II and WordStar. You do of course have to get out of dBASE II and into WordStar to do this – so I'm not pretending that it is in any way integrated.

10.5 Loops

I introduced the idea of loops and gave an example of a dBASE II program to demonstrate the ASCII code in Chapter 6. You will now appreciate sight of the full program which generated the earlier printout.
If you omitted the SET ECHO OFF you would find that the commands themselves in the DO . . . . ENDDO loop will appear on the screen each time the program goes through the loop, i.e. 11 times. The results will also appear in the middle of these collections of commands. If you are in any doubt about the effect of this command then run the program omitting SET ECHO OFF, and you will soon appreciate their function. Even then you are not out of the trees, because you will recall that SET TALK ON is the default state, and that it controls the program reporting on the state of its variables. So, if you leave this ON, then COUNT will report its state each time round the loop — 11 times! Again if in doubt, try the program yourself without SET TALK OFF, and see!

```
** TO GENERATE THE ASCII CODE **
SET ECHO OFF
SET TALK OFF
SET ALTERNATE TO B:ASCII.TXT
SET ALTERNATE ON
?
?
? 'ASCII CHARACTER SET '
?
STORE 40 TO COUNT
DO WHILE COUNT < 51
? STR(COUNT,3),'---',CHR(COUNT)
STORE COUNT+1 TO COUNT
ENDDO
?
SET ALTERNATE OFF
RETURN
```

Fig. 10.6 Full program for ASCII code generation

I called the command file ASCII, so it is stored as ASCII.PRG, and you can see from Figure 10.6 that the results are stored as ASCII.TXT. To generate the text for Chapter 6, I loaded into my WordStar document ASCII.PRG followed by ASCII.TXT. Well no — it was not quite as simple as that!

If you look back you will see that I generated three sections of the code by starting the loop at 40 and ending it at < 51, then started at 60 and ended at < 71, and started at 90 and ended at < 101. I had to change two lines only:

STORE 40 TO COUNT   became   STORE 60 TO COUNT   and later
STORE 90 TO COUNT

At the same time

DO WHILE COUNT < 51   became   DO WHILE COUNT < 71 and
DO WHILE COUNT < 101.

But each time I ran the program ASCII.TXT would have been overwritten with the next new set of data. So, when I changed the program I changed the two lines which I have indicated, and the 'SET ALTERNATE TO' file, to ASC1.TXT, ASC2.TXT and ASC3.TXT. Then I could read in the three runs of the program as required for my text.

This description has also emphasized the main characteristics of loops — they should have a beginning, middle and end! The starting point in the ASCII example was in the first instance STORE 40 TO COUNT, or put the number 40 into the store location named COUNT. The finishing point was determined by the statement DO WHILE COUNT < 51, which meant that 50 was the finishing post, because inside the loop the number in COUNT was increasing by 1. COUNT = 50 would thus be the last pass through the loop as 50 is the last integer < 51 (and not = 51).

The middle of the loop is the power–house, where ? means 'print'

```
? STR(COUNT,3),'---',CHR(COUNT)
STORE COUNT+1 TO COUNT
```

The first line displays the value of the number in COUNT as a string value in the right–hand side of a column of three spaces - STR(COUNT,3). Then the three dashes --- are just literally displayed, followed by the ASCII code for the number in COUNT which is given by CHR(COUNT).

The second line says put COUNT+1 into the store location COUNT. In other words replace the old value of COUNT with the old value plus 1.

So, a loop must have a beginning, middle and end — true enough; but the middle must also in some way change things to make the processing change each time the loop is executed. In the above example the change is an increment of 1 in the value of COUNT.

The main characteristics of loops are typified and summarised in figure 10.7.

```
STORE 40 TO COUNT                        .... start
DO WHILE COUNT < 51                      .... condition to end the loop
? STR(COUNT,3),'---',CHR(COUNT)          .... do some 'printing'
STORE COUNT+1 TO COUNT                   .... increment COUNT by 1
ENDDO                                    .... end of loop instructions
```

Fig. 10.7 Main features of a loop

10.6 Numbers

I am still concerned with loops, but will use them to explore just a little further some of the ideas and warnings about numbers which I touched upon in Chapter 6. You will recall that you should be cautious about the accuracy of large and small numbers, and those lurking about zero. There are several lessons to be learned from the program.

```
** RECIPROCALS OF NUMBERS AND DIVIDE BY ZERO**
SET ECHO OFF
SET TALK OFF
SET ALTERNATE TO B:NUMB1.TXT
SET ALTERNATE ON
?
STORE 1 TO COUNT                  .... start at 1
DO WHILE COUNT >= -1              .... end at -1
? COUNT, 1/COUNT                  .... show COUNT and 1/COUNT
STORE COUNT-0.1 TO COUNT          .... increment COUNT by -0.1
ENDDO
?
SET ALTERNATE OFF
RETURN
```

If the program is now run, you will see:

```
          1              1
        0.9            1.1
        0.8            1.2
        0.7            1.4
        0.6            1.6
        0.5            2.0
        0.4            2.5
        0.3            3.3
        0.2            5.0
        0.1           10.0
        0.0
*** ZERO DIVIDE
        -.1          -10.0
        -.2           -5.0
        -.3           -3.3
        -.4           -2.5
        -.5           -2.0
        -.6           -1.6
        -.7           -1.4
        -.8           -1.2
        -.9           -1.1
       -1.0           -1.0
```

Fig. 10.8 Reciprocals of numbers and division by zero

If you are in any doubt — you will recall that the reciprocal of a number is 1 divided by the number. I have shown the features of a loop with comments to the right of the program — beginning, end and middle with increment. The increment in this case is negative −0.1. So, the effect is to start at 1 and reduce by steps of −0.1 to −1. dBASE II is so well behaved that it warns us that the program tried to divide by zero at the appropriate point — it did not stop processing though!

Why did it give the results limited to one decimal place only? If you have programmed in BASIC before you would not have expected that. Let's give it the data in a 'more accurate' form!

```
STORE 1.000 TO COUNT
DO WHILE COUNT >= -1.000
? COUNT, 1.000/COUNT
STORE COUNT-0.100 TO COUNT
ENDDO
```

```
      1.000            1.000
      0.900            1.111
      0.800            1.250
      0.700            1.428
      0.600            1.666
      0.500            2.000
      0.400            2.500
      0.300            3.333
      0.200            5.000
      0.100           10.000
      0.000
*** ZERO DIVIDE
      -.100          -10.000
```

Fig. 10.9 'More accurate' reciprocals

and so on, you've got the message by now!

I've only shown the loop section of the program to save a little space, the only difference was the name of the Text file and that is not relevant to the solution of the problem. You can see that the accuracy which we get out, is a mirror image of that which we put in — in this case to three decimal places. This is not the place to explore all of the number crunching techniques provided by dBASE II, but you have seen enough to realise that you have to proceed carefully if you want to do arithmetic using the package — in addition to being careful about possible division by zero at all times. Compare the above printouts with those obtained using BASIC and SuperCalc shown in Appendix 2.

We've looked at small numbers, now let's get dBASE II to show us how it handles large numbers. The following program takes the number 123.45 and squares it, and cubes it and so on until ending at the 10th power.

```
** LARGE NUMBERS **
SET ECHO OFF
SET TALK OFF
SET ALTERNATE TO B:NUMB3.TXT
SET ALTERNATE ON
?
?
?
STORE 1 TO COUNT
STORE 123.45 TO NUMBER
? '           C','  123.45 RAISED TO THE POWER C'
?
DO WHILE COUNT < 11
? COUNT, NUMBER
STORE COUNT+1 TO COUNT
STORE 123.45*NUMBER TO NUMBER
ENDDO
?
SET ALTERNATE OFF
RETURN
```

When run this program gives:

```
 C   123.45 RAISED TO THE POWER C

 1      123.45
 2   15239.9025
 3   1881365.963000
 4   232254628.10000000
 5   28671833830.0000000000
 6   3539537880000.000000000000
 7   436955951000000.00000000000000
 8   53942212100000000.0000000000000000
 9   6659166080000000000.000000000C0000000
10   822074052000000000000.000000000C0000000000
```

Fig. 10.10 Large numbers program

The shape of the output should surprise you, but the program itself needs little explanation except to comment on the line which does all of the work: STORE 123.45*NUMBER TO NUMBER

Before entering the loop we had made the store location called NUMBER hold 123.45, at the line STORE 123.45 TO NUMBER. First time round the loop 123.45*NUMBER just means 123.45*123.45 or 123.45 squared, and then this square is stored in NUMBER. So, next time round the loop the square is in NUMBER, and is eventually multiplied by 123.45 giving the cube in NUMBER, and so on.

Two things should strike you from the run of the program. The first is that dBASE II does not automatically break into the E notation for numbers above a certain magnitude, as SuperCalc and BASIC do. The second is that it is not consistent about the number of significant figures to which it rounds the product. There are of course ways in which you the programmer can control the accuracy to meet the needs of your particular application, but this is not the place to go into such details. Suffice it to say again that you have to be very careful about how you interpret the results of arithmetic processing, and you should always check that programs are giving what you would expect.

10.7 Address labels

If you have WordStar with Mailmerge then you can produce envelope labels using that combination, even if your address data is held on dBASE II files. As an example I am going to assume that you do not have these facilities, and that you wish to produce labels for data held in a dBASE II data file. You can use a program in a command file to do this job for you.

The labels usually come on continuous sheets of perforated computer paper, are self–adhesive and distributed over the sheet in set predetermined positions. So the task of the program is to type the address in say five lines, then skip five lines to the next label and print the next address, and so on down the sheet. I have oversimplified and omitted some points of detail, but this is the core of the task.

In the programs I simplify again by using the STAFF file and the 'addresses' consist of Name, Office and Region for the personnel in that file. Nothing is lost by this and a lot of paper is saved. So, the task becomes three lines of address followed by three blank lines. I work up to the final program in easy stages which should speak for themselves, see figure 10.11.

The rows of asterisks ********** divide the DO loop from the rest of the program. The upper and lower sections will appear very standard to you by now. In fact if you try some programming for yourself and follow the examples in this chapter, it will pay you to save these lines in a separate file and just copy them into the new command file which you wish to create. Then all you have to do is to change to the new file names in the upper section, and type in the middle section each time.

```
** TO PRINT OUT ADDRESS LABELS **
SET ECHO OFF
SET TALK OFF
USE A:STAFF
SET ALTERNATE TO B:ADDLAB1.TXT
SET ALTERNATE ON
GO TOP
**********
DO WHILE .NOT. EOF
? FNAME,SNAME
? OFFICE
? REGION
?
?
?
SKIP
ENDDO
***********
SET ALTERNATE OFF
RETURN
```

Fig. 10.11 First address label program

The copying is done by exiting dBASE II and using the MS–DOS COPY command. I have left in the creation of the ADDLAB1.TXT file, to remind you that if you had created a disk file of the labels, and if your micro system is sufficiently sophisticated, then you could print the labels from the disk file in the 'background' while still using your micro to carry out a completely unrelated task.

The last line of the upper section GO TOP sends you to the first record of the file. The first line of the DO loop says 'do while not at the end of the file' — EOF stands for 'end of file'. Then you have three print statements to print Name, Office and Region on separate lines; followed by three blank lines. SKIP moves you on to the next record, before returning back through the loop. Let's see what this gives us.

```
CHARLOTTE    SMITH
BRISTOL
S



DORIS        JONES
LEEDS
N



HAROLD       HOBBINS
BIRMINGHAM
C
```

and so on through the 20 members of staff.

Fig. 10.12 First attempt at labels

The gaps appear between the names because the dBASE II stores them in the space allowed by the structure of the file, which in this case is 12 spaces for FNAME and SNAME. If the name does not fill the allotted space then it will carry round with it the remaining blank spaces. You can trim off these blank spaces with the TRIM command. The next attempt at the program gives an improved appearance.

```
GO TOP
**********
DO WHILE .NOT. EOF
? TRIM(FNAME),SNAME
? TRIM(OFFICE),'OFFICE'
? TRIM(REGION),'REGION'
?
?
?
SKIP
ENDDO
***********
```

and when this is run you will get

```
CHARLOTTE SMITH
BRISTOL OFFICE
S REGION



DORIS JONES
LEEDS OFFICE
N REGION



HAROLD HOBBINS
BIRMINGHAM OFFICE
C REGION
```

Trimming and adding the words OFFICE and REGION has made the label look more acceptable. I am of course assuming that the labels are for internal post purposes, within the company itself. If they are to be circulated within the firm it will obviously be of help if they were sorted into alphabetical order of Name and Office. The next program would do this job automatically.

and when run now would give you:

```
** TO PRINT OUT ADDRESS LABELS **
SET ECHO OFF
SET TALK OFF
USE A:STAFF
INDEX ON OFFICE + SNAME TO B:LABOFF
SET ALTERNATE TO B:ADDLAB3.TXT
SET ALTERNATE ON
GO TOP
**********
DO WHILE .NOT. EOF
? TRIM(FNAME),SNAME
? TRIM(OFFICE),'OFFICE'
? TRIM(REGION),'REGION'
?
?
?
SKIP
ENDDO
***********
SET ALTERNATE OFF
RETURN
```

Fig 10.13 To tidy up the label output with TRIM

```
BILL ADAMS
BIRMINGHAM OFFICE
C REGION


HAROLD HOBBINS
BIRMINGHAM OFFICE
C REGION


SUSAN SMALL
BIRMINGHAM OFFICE
C REGION


CLIVE JANES
BRISTOL OFFICE
S REGION
```

and so on for the rest of the Offices.

Fig. 10.14 The label program with office and name sorting

10.8 Decisions

We used the basic idea of decision making in the chapter Logic and Databases and in the dBASE II worksheets. The 'logic' was

> IF (condition is true) THEN select the record
> otherwise ignore it

The following method of decision making will hold no surprises. Assume that the company wishes to mail only those staff who are over 45 years of age on the 1st January 1989. I just show the section inside the loop, and leave the rest of the program as above apart from the text filename.

```
**********
DO WHILE .NOT. EOF
     IF DOB < 430101
          ? TRIM(FNAME),SNAME
          ? TRIM(OFFICE),'OFFICE'
          ? TRIM(REGION),'REGION'
          ?
          ?
          ?
     ENDIF
SKIP
ENDDO
***********
```

Fig. 10.15 The IF . . . . ENDIF section for making decisions

I have indented the section of the loop starting with IF and ending with ENDIF. This section is obeyed in the following way: if the DOB is earlier than 430101 then the rest of the statements in that section are carried out, if not

just jump over them and go on to the ENDIF point of the program.
IF (condition is true) THEN go through the statements to ENDIF otherwise just jump over the statements to ENDIF.

As I said at the start of the chapter, decisions are made by providing two alternative paths in the program — do the commands in the IF section or ignore them.

When the program is run you get the following results — remember that the program indexes on Name with Office.

```
HAROLD HOBBINS
BIRMINGHAM OFFICE
C REGION


SUSAN SMALL
BIRMINGHAM OFFICE
C REGION


JOAN BULL
CROYDON OFFICE
S REGION


JOHN APRON
LEEDS OFFICE
N REGION


DORIS JONES
LEEDS OFFICE
N REGION


KATIE SMALES
LEEDS OFFICE
N REGION


BERT JOHNSON
MANCHESTER OFFICE
N REGION
```

Fig. 10.16 Over 45s: indexed on name within office

10.9 Postscript

I hope that this very brief and incomplete introduction to programming in dBASE II has encouraged you to write a few command files to carry out tasks which are useful to you. Only if you are a very experienced programmer should you embark on large scale programs. Limit yourself for a start to a number of simple, but useful routines. One such program could be to sort a data file, which gives you the option to state which field you want the file sorted on, and then gets on and sorts for you, first having automatically made that vital copy of the original file so that there is no fear of the original data being lost in the sorting process. Another could be to allow you to append data from one file to another using the Modify Structure command, but which also makes that essential copy for you before you start, because this command can easily lead you into losing all of your data. This particular routine is given in my version of the dBASE II manual which came with the package. These programs which carry out file related chores carefully for you are often referred to as 'utilities'.

It is tempting to go on and on adding more programs to introduce the rest of the dBASE II commands, and leave you with an arsenal of utilities; but that would require a whole book on its own. I hope I have achieved what I set out to do, namely to whet your appetite. I have only introduced you to the surface of the package, I hope you delve deeper into it, or feel inspired to start on dBASE III and its upgrades.

Appendices

Appendix 1

Solutions to dBASE II exercises

Inspecting a data file

If you simply repeated the sequence of commands which were suggested in the worksheet, but now with the HOLIDAY file you would get results on the screen very similar to the following.

```
 .USE A:HOLIDAY
 .LIST
00001   FR072 FRANCE      FULL   OBCD   EAT       195
00002   FR211 FRANCE      HALF   OBCD   EAT       225
00003   FR382 FRANCE      APT    OOCD   MAN       255
00004   IT229 ITALY       FULL   ABCD   LUT       210
00005   IT365 ITALY       HALF   OBCD   EAT       205
00006   IT509 ITALY       HALF   OOCD   ELAS      215
00007   IT882 ITALY       FULL   ABCD   EAT       265
00008   MA078 MAJORCA     HALF   OOCD   EIRM      185
00009   MA147 MAJORCA     FULL   OBCD   EAT       205
00010   MA364 MAJORCA     FULL   OOCO   EAT       175
00011   MA662 MAJORCA     APT    ABOD   MAN       190
00012   MA771 MAJORCA     HALF   ABCD   EAT       215
00013   PO339 PORTUGAL    HALF   OBOD   EAT       265
00014   PO887 PORTUGAL    HALF   OBCO   EIRM      245
00015   SP137 SPAIN       FULL   ABOD   ELAS      190
00016   SP258 SPAIN       FULL   ABOO   LUT       205
00017   SP481 SPAIN       HALF   ABCO   EAT       170
00018   SP551 SPAIN       FULL   OBCO   EIRM      195
00019   SP722 SPAIN       APT    OBCD   EAT       190
00020   SP901 SPAIN       HALF   ABCD   ELAS      210
 .LIST STRUCTURE
STRUCTURE FOR FILE:   A:HOLIDAY .DBF
NUMBER OF RECORDS:    00020
DATE OF LAST UPDATE: 05/05/87
PRIMARY USE DATABASE
FLD        NAME       TYPE WIDTH   DEC
001      REFNO         C     005
002      COUNTRY       C     010
003      TYPE          C     005
004      WEEKS         C     005
005      AIRPORT       C     005
006      PRICE         N     004
** TOTAL **                00035
```

```
 .DISPLAY
00020  SP901 SPAIN        HALF   ABCD   GLAS      210
 .GO TOP
 .DISPLAY
00001  FR072 FRANCE       FULL   OBCD   GAT       195
 .DISPLAY NEXT 5
00001  FR072 FRANCE       FULL   OBCD   GAT       195
00002  FR211 FRANCE       HALF   OBCD   GAT       225
00003  FR382 FRANCE       APT    OOCD   MAN       255
00004  IT229 ITALY        FULL   ABCD   LUT       210
00005  IT365 ITALY        HALF   OBCD   GAT       205
 .GOTO 7
 .DISPLAY
00007  IT882 ITALY        FULL   ABCD   GAT       265
 .DISPLAY NEXT 4
00007  IT882 ITALY        FULL   ABCD   GAT       265
00008  MA078 MAJORCA      HALF   OOCD   BIRM      185
00009  MA147 MAJORCA      FULL   OBCD   GAT       205
00010  MA364 MAJORCA      FULL   OOCO   GAT       175
 .DISPLAY ALL
00001  FR072 FRANCE       FULL   OBCD   GAT       195
00002  FR211 FRANCE       HALF   OBCD   GAT       225
00003  FR382 FRANCE       APT    OOCD   MAN       255
00004  IT229 ITALY        FULL   ABCD   LUT       210
00005  IT365 ITALY        HALF   OBCD   GAT       205
00006  IT509 ITALY        HALF   OOCD   GLAS      215
00007  IT882 ITALY        FULL   ABCD   GAT       265
00008  MA078 MAJORCA      HALF   OOCD   BIRM      185
00009  MA147 MAJORCA      FULL   OBCD   GAT       205
00010  MA364 MAJORCA      FULL   OOCO   GAT       175
00011  MA662 MAJORCA      APT    ABOD   MAN       190
00012  MA771 MAJORCA      HALF   ABCD   GAT       215
00013  PO339 PORTUGAL     HALF   OBOD   GAT       265
00014  PO887 PORTUGAL     HALF   OBCO   BIRM      245
00015  SP137 SPAIN        FULL   ABOD   GLAS      190
WAITING
00016  SP258 SPAIN        FULL   ABOO   LUT       205
00017  SP481 SPAIN        HALF   ABCO   GAT       170
00018  SP551 SPAIN        FULL   OBCO   BIRM      195
00019  SP722 SPAIN        APT    OBCD   GAT       190
00020  SP901 SPAIN        HALF   ABCD   GLAS      210
```

Interrogating a data file

```
 .USE A:HOLIDAY
 .LIST FOR AIRPORT = 'GAT'
00001  FR072 FRANCE       FULL   OBCD   GAT       195
00002  FR211 FRANCE       HALF   OBCD   GAT       225
00005  IT365 ITALY        HALF   OBCD   GAT       205
00007  IT882 ITALY        FULL   ABCD   GAT       265
00009  MA147 MAJORCA      FULL   OBCD   GAT       205
00010  MA364 MAJORCA      FULL   OOCO   GAT       175
00012  MA771 MAJORCA      HALF   ABCD   GAT       215
00013  PO339 PORTUGAL     HALF   OBOD   GAT       265
00017  SP481 SPAIN        HALF   ABCO   GAT       170
00019  SP722 SPAIN        APT    OBCD   GAT       190
 .LIST FOR COUNTRY = 'SPAIN'
00015  SP137 SPAIN        FULL   ABOD   GLAS      190
00016  SP258 SPAIN        FULL   ABOO   LUT       205
00017  SP481 SPAIN        HALF   ABCO   GAT       170
00018  SP551 SPAIN        FULL   OBCO   BIRM      195
00019  SP722 SPAIN        APT    OBCD   GAT       190
00020  SP901 SPAIN        HALF   ABCD   GLAS      210
 .LIST FOR 'SP' $ COUNTRY
00015  SP137 SPAIN        FULL   ABOD   GLAS      190
```

```
00016  SP258 SPAIN      FULL  ABOO  LUT    205
00017  SP481 SPAIN      HALF  ABCO  GAT    170
00018  SP551 SPAIN      FULL  OBCO  BIRM   195
00019  SP722 SPAIN      APT   OBCD  GAT    190
00020  SP901 SPAIN      HALF  ABCD  GLAS   210
 .LIST FOR PRICE < 200
00001  FR072 FRANCE     FULL  OBCD  GAT    195
00008  MA078 MAJORCA    HALF  OOCD  BIRM   185
00010  MA364 MAJORCA    FULL  OOCO  GAT    175
00011  MA662 MAJORCA    APT   ABOD  MAN    190
00015  SP137 SPAIN      FULL  ABOD  GLAS   190
00017  SP481 SPAIN      HALF  ABCO  GAT    170
00018  SP551 SPAIN      FULL  OBCO  BIRM   195
00019  SP722 SPAIN      APT   OBCD  GAT    190
 .LIST FOR TYPE <> 'FULL'
00002  FR211 FRANCE     HALF  OBCD  GAT    225
00003  FR382 FRANCE     APT   OOCD  MAN    255
00005  IT365 ITALY      HALF  OBCD  GAT    205
00006  IT509 ITALY      HALF  OOCD  GLAS   215
00008  MA078 MAJORCA    HALF  OOCD  BIRM   185
00011  MA662 MAJORCA    APT   ABOD  MAN    190
00012  MA771 MAJORCA    HALF  ABCD  GAT    215
00013  PO339 PORTUGAL   HALF  OBOD  GAT    265
00014  PO887 PORTUGAL   HALF  OBCO  BIRM   245
00017  SP481 SPAIN      HALF  ABCO  GAT    170
00019  SP722 SPAIN      APT   OBCD  GAT    190
00020  SP901 SPAIN      HALF  ABCD  GLAS   210
 .LIST FOR 'AB' $ WEEKS
00004  IT229 ITALY      FULL  ABCD  LUT    210
00007  IT882 ITALY      FULL  ABCD  GAT    265
00011  MA662 MAJORCA    APT   ABOD  MAN    190
00012  MA771 MAJORCA    HALF  ABCD  GAT    215
00015  SP137 SPAIN      FULL  ABOD  GLAS   190
00016  SP258 SPAIN      FULL  ABOO  LUT    205
00017  SP481 SPAIN      HALF  ABCO  GAT    170
00020  SP901 SPAIN      HALF  ABCD  GLAS   210
 .COUNT FOR 'GAT' $ AIRPORT
COUNT = 00010
 .COUNT FOR PRICE < 200
COUNT = 00008
```

Logic and interrogation

```
 .USE A:HOUSES
 .LIST FOR AREA = 'BROMLEY' .AND. GARDEN = 'L'
00013  BR29  BROMLEY          D   3   2   1 L    75000
 .LIST FOR TYPE = 'D' .AND. BEDROOMS >=4
00002  CI23  CHISLEHURST      D   5   3   2 M   168000
00005  BE73  BEXLEY           D   4   2   1 M    52750
00009  CI50  CHISLEHURST      D   5   3   2 M    95000
00016  FA32  FARNBOROUGH      D   6   2   3 L   200000
00022  BR62  BROMLEY          D   4   2   0 M    69995
 .LIST FOR GARDEN = 'L' .AND. PRICE < 75000
00001  WW14  WEST WICKHAM     D   3   2   0 L    55000
00007  PW19  PETTS WOOD       D   3   2   1 L    69950
00011  OR57  ORPINGTON        S   4   1   1 L    50000
00012  SE72  SEVENOAKS        B   2   1   1 L    35000
00015  BE79  BEXLEY           S   3   1   2 L    51000
00018  BE88  BEXLEY           S   2   1   1 L    33500
 .LIST FOR AREA = 'ORPINGTON' .OR. AREA = 'PETTS WOOD'
00003  PW48  PETTS WOOD       D   3   1   1 M    69995
00004  OR09  ORPINGTON        T   3   1   0 S    28500
00007  PW19  PETTS WOOD       D   3   2   1 L    69950
00008  OR63  ORPINGTON        M   3   1   1 M    29950
00011  OR57  ORPINGTON        S   4   1   1 L    50000
```

```
00017  OR35  ORPINGTON         M    2   1   1 N     31000
00019  OR40  ORPINGTON         B    2   1   1 M     64500
 .LIST FOR BEDROOMS >=3 .OR. RECROOMS >=2
00001  WW14  WEST WICKHAM      D    3   2   0 L     55000
00002  CI23  CHISLEHURST       D    5   3   2 M    168000
00003  PW48  PETTS WOOD        D    3   1   1 M     69995
00004  OR09  ORPINGTON         T    3   1   0 S     28500
00005  BE73  BEXLEY            D    4   2   1 M     52750
00007  PW19  PETTS WOOD        D    3   2   1 L     69950
00008  OR63  ORPINGTON         M    3   1   1 N     29950
00009  CI50  CHISLEHURST       D    5   3   2 M     95000
00010  BR82  BROMLEY           S    4   3   0 S     36250
00011  OR57  ORPINGTON         S    4   1   1 L     50000
00013  BR29  BROMLEY           D    3   2   1 L     75000
00014  CE05  CHELSFIELD        B    3   2   2 L     75000
00015  BE79  BEXLEY            S    3   1   2 L     51000
00016  FA32  FARNBOROUGH       D    6   2   3 L    200000
00021  SI30  SIDCUP            S    4   2   2 M     55000
00022  BR62  BROMLEY           D    4   2   0 M     69995
00023  BR12  BROMLEY           T    3   1   1 S     42000
00024  WW43  WEST WICKHAM      S    3   2   1 M     49750
 .LIST FOR TYPE = 'D' .OR. GARDEN = 'L'
00001  WW14  WEST WICKHAM      D    3   2   0 L     55000
00002  CI23  CHISLEHURST       D    5   3   2 M    168000
00003  PW48  PETTS WOOD        D    3   1   1 M     69995
00005  BE73  BEXLEY            D    4   2   1 M     52750
00007  PW19  PETTS WOOD        D    3   2   1 L     69950
00009  CI50  CHISLEHURST       D    5   3   2 M     95000
00011  OR57  ORPINGTON         S    4   1   1 L     50000
00012  SE72  SEVENOAKS         B    2   1   1 L     35000
00013  BR29  BROMLEY           D    3   2   1 L     75000
00014  CE05  CHELSFIELD        B    3   2   2 L     75000
00015  BE79  BEXLEY            S    3   1   2 L     51000
00016  FA32  FARNBOROUGH       D    6   2   3 L    200000
00018  BE88  BEXLEY            S    2   1   1 L     33500
00022  BR62  BROMLEY           D    4   2   0 M     69995
 .LIST FOR .NOT.(GARDEN = 'L')
00002  CI23  CHISLEHURST       D    5   3   2 M    168000
00003  PW48  PETTS WOOD        D    3   1   1 M     69995
00004  OR09  ORPINGTON         T    3   1   0 S     28500
00005  BE73  BEXLEY            D    4   2   1 M     52750
00006  BI37  BICKLEY           F    1   1   0 N     22950
00008  OR63  ORPINGTON         M    3   1   1 N     29950
00009  CI50  CHISLEHURST       D    5   3   2 M     95000
00010  BR82  BROMLEY           S    4   3   0 S     36250
00017  OR35  ORPINGTON         M    2   1   1 N     31000
00019  OR40  ORPINGTON         B    2   1   1 M     64500
00020  SI24  SIDCUP            F    2   1   1 N     32500
00021  SI30  SIDCUP            S    4   2   2 M     55000
00022  BR62  BROMLEY           D    4   2   0 M     69995
00023  BR12  BROMLEY           T    3   1   1 S     42000
00024  WW43  WEST WICKHAM      S    3   2   1 M     49750
 .LIST FOR .NOT.(BEDROOMS >3 .OR. RECROOMS > 1)
00003  PW48  PETTS WOOD        D    3   1   1 M     69995
00004  OR09  ORPINGTON         T    3   1   0 S     28500
00006  BI37  BICKLEY           F    1   1   0 N     22950
00008  OR63  ORPINGTON         M    3   1   1 N     29950
00012  SE72  SEVENOAKS         B    2   1   1 L     35000
00015  BE79  BEXLEY            S    3   1   2 L     51000
00017  OR35  ORPINGTON         M    2   1   1 N     31000
00018  BE88  BEXLEY            S    2   1   1 L     33500
00019  OR40  ORPINGTON         B    2   1   1 M     64500
00020  SI24  SIDCUP            F    2   1   1 N     32500
00023  BR12  BROMLEY           T    3   1   1 S     42000
 .LIST FOR .NOT.(GARDEN = 'L' .AND. PRICE > 75000)
00001  WW14  WEST WICKHAM      D    3   2   0 L     55000
00002  CI23  CHISLEHURST       D    5   3   2 M    168000
```

```
00003  PW48  PETTS WOOD        D   3   1   1 M    69995
00004  OR09  ORPINGTON         T   3   1   0 S    28500
00005  BE73  BEXLEY            D   4   2   1 M    52750
00006  BI37  BICKLEY           F   1   1   0 N    22950
00007  PW19  PETTS WOOD        D   3   2   1 L    69950
00008  OR63  ORPINGTON         M   3   1   1 N    29950
00009  CI50  CHISLEHURST       D   5   3   2 M    95000
00010  BR82  BROMLEY           S   4   3   0 S    36250
00011  OR57  ORPINGTON         S   4   1   1 L    50000
00012  SE72  SEVENOAKS         B   2   1   1 L    35000
00013  BR29  BROMLEY           D   3   2   1 L    75000
00014  CE05  CHELSFIELD        B   3   2   2 L    75000
00015  BE79  BEXLEY            S   3   1   2 L    51000
00017  OR35  ORPINGTON         M   2   1   1 N    31000
00018  BE88  BEXLEY            S   2   1   1 L    33500
00019  OR40  ORPINGTON         B   2   1   1 M    64500
00020  SI24  SIDCUP            F   2   1   1 N    32500
00021  SI30  SIDCUP            S   4   2   2 M    55000
00022  BR62  BROMLEY           D   4   2   0 M    69995
00023  BR12  BROMLEY           T   3   1   1 S    42000
00024  WW43  WEST WICKHAM      S   3   2   1 M    49750
```

Editing a data file

```
 .USE A:HOUSES
 .COPY TO B:TEMP
 00024 RECORDS COPIED
 .USE B:TEMP
 .EDIT
ENTER RECORD # : 4
```

The change to the price data was made to this record, and to records 8, 11, 17 and 19. Details of the changes are not shown here.

```
 .DELETE RECORD 5
 00001 DELETION(S)
 .DELETE RECORD 15
 00001 DELETION(S)
 .DELETE RECORD 18
 00001 DELETION(S)
 .DELETE RECORD 20
 00001 DELETION(S)
 .DELETE RECORD 21
 00001 DELETION(S)
 .PACK
PACK COMPLETE, 00019 RECORDS COPIED
 .GOTO 17
 .INSERT BEFORE
 .GOTO 18
 .INSERT BEFORE
 .LIST
00001  WW14  WEST WICKHAM      D   3   2   0 L    55000
00002  CI23  CHISLEHURST       D   5   3   2 M   168000
00003  PW48  PETTS WOOD        D   3   1   1 M    69995
00004  OR09  ORPINGTON         T   3   1   0 S    30500
00005  BI37  BICKLEY           F   1   1   0 N    22950
00006  PW19  PETTS WOOD        D   3   2   1 L    69950
00007  OR63  ORPINGTON         M   3   1   1 N    31950
00008  CI50  CHISLEHURST       D   5   3   2 M    95000
00009  BR82  BROMLEY           S   4   3   0 S    36250
00010  OR57  ORPINGTON         S   4   1   1 L    52000
00011  SE72  SEVENOAKS         B   2   1   1 L    35000
00012  BR29  BROMLEY           D   3   2   1 L    75000
```

```
00013  CE05  CHELSFIELD       B    3   2   2 L     75000
00014  FA32  FARNBOROUGH      D    6   2   3 L    200000
00015  OR35  ORPINGTON        M    2   1   1 N     33000
00016  OR40  ORPINGTON        B    2   1   1 M     66500
00017  BR77  BROMLEY          D    5   2   1 S     57900
00018  WW27  WEST WICKHAM     S    4   2   2 L     67500
00019  BR62  BROMLEY          D    4   2   0 M     69995
00020  BR12  BROMLEY          T    3   1   1 S     42000
00021  WW43  WEST WICKHAM     S    3   2   1 M     49750
```

Sorting and indexing

```
 .USE A:HOUSES
 .COPY TO B:HOUSTEMP
00024 RECORDS COPIED
 .USE B:HOUSTEMP
 .SORT ON PRICE TO B:HOUSPRI
SORT COMPLETE
 .USE B:HOUSPRI
 .GO TOP
 .DISPLAY NEXT 7
00001  BI37  BICKLEY          F    1   1   0 N     22950
00002  OR09  ORPINGTON        T    3   1   0 S     28500
00003  OR63  ORPINGTON        M    3   1   1 N     29950
00004  OR35  ORPINGTON        M    2   1   1 N     31000
00005  SI24  SIDCUP           F    2   1   1 N     32500
00006  BE88  BEXLEY           S    2   1   1 L     33500
00007  SE72  SEVENOAKS        B    2   1   1 L     35000
 .USE B:HOUSTEMP
 .GO TOP
 .DISPLAY NEXT 7
00001  WW14  WEST WICKHAM     D    3   2   0 L     55000
00002  CI23  CHISLEHURST      D    5   3   2 M    168000
00003  PW48  PETTS WOOD       D    3   1   1 M     69995
00004  OR09  ORPINGTON        T    3   1   0 S     28500
00005  BE73  BEXLEY           D    4   2   1 M     52750
00006  BI37  BICKLEY          F    1   1   0 N     22950
00007  PW19  PETTS WOOD       D    3   2   1 L     69950
 .INDEX ON PRICE TO B:PRICIND
00024 RECORDS INDEXED
 .GO TOP
 .DISPLAY NEXT 7
00006  BI37  BICKLEY          F    1   1   0 N     22950
00004  OR09  ORPINGTON        T    3   1   0 S     28500
00008  OR63  ORPINGTON        M    3   1   1 N     29950
00017  OR35  ORPINGTON        M    2   1   1 N     31000
00020  SI24  SIDCUP           F    2   1   1 N     32500
00018  BE88  BEXLEY           S    2   1   1 L     33500
00012  SE72  SEVENOAKS        B    2   1   1 L     35000
 .INDEX ON AREA TO B:ARIND
00024 RECORDS INDEXED
 .GO TOP
 .DISPLAY NEXT 7
00005  BE73  BEXLEY           D    4   2   1 M     52750
00015  BE79  BEXLEY           S    3   1   2 L     51000
00018  BE88  BEXLEY           S    2   1   1 L     33500
00006  BI37  BICKLEY          F    1   1   0 N     22950
00010  BR82  BROMLEY          S    4   3   0 S     36250
00013  BR29  BROMLEY          D    3   2   1 L     75000
00022  BR62  BROMLEY          D    4   2   0 M     69995
 .INDEX ON TYPE TO B:TYPIND
00024 RECORDS INDEXED
```

```
 .GO TOP
 .DISPLAY NEXT 7
00012  SE72  SEVENOAKS          B     2     1     1 L      35000
00014  CE05  CHELSFIELD         B     3     2     2 L      75000
00019  OR40  ORPINGTON          B     2     1     1 M      64500
00001  WW14  WEST WICKHAM       D     3     2     0 L      55000
00002  CI23  CHISLEHURST        D     5     3     2 M     168000
00003  PW48  PETTS WOOD         D     3     1     1 M      69995
00005  BE73  BEXLEY             D     4     2     1 M      52750
 .INDEX ON AREA + TYPE TO B:ARTYP
00024 RECORDS INDEXED
 .GO TOP
 .DISPLAY NEXT 7
00005  BE73  BEXLEY             D     4     2     1 M      52750
00015  BE79  BEXLEY             S     3     1     2 L      51000
00018  BE88  BEXLEY             S     2     1     1 L      33500
00006  BI37  BICKLEY            F     1     1     0 N      22950
00013  BR29  BROMLEY            D     3     2     1 L      75000
00022  BR62  BROMLEY            D     4     2     0 M      69995
00010  BR82  BROMLEY            S     4     3     0 S      36250
 .INDEX ON BEDROOMS + PRICE TO B:BEDPRI
00024 RECORDS INDEXED
 .GO TOP
 .DISPLAY NEXT 7
00006  BI37  BICKLEY            F     1     1     0 N      22950
00004  OR09  ORPINGTON          T     3     1     0 S      28500
00008  OR63  ORPINGTON          M     3     1     1 N      29950
00017  OR35  ORPINGTON          M     2     1     1 N      31000
00020  SI24  SIDCUP             F     2     1     1 N      32500
00018  BE88  BEXLEY             S     2     1     1 L      33500
00012  SE72  SEVENOAKS          B     2     1     1 L      35000
 .INDEX ON TYPE + STR(PRICE,6,0) TO B:TYPRI
00024 RECORDS INDEXED
 .GO TOP
 .DISPLAY NEXT 7
00012  SE72  SEVENOAKS          B     2     1     1 L      35000
00019  OR40  ORPINGTON          B     2     1     1 M      64500
00014  CE05  CHELSFIELD         B     3     2     2 L      75000
00005  BE73  BEXLEY             D     4     2     1 M      52750
00001  WW14  WEST WICKHAM       D     3     2     0 L      55000
00007  PW19  PETTS WOOD         D     3     2     1 L      69950
00003  PW48  PETTS WOOD         D     3     1     1 M      69995
 .INDEX ON AREA + STR(PRICE,6,0) TO B:ARPRI
00024 RECORDS INDEXED
 .GO TOP
 .DISPLAY NEXT 7
00018  BE88  BEXLEY             S     2     1     1 L      33500
00015  BE79  BEXLEY             S     3     1     2 L      51000
00005  BE73  BEXLEY             D     4     2     1 M      52750
00006  BI37  BICKLEY            F     1     1     0 N      22950
00010  BR82  BROMLEY            S     4     3     0 S      36250
00023  BR12  BROMLEY            T     3     1     1 S      42000
00022  BR62  BROMLEY            D     4     2     0 M      69995
```

List layouts and reports

Exercise 1 (a)

```
 .LIST OFF REFNO AREA TYPE BEDROOMS FOR PRICE < 50000

OR09  ORPINGTON         T     3
BI37  BICKLEY           F     1
OR63  ORPINGTON         M     3
BR82  BROMLEY           S     4
```

```
SE72  SEVENOAKS          B    2
OR35  ORPINGTON          M    2
BE88  BEXLEY             S    2
SI24  SIDCUP             F    2
BR12  BROMLEY            T    3
WW43  WEST WICKHAM       S    3
```

Exercise 1 (b)

```
.LIST OFF REFNO TYPE BEDROOMS PRICE FOR 'ORP' $ AREA

OR09  T    3    28500
OR63  M    3    29950
OR57  S    4    50000
OR35  M    2    31000
OR40  B    2    64500
```

Exercise 2 (a)

```
.LIST OFF REFNO TYPE WEEKS PRICE FOR PRICE < 200

FR072 FULL  OBCD     195
MA078 HALF  OOCD     185
MA364 FULL  OOCO     175
MA662 APT   ABOD     190
SP137 FULL  ABOD     190
SP481 HALF  ABCO     170
SP551 FULL  OBCO     195
SP722 APT   OBCD     190
```

Exercise 2 (b)

```
.LIST OFF COUNTRY TYPE PRICE FOR 'AB' $ WEEKS

ITALY       FULL    210
ITALY       FULL    265
MAJORCA     APT     190
MAJORCA     HALF    215
SPAIN       FULL    190
SPAIN       FULL    205
SPAIN       HALF    170
SPAIN       HALF    210
```

Exercise 2 (c)

```
.LIST OFF REFNO TYPE WEEKS PRICE FOR 'GAT' $ AIRPORT

FR072 FULL  OBCD     195
FR211 HALF  OBCD     225
IT365 HALF  OBCD     205
IT882 FULL  ABCD     265
MA147 FULL  OBCD     205
MA364 FULL  OOCO     175
MA771 HALF  ABCD     215
PO339 HALF  OBOD     265
SP481 HALF  ABCO     170
SP722 APT   OBCD     190
```

Exercise 3 (a)

```
 .REPORT FORM B:HOUSREP2.FRM FOR PRICE < 50000
ENTER OPTIONS, M=LEFT MARGIN, L=LINES/PAGE, W=PAGE WIDTH M=5,W=60
PAGE HEADING? (Y/N) Y
ENTER PAGE HEADING: HOUSES FOR LESS THAN #50,000
DOUBLE SPACE REPORT? (Y/N) N
ARE TOTALS REQUIRED? (Y/N) N
COL     WIDTH,CONTENTS
001      4,TYPE
ENTER HEADING: TYPE
002      4,BEDROOMS
ENTER HEADING: BEDS
003      18,AREA
ENTER HEADING: LOCATION
004      5,PRICE
ENTER HEADING: PRICE
005      5,REFNO
ENTER HEADING: REFNO
006

     PAGE NO. 00001
     12/18/87

               HOUSES FOR LESS THAN #50,000

     TYPE BEDS LOCATION           PRICE REFNO

     T       3 ORPINGTON          28500 OR09
     F       1 BICKLEY            22950 BI37
     M       3 ORPINGTON          29950 OR63
     S       4 BROMLEY            36250 BR82
     B       2 SEVENOAKS          35000 SE72
     M       2 ORPINGTON          31000 OR35
     S       2 BEXLEY             33500 BE88
     F       2 SIDCUP             32500 SI24
     T       3 BROMLEY            42000 BR12
     S       3 WEST WICKHAM       49750 WW43

 .INDEX ON PRICE TO B:HOUPRIND1
00024 RECORDS INDEXED
 .USE A:HOUSES INDEX B:HOUPRIND1
 .REPORT FORM B:HOUSREP2 FOR PRICE < 50000

     PAGE NO. 00001
     12/18/87

               HOUSES FOR LESS THAN #50,000

     TYPE BEDS LOCATION           PRICE REFNO

     F       1 BICKLEY            22950 BI37
     T       3 ORPINGTON          28500 OR09
     M       3 ORPINGTON          29950 OR63
     M       2 ORPINGTON          31000 OR35
     F       2 SIDCUP             32500 SI24
     S       2 BEXLEY             33500 BE88
     B       2 SEVENOAKS          35000 SE72
     S       4 BROMLEY            36250 BR82
     T       3 BROMLEY            42000 BR12
     S       3 WEST WICKHAM       49750 WW43
```

Exercise 3 (b)

```
 .REPORT FORM B:HOLREP1.FRM FOR 'GAT' $ AIRPORT
ENTER OPTIONS, M=LEFT MARGIN, L=LINES/PAGE, W=PAGE WIDTH M=10,W=60
PAGE HEADING? (Y/N) N^Y
ENTER PAGE HEADING: FLY FROM GATWICK
DOUBLE SPACE REPORT? (Y/N) N
ARE TOTALS REQUIRED? (Y/N) N
COL     WIDTH,CONTENTS
001      10,COUNTRY
ENTER HEADING: COUNTRY
002       5,TYPE
ENTER HEADING: TYPE
003       4,PRICE
ENTER HEADING: COST
004       5,REFNO
ENTER HEADING: REFNO
005
          PAGE NO. 00001
          12/18/87
                    FLY FROM GATWICK

          COUNTRY     TYPE  COST REFNO

          FRANCE      FULL   195 FR072
          FRANCE      HALF   225 FR211
          ITALY       HALF   205 IT365
          ITALY       FULL   265 IT882
          MAJORCA     FULL   205 MA147
          MAJORCA     FULL   175 MA364
          MAJORCA     HALF   215 MA771
          PORTUGAL    HALF   265 PO339
          SPAIN       HALF   170 SP481
          SPAIN       APT    190 SP722

 .INDEX ON PRICE TO B:HOLPRIND1
00020 RECORDS INDEXED
 .USE A:HOLIDAY INDEX B:HOLPRIND1
 .REPORT FORM B:HOLREP1 FOR 'GAT' $ AIRPORT

          PAGE NO. 00001
          12/18/87
                    FLY FROM GATWICK

          COUNTRY     TYPE  COST REFNO

          SPAIN       HALF   170 SP481
          MAJORCA     FULL   175 MA364
          SPAIN       APT    190 SP722
          FRANCE      FULL   195 FR072
          ITALY       HALF   205 IT365
          MAJORCA     FULL   205 MA147
          MAJORCA     HALF   215 MA771
          FRANCE      HALF   225 FR211
          ITALY       FULL   265 IT882
          PORTUGAL    HALF   265 PO339
```

Appendix 2

Numbers great and small

We looked at how numbers are represented in computers in Chapter 6, where I introduced the E notation for large numbers, and warned about the care which needs to be taken with small numbers which lurk about zero. We looked at how dBASE II addresses these problems in Chapter 10, and now let's look at how SuperCalc copes, and finally a different solution to the same problem in BBC BASIC — just to round things off!

I used the Replicate command to set up the following sheet in SuperCalc3.

```
   :    A    ::    B    ::    C    :
 1: 1                  1/A1
 2: A1-0.1             1/A2
 3: A2-0.1             1/A3
 4: A3-0.1             1/A4
 5: A4-0.1             1/A5
 6: A5-0.1             1/A6
 7: A6-0.1             1/A7
 8: A7-0.1             1/A8
 9: A8-0.1             1/A9
10: A9-0.1             1/A10
11: A10-0.1            1/A11
12: A11-0.1            1/A12
13: A12-0.1            1/A13
14: A13-0.1            1/A14
15: A14-0.1            1/A15
```

The following set of values appeared on the sheet.

```
   :    A    ::    B    ::    C    :
 1:         1                    1
 2:        .9            1.111111
 3:        .8                1.25
 4:        .7            1.428571
 5:        .6            1.666667
 6:        .5                   2
 7:        .4                 2.5
 8:        .3            3.333333
 9:        .2                   5
10:        .1                  10
11:         0               ERROR
12:       -.1                 -10
13:       -.2                  -5
14:       -.3            -3.33333
15:       -.4                -2.5
```

Like dBASE II we get an error message at 1/0.

The following replicated set of commands were used to look at large numbers.

```
   |   A    ||   B   ||     C      ||   D   ||      E
 1|  1                 123.45^A1             123.45^A1
 2|  A1+1              123.45^A2             123.45^A2
 3|  A2+1              123.45^A3             123.45^A3
 4|  A3+1              123.45^A4             123.45^A4
 5|  A4+1              123.45^A5             123.45^A5
 6|  A5+1              123.45^A6             123.45^A6
 7|  A6+1              123.45^A7             123.45^A7
 8|  A7+1              123.45^A8             123.45^A8
 9|  A8+1              123.45^A9             123.45^A9
10|  A9+1              123.45^A10            123.45^A10
```

And the following set of values resulted.

```
   |   A    ||   B   ||     C      ||   D   ||          E        |
 1|         1             123.45                         123.45
 2|         2           15239.90                     15239.9025
 3|         3           1881366.                 1881365.963625
 4|         4           2.3225e8                 232254628.2095
 5|         5           2.867e10                 28671833852.46
 6|         6           3.540e12                 3539537889087.
 7|         7           4.370e14                 4.369559524e14
 8|         8           5.394e16                 5.394221232e16
 9|         9           6.659e18                 6.659166111e18
10|        10           8.221e20                 8.220740565e20
```

SuperCalc3 expresses its values to a different precision from dBASE II, as you can see and uses 'e' instead of 'E'.

Finally look at a BASIC program loop which deals with small numbers near zero, which neither says 0 nor warns about the approximation it is making to 0. The lesson which I'm sure I have conveyed by now is take care with how you interpret the results from calculations where the numbers may be very large or very small.

```
10 FOR NUMBER=-1 TO 1 STEP(.2)
20 PRINT TAB(1);NUMBER;TAB(15);1/NUMBER
30 NEXT NUMBER

RUN

-1               -1
-.8              -1.25
-.6              -1.66667
-.4              -2.5
-.2              -5
-2.98023E-08     -3.35544E+07
 .2               5
 .4               2.5
 .6               1.66667
 .8               1.25
 1                1
```

Zero ?!

I divided by Zero ?!

Appendix 3

The ASCII Code

Code	ASCII Character	Code	ASCII Character	Code	ASCII Character
000	NUL	043	+	086	V
001	SOH	044	'	087	W
002	STX	045	–	088	X
003	ETX	046	.	089	Y
004	EOT	047	/	090	Z
005	ENQ	048	0	091	[
006	ACK	049	1	092	
008	BS	051	3	094	^
009	HT	052	4	095	–
010	LF	053	5	096	´
011	VT	054	6	097	a
012	FF	055	7	098	b
013	CR	056	8	099	c
014	SO	057	9	100	d
015	SI	058	:	101	e
016	DLE	059	;	102	f
017	DC1	060	<	103	g
018	DC2	061	=	104	h
019	DC3	062	>	105	i
020	DC4	063	?	106	j
021	NAK	064	@	107	k
022	SYN	065	A	108	l
023	ETB	066	B	109	m
024	CAN	067	C	110	n
025	EM	068	D	111	o
026	SUB	069	E	112	p
027	ESCAPE	070	F	113	q
028	FS	071	G	114	r
029	GS	072	H	115	a
030	RS	073	I	116	t
031	US	074	J	117	u
032	SPACE	075	K	118	v
033	!	076	L	119	w
034	″	077	M	120	x
035	#	078	N	121	y
036	$	079	O	122	z
037	%	080	P	123	{
038	&	081	Q	124	|
039	'	082	R	125	}
040	(	083	S	126	~
041	)	084	T	127	DEL
042	*	085	U		

Glossary

Analogue/Digital Converter
A hardware device which converts analogue information, e.g. time, temperature or distance moved by a robot arm, into digital or numeric form. These converters allow digital computers to interact with real world analogue quantities.

Applications Software
A program or suite of programs designed to solve a specific class of problems, or perform a particular application e.g. accounts, sales ledger or stock control. It is assumed that such a package will need only minor modifications to cope with your particular sales ledger or stock control requirements.

Assembler (Assembly Code)
The most convenient form of machine code, available in alphanumeric form, and used by systems' programmers to write their software. Each type of chip has its own 'assembly code' and so the programs written are very machine or hardware dependent.

ASCII Code
American Standard Code for Information Interchange, an internationally accepted system for coding alphanumeric characters for use in computers, see Appendix 3.

Authoring Language
A very high level programming language designed to speed up and simplify the job of writing applications software. Authoring languages can be especially useful to enable people who are not professional programmers to write their own software.

Bar–Code
A pattern of printed lines common on books and groceries, which contains coded information and allows data to be read from these items directly into a computer.

BASIC
Beginners' All-purpose Symbolic Instruction Code. At present, the most popular programming language for beginners and education generally, and

almost universally available on microcomputers. It exists in many dialects, with minor incompatibilities. Over the years it has been upgraded and is used now quite widely for business applications.

Baud
A measure of the rate of transmitting information within or between computer systems; 1 baud is approximately 1 bit per second. Telex operates at 50 baud; programs are often loaded from cassette at 300 baud; teletext operates at 1200 to 2400 baud.

Benchmark
A standard against which computer functions are compared. For example, the speed with which a computer executes a certain program could be used on different computers to compare their relative speeds of processing.

Bespoke Software
Software which has been designed for a specific application for a specific customer, in contrast with off–the–shelf general application packages which have to be adapted to suit particular user requirements.

Bi–directional Printers
Printers which strike as they pass both left–to–right and right–to–left are called bi–directional. The characters are automatically printed out in reverse order on the right–to–left traverses.

Centronics Interface
A standard parallel interface widely used by microcomputer manufacturers for connecting printers to processors.

COBOL
Common Business Orientated Language. A high level programming language used widely in business computing, but usually on mainframe computers although versions of the language are available for micros.

Command Mode
A style of interaction with a software package in which the user controls the program by typing in commands, by contrast to choosing control options from a menu.

Compiler
A program which translates the code of a high level language into machine code. When a program in high level language is compiled it is translated all in one go, and when the program is run it is run all in machine code. Contrast this with an interpreter which translates a high level program into code line by line as the program is run, each time it is run.

Control Codes
The codes used in software packages to make printers produce a variety of effects, like margins, bold face and underlining.

CP/M
Control Program for Microcomputers. A virtual standard disk operating system for 8-bit microcomputers. There are several different versions of CP/M. The 16-bit version is called CP/M-86 and the multi-user version MP/M. CP/M Plus is another name for CP/M Version 3.

CPI
Characters per inch; used to measure the number of characters of printer typefaces.

CPS
Characters per second; used to measure printer speed.

Data–base
A collection of data stored in files usually in some magnetic medium and organized systematically to make processing easy, usually offering a procedural or enquiry language to let you interrogate the data–base automatically.

Default
The value or state which a computer system assumes unless it is otherwise instructed. For example a word processing package may take as a default value a page length of 66 lines until instructed otherwise, or a disk operating system may default to one particular drive unless instructed to address another drive.

Desk Top Publishing
The facility to produce professional looking documents without the need for typesetters and graphic artists: you write the text, edit it, draw the illustrations, add in photographs, design page layouts and print the final document using a relatively inexpensive computer with a laser printer.

Dialogue
An exchange of questions and answers between a computer program or software package and the user.

Disk Operating System (DOS)
A program which controls the storage and retrieval of programs and data to and from disks. See also CP/M and MS–DOS.

Electronic Mail
The electronic transmission and reception of messages or data across a distance using telephone lines, or radio waves.

Enquiry Language
A high level language designed specifically for interrogating a database.

Fax
Facsimile transmission: the entire contents of a sheet of paper (including letterhead, signature, etc. of a letter) are scanned optically and coded

electronically, and sent to a remote terminal connected by a telecommunications link. Pictures can also be transmitted.

Function Keys
Keys on a computer keyboard which carry out specific operations with one key stroke. Their use can be defined by the user or software, so that the same key which justifies text while using a word processing package for example, may also be used on another occasion to reformat a spreadsheet.

Graphics
Picture, diagram or graph which the computer can produce on the screen or print on to paper. The higher the resolution (see Resolution) the clearer the picture.

Graphics Tablet
An input device on which the user traces a shape with a wand or pen, and the trace is then coded in digital form for the computer to process.

High–level Language
A programming language e.g. BASIC, COBOL, FORTRAN, LISP, LOGO, PASCAL or PROLOG, in which instructions are written in words or codes closely resembling English phrases or mathematical equations, for subsequent translation into machine language.

Integrated Software
A suite of programs which are designed as a collection, so that the data output from one can automatically be fed into another. True integration would mean that the different programs could cohabit the same RAM, but RAMs of that size are not generally yet available.

Interface
Junction between two devices in a computer system, e.g. between processor and printer. Computer interfaces consist of not only the hardware (plugs and cables etc.), but must include specially written software as well, to allow the passage of electronic information between the two devices.

Interpreter
A system's program which translates software written in high–level language into machine code. Each line of an interpreted program has to be retranslated every time it is executed — compare this with Compiler above.

KIPS
Knowledge Information Processing Systems. The name given by the Japanese to the proposed Fifth Generation computers to distinguish between the digital/numeral basis of our current methods of data processing, and what is expected of the new generation of machines.

List Processing
The processing of data arranged in the form of lists; on the one hand forming the theoretical basis of the high level language LISP (LISt Processing), and

on the other in word processing, where it is sometimes used to describe the insertion of standard information into mail shots.

MailMerge
A word processing facility where details from a file are merged into a standard letter.

Master File
A file containing standard information which changes very infrequently, being updated only from time to time, e.g. a customer name and address file which remains relatively constant, changing only when the customer moves home; contrast this with the transaction file, which changes every time the customer is involved in a transaction.

Menu–driven
Describes software in which the user controls the package by choosing options from a menu presented on the screen of the system.

Modem
MOdulator/DEModulator. A device which allows computers to transmit information through a telecommunications link, by converting digital information into an analogue signal and vice versa.

Mouse
A small input device (see Figure 1.1 in Chapter 1) which may be rolled around on a desk top to control the movement of a pointer on the screen of a computer. Choices are made by moving this pointer to menu options on the screen and then pressing a switch on the mouse.

MS–DOS
The standard 16-bit disk operating system designed by Microsoft Inc., originally commissioned by IBM for its Personal Computer (on which it is known as PC–DOS) but available on many other machines in addition to straight IBM PC clones.

Multi-tasking
A computer system which can cope with more than one program at a time.

Multi-user
A system which can cope with more than one user at a time.

Optical Character Recognition (OCR)
A method whereby a printed document can be scanned by a machine which 'recognises' special printed characters by their shape, thus allowing them to be 'read' into a computer system.

Parallel Interface
A connection between two devices which allows digital information to be passed from one to the other in packets of 8-, 16- or 32- bits simultaneously.

Thus the bits within the packets are said by engineers to be passed 'in parallel'. Contrast this with the serial interface, below.

Pixel
Picture element: the tiny area of fluoresence on the VDU or TV screen, when grouped make up the pictures seen. The more pixels to a given area of the screen the higher the resolution, and the sharper and clearer the picture.

Prompt
Any sign by the computer (a signal on the screen or an audible bleep) to indicate that it is waiting for a response from the user.

Query Language
A high level language designed specifically for interrogating a data–base.

Random Access
A method by which data can be read directly and therefore quickly from any sector of a floppy disk, rather than having to read one by one through all of the records until the particular data record is found. Contrast with Serial Access below.

Random Access Memory (RAM)
The memory space of the processor of a micro which is freely available to the user to read from and write to as required, where programs and data may be stored while they are processed. When the computer is switched off the contents of the RAM are lost.

Read Only Memory (ROM)
Part of the processor's memory which stores programs which cannot be changed, e.g. the BASIC interpreter, or the operating system. Unlike RAM, the contents cannot be changed by the user who can read from ROM but not write to it. When the machine is switched off the contents of ROM are not lost.

Resolution
A concept derived from the 'resolving power' of an optical system, which is the ability of an optical system (microscope or telescope) to produce separate images of objects which are very close together. 'Resolution' is used in computing to indicate the efficiency with which a system produces a clear 'image', on screen, printer or graphics plotter, or even how efficiently accurate information is transmitted round an electronic system.

RS-232
A standard interface developed by the Electronics Industry Association for telecommunications equipment. Transmission is serial, at one of a standard range of speeds. The standard has been widely adopted by computer manufactures, so that most computers have an RS-232 'port' (output socket plus software) for connecting processors to peripherals.

Screen Dump
This is when the contents of a complete screen are output to printer or disk (usually the former). Your system needs software to be able to do this, and MS–DOS machines can usually perform this function simply by using the **Shift/PrtSc** key combination which triggers off the software.

Serial Access
When a data file must be accessed (searched or interrogated) in the sequence in which it is physically stored, byte by byte, field by field or record by record, until the required item of data is found. When data is stored on magnetic tape, this is the only way in which you can locate an item of data. Contrast with Random Access above.

Serial Interface
A connection between two devices of a micro's system which allows digital information to be passed from one device to another one bit at a time. Contrast with Parallel Interface.

Stand–alone
A computer used on its own, as opposed to being part of a network, or telecommunications link, or terminal of a main frame computer.

Systems Software
Software such as disk operating systems and programming languages which the computer needs to allow it to run applications software.

Telesoftware
Software that is sent straight into a computer's memory from a distance, using telephone or radio communication methods.

Teletext
Information broadcast as part of a television transmission, e.g. in the UK CEEFAX (BBC) or ORACLE (IBA). Teletext televisions have built in teletext decoders.

Telex
World telegraphic system which allows communications between special printers. By modern computing standards it is slow and lacks flexibility, but it is well established and internationally available, and widely used in the world's business community.

Toggle
A switch or key which reserves an effect when pressed, such as a pull light switch which you pull once for 'on' and then pull again for 'off'. In MS DOS an initial **Ctrl/P** will switch the printer ON, the next occurrence of **Ctrl/P** will switch the printing facility OFF.

Transaction File
A file containing data to be processed for a particular purpose; it may have to be combined with data from a Master file. For example, to do a payroll, the

Transaction file might contain details of hours worked per week or month for a specific period, while the Master file would have more permanent details of the employees, such as their rates of pay, tax codes, National Insurance details and so on.

UNIX
A sophisticated disk operating system originally designed for microcomputers at Bell Laboratories, which has been adapted for 16– and 32–bit microcomputers, and allows multi–users and multi–tasking.

Upgrade
The process of improving or adding to the original hardware or software of your system. A good system will have well–planned 'upgrade path' so that software can be transferred to the new expanded hardware or software system without wasted effort on loss of facilities or data.

Utilities
Collections of programs which allow you to carry out useful housekeeping operations for your system, like copying or formating disks, or recovering deleted files.

Videodisk
A coated plastic disc which can store large numbers of television pictures together with the associated sound. Unlike videotape, videodisks can be accessed randomly. They have great potential as a medium for a computer data storage because of their enormous capacities, and capability of mixing visual and computer generated information. The reading and writing mechanism involves laser optics, and is currently very expensive, but inevitably prices are dropping, and the systems will be generally available within a few years, and will represent the next major advance in storage media.

Videotex
An electronic method of receiving information from a distance and displaying it on a screen. Videotex may use television transmission (teletext) or telephone lines (viewdata). Teletext is receive–only or one–way videotex, but viewdata is receive–send, or two–way, interactive videotex.

Viewdata
Two–way transmission of electronic information, using telephone lines. Users can, not only retrieve information from large databases, but also send messages and instructions back. Prestel was the world's first public viewdata system.

Winchester Disk
A type of sealed hard disk unit becoming very popular for use with microcomputers. Originally 14 inches in diameter and used on mainframe computers, Winchesters have become progressively smaller matching the shrinking diameter of floppy disks. They are capable of storing large quantities of data, 10 to 40 Megabytes and upwards.

Word Wrap
On a typewriter, the user has to press a carriage return key or lever at the end of each line. Wordprocessing software avoids this interruption by taking care of new line automatically — a process known as a word wrap, or wrap around.

Work File
See Transaction File.

Write Protected
A disk made 'read only', so that nothing can be recorded on to it. With 5¼ inch floppy disks this is achieved by covering its write–protect notch with tape or foil.

Index